ASEAN
and the Diplomacy
of Accommodation

Association of South East Asian Nations (ASEAN)

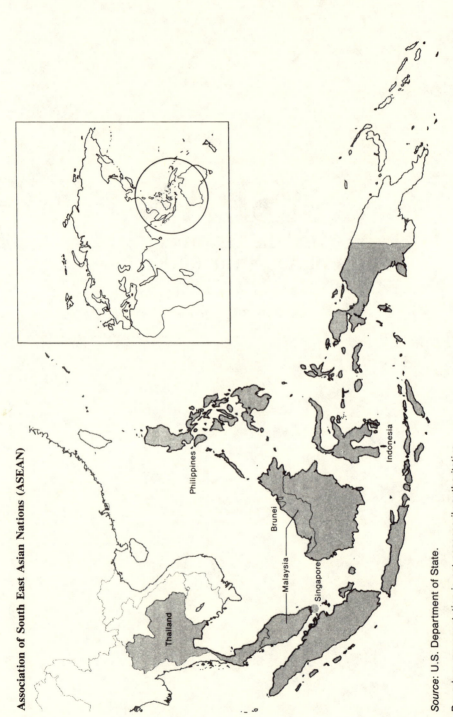

Thailand

Philippines

Brunei

Malaysia

Singapore

Indonesia

Source: U.S. Department of State.

Boundary representation is not necessarily authoritative.

ASEAN
and the Diplomacy
of Accommodation

Michael Antolik

An East Gate Book

M. E. Sharpe, Inc.
Armonk, New York
London, England

An East Gate Book

Copyright © 1990 by M. E. Sharpe, Inc.
80 Business Park Drive, Armonk, New York 10504.

Available in the United Kingdom and Europe from M. E. Sharpe,
Publishers, 3 Henrietta Street, London WC2E 8LU.

Library of Congress Catologing-in-Publication Data

Antolik, Michael, 1948–
    Asean and the diplomacy of accommodation / by Michael
Antolik
        p.   cm.
    Includes bibliographical references.
    ISBN 0-87332-630-X
    1. Asia, Southeastern—Politics and government—1945– .
  2. Asia, Southeastern—Foreign relations. 3. ASEAN. I. Title.
DS526.7.A59 1990
327′.0959—dc20   89-49026
                                                                              CIP

Printed in the United States of America

                                    ∞

TS   10   9   8   7   6   5   4   3   2   1

To John Baptist De La Salle

Contents

Preface

THE ASEAN logo represents a rice bowl, a cultural commonality to all its members, with six vertical lines to toll the membership. When taken together, these elements remind that ASEAN stands for a grouping of individual states whose record of coordinated policy suggests commonality and solidarity. Interestingly, this logo also summons up an important question about the Association: Just as the absence of a horizontal band prompts the observer to ask what holds the bowl together, so too one asks—What holds the ASEAN states together?

In 1984 a Malaysian diplomat offered this explanation: "Asean is just a club." At first glance the description of the Association of Southeast Asian Nations (ASEAN) as a "club" may not appear very useful or scientifically rigorous; but consider the dictionary meanings of "club": "a group organized for a purpose; an organization which offers its subscribers benefits." These two dimensions, organization and securing benefits, are intrinsic dynamics of institution formation in particular and politics in general. That a member describes the institution as a "club" signifies the informality characteristic of ASEAN interactions, as well as the good feelings, sense of trust, and even smiles that the member diplomats are often so careful to project to outsiders. Consequently, ASEAN can be investigated along all these lines suggested by the metaphor of a "club."

The ASEAN phenomenon invites investigation because it has remained effective and valued for over twenty years; other regional associations have come and gone over this time. ASEAN's success invites comparison both to help it avoid pitfalls and to aid other groupings in their search for improved multilateral cooperation processes. Comparison, however, has sometimes proved to be confusing. While ASEAN stands tall compared to several defunct or paralyzed regional organizations, its stature next to the progress of the European Community is less imposing.

In particular, the recent steps announced by the EC to integrate more fully members' economies contrast dramatically with the small number of ASEAN joint-economic projects—on this level, ASEAN deserves the label paralyzed, if not defunct. (It was such an indictment that evoked the description of "club" and continued, "it can't do wonders overnight.") ASEAN's own articulations invite such charges, however; declarations and policy statements could easily lead one to believe that the acronym also stands for Always Stress Economics And Neutrality. In fairness, one should note that the ASEAN position has evolved from its founding days, when it appeared that governments were entering into a multilateral approach to economic cooperation, to the contemporary approach which views the Association as an enabler to private-sector economic cooperation. Nevertheless, when trying to explain the nature and functions of the Association, the ASEAN paradox often arises. Why have states maintained membership in a club that has not produced the benefits offered in its charter?

The invocation of neutrality suggests that ASEAN perhaps provides a benefit in that other area important to states, security; but this benefit is even more deeply shrouded by the mists of ASEAN. Security activity or cooperation is officially eschewed by the ASEAN organization; yet things are somewhat more flexible in reality, as much is done "under the ASEAN umbrella" or "in the spirit of ASEAN." The role that security interests play is obfuscated by an all-too-frequent identification of ASEAN with another organization, SEATO. Though years departed, SEATO still seems to have more name-recognition than ASEAN in all circles but those familar with Asian politics. Comparing ASEAN with SEATO makes clear that ASEAN is not a formal, collective defense organization; however, ASEAN members' bilateral security-related cooperation continues the confusion. This cooperation creates the impression of an alliance despite denials, explanations, or rationalizations that such activity is not an ASEAN activity, only done in "the spirit of ASEAN."

So perhaps discerning this spirit is central to understanding what holds this association together. Indeed, ASEAN has many characteristics of a spirit—one is never sure when it is present, but its presence is often felt and influences decisions. Many gatherings are held and individual sacrifices are made in its name. Many claim to know its will and speak accordingly. Most telling, ASEAN is hard to define.

To illustrate, a first challenge concerns the style of the acronym; should it be "ASEAN" or "Asean"? Though the practice in Southeast Asia favors the latter and many style books advocate lower case for acronyms of more than four letters, I have chosen ASEAN because the Association is not widely recognized outside its home region, and Asean is often taken for a typing error for "Asian."

This study of the many activities undertaken by these ASEAN states reflects the inspiration and support of many individuals. In my quest to break ASEAN down into parts, Professor James Morley kept alive the importance of the environment in which the action was taking place. Professor Howard Wriggins more than once kept me from succumbing to the lure of reification. For their comments on this text I am most appreciative to Professors Chai-Anan Samudavanija and Juwuno Sudarsono. I am particularly grateful to the Visiting Fellows program of the Institute of Southeast Asian Studies, Singapore, whose hospitality was only exceeded by the generosity of individual scholars there. At the National University of Singapore, I thank in particular professors Lau Teik Soon, Leo Suryadinata, and Kernail Singh Sanhu, director of ISEAS. Likewise, the Institute of Security and International Studies at Chulalongkorn University has several times been most helpful; my thanks go especially to Professors Chayachoke Chulasiriwongs, Kusuma Snitwongse, and Sukhumbhand Paribatra. I would also like to thank the Faculty of Political Science at Thammasat University for hosting a discussion that raised my insights into indigenous perspectives on political interaction. Several other scholars deserve my appreciation: Hadi Soesastro of Jakarta's Centre for Strategic and International Studies; Zacharia Ahmad and Noordin Sopiee of Kuala Lumpur's Institute of Strategic and International Studies; Wilfredo Villacorta and Andrew Gonzalez of Manila's De La Salle University; and Carolina Hernandez and Estrella Solidum of the University of the Philippines.

For the time, facilities, and funding to research and write I am most grateful to Manhattan College, Christian Brothers Center, Lloyd Hall community, and the Uralic and Altaic Studies program, directed by

Professor Denis Sinor, under the auspices of the National Endowment for the Humanities. To the helpful and cordial people at M. E. Sharpe, headed by Douglas Merwin, I extend my appreciation. For both editorial advice and general encouragement, my thanks to David J. Larkin, Jr.

Abbreviations

AMM	Annual Ministerial Meeting
ASA	Association of Southeast Asia
ASEAN	Association of Southeast Asian Nations
CGDK	Coalition Government of Democratic Kampuchea
CPM	Communist Party of Malaya
CPT	Communist Party of Thailand
DAP	Democratic Action Party
DMZ	demilitarized zone
EC	European Community
ICK	International Conference on Kampuchea
ISEAS	Institute of Southeast Asian Studies
JIM	Jakarta Informal Meeting
KPNLF	Khmer People's National Liberation Front
MCA	Malaysian Chinese Association
MIC	Malaysian Indian Congress
MNLF	Mindanao National Liberation Front
NEP	New Economic Policy
Pas	Parti Islam
PAP	People's Action Party
PKI	Communist Party of Indonesia
PLO	Palestine Liberation Organization
PMM	Post-Ministerial Meeting
PPP	Muslim United Development Party
PRB	Party Rakyat Brunei
PULO	Patani United Liberation Organization
SEATO	Southeast Asian Treaty Organization
SOM	Senior Officials Meeting
UMNO	United Malays National Organization

ASEAN
and the Diplomacy
of Accommodation

1
The Meanings of ASEAN

Will the real Asean please stand up? Is it the meek, inward-looking grouping that hangs together without real cohesion, that has achieved all too little in its internal arrangements, or the dynamic, confident, solid front that fears no one, can face the world with confidence and is even now becoming a pacesetter and former of world opinion?

—Singapore *Monitor*

THE Association of Southeast Asian Nations (ASEAN)—a group founded in 1967, comprising Indonesia, Malaysia, the Philippines, Singapore, Thailand, and since 1985 Brunei—has impressed observers with its members' ability both to maintain good relations and to coordinate their foreign policies. It has disappointed them with little or no progress toward its declared economic goals. There is little wonder, then, that the real ASEAN is asked to stand up. ASEAN's own statesmen admit that it has several faces or dimensions; Foreign Minister Dhanabalan of Singapore reminds that "we should not lose sight of the fact that Asean is not exclusively an economic organization, but a more rounded collectivity encompassing political, cultural and social dimensions. It is a collective instrument to meet common external problems. . . . But Asean is more than the sum total of its projects. Asean is also an emerging regional consciousness."[1]

The Philippines' Carlos P. Romulo addressed the point this way: "Though the ASEAN is not a political bloc, it has to fulfill its role as an element for peace and balance in the area."[2] Malaysia's Ghazalie Shafie adds that ASEAN "has become more than just a regional intergovernmental organization but a habit of mind among its citizenries. It is an entente of a special kind which transcends boundaries, governments and peoples. Here lies the greatest difference between Asean and other regional groups before and now including the EEC."[3]

These commentaries suggest that there are several ASEANs: one is an economic grouping, one deals with diplomacy, and one expresses a collective consciousness.

In other words, "ASEAN" can refer to an intergovernmental organization, a consultative process among members, and a geographic expression. Most clearly, it is an intergovernmental organization that includes the institutions and projects created to foster economic and cultural cooperation. The progress made toward economic cooperation has been limited, however; in the twenty years of its existence, the ASEAN organization has succeeded in carrying out only two joint industrial projects. Trade tariffs between members have been lowered, but only slightly. This lack of progress is not surprising because the ingredients for economic integration have long been seen to be lacking. Michael Leifer's 1972 observation still holds today: "the various economies of the region, based as they are, in the main, on the production and export of primary goods, do not stand in practical complementary relationship to each other.... The respective countries of the area can offer each other much less than can be gained from bilateral arrangements with a country like Japan."[4] Consequently, a more recent analysis concurs that a "proposal for a free trade zone and customs union would be unacceptable to the member states."[5]

Progress toward cultural cooperation has been more dramatic, however. Social and artistic exchanges have given member nations an increased awareness of their own regional identity. Many cultural and professional transnational organizations located in these five nations have incorporated "ASEAN" in their title. This proliferation of ASEAN-affiliated groups has strengthened the concept of community and regionalism and at the same time enhanced the recognition of the mother intergovernmental organization, which must authorize the use of "ASEAN" by these affiliated groups.

This group awareness has given "ASEAN" its second use as a

geographic expression or "convenient acronym"[6] to group open-market, non-Communist countries of Southeast Asia—all of which are members of ASEAN—even when not referring to the ASEAN organization itself. "ASEAN countries" is a phrase used by outsiders and members to group these high growth-rate, open-market economies in much the same way that Central America is used to identify the countries between Mexico and Colombia.

But ASEAN goes beyond passive geographical codification, evidencing a more vibrant cooperative dimension; "ASEAN" refers to the successful consultative process that these states have used in managing tensions among themselves and in dealing with the external environment. This process toward accommodation began with the ASEAN membership treaty, which these states used as an indirect nonaggression pact and has since been enhanced by the "spirit of ASEAN," which, like "ASEAN," represents the record of good faith and good neighborliness. Operating on bilateral and multilateral levels, the ASEAN process is acknowledged in the oft-used formulas "ASEAN members," "ASEAN states," or "ASEAN partners," which distinguish the consultative process from the ASEAN organization and the ideal of regional community, "ASEAN." Finally, ASEAN used alone aggregates all dimensions: institutions, identity, and interactions.

The ASEAN Symbol

The ASEAN process, which has appeared dynamic, confident, and solid, stands on members' shared values and ideals, which they often cite as "the spirit of ASEAN" and which can be summarized in their perceptions that the process has brought peace and stability to their subregion. While the two decades of cooperation and apparent cordiality among ASEAN members now overshadow the antagonisms and strife present at the foundation of the Association, the local leaders, especially those who remember the mid-1960s, know that founding ASEAN was a breakthrough. For example, President Suharto of Indonesia, a leading force in the creation of the ASEAN process, looked back on the origins of ASEAN and commented that the founders hoped that it was to play a constructive role in solving all problems in Southeast Asia because "the objective of peace was the basic factor that gave birth to ASEAN."[7] Another founder, Singapore's Prime Minister Lee Kwan Yew, reviewed and explained the ASEAN process in an address to the ASEAN Annual Ministerial Meeting (AMM) in 1982: "In 1967 [we] set about building a framework for our cooperation. Thus were Asean members spared from feuding. Of course, we are not without problems and differences. However, we have learned to manage these differences and to contain them. Most important, we have made a habit of working together, of consulting each other over common problems."[8]

The importance and the success of the process is clear when viewed from a conflict-management perspective: "The potential for conflict between ASEAN members will exist for a long time. Perhaps it is surprising that not more disputes reached the boiling point in the first decade."[9] Finally, the address of Prime Minister Prem of Thailand shows that peace, the motivating concept behind the symbol, has been transmitted over the years and administrations. He opened the 1983 annual meeting with this definition: "What Asean stands for is absolutely clear. It stands for peace and prosperity for Southeast Asia."[10]

A conflict-managing process institutionalized by membership in the ASEAN organization is an example of what Joseph Nye called the derivative use of regional organizations: "Shared membership in a regional organization may be considered comparable to statements of good will or nonaggression treaties."[11] Similarly, John Stremlau describes some likely tangible advantages of regional cooperation germane to the ASEAN experience: assistance in the resolution of local disputes; deterrence of secession; help in coordinating domestic policies so that one does not destabilize another; reinforcement of norms of behavior, especially concerning larger members; bolstering a sense of cultural affinity, racial pride, or shared grievances; conference of stature and publicity; lending the appearance of influence with the major powers.[12]

These utilities define the benefits derived from the ASEAN peace; they serve members' national and regime interests, and so create the political will to cooperate. Stremlau emphasizes regime interests, and they are salient to an analysis of ASEAN politics: "The primary and prevalent concerns of Third World governments are with threats to their security that are domestic in origin or emanate in neighboring countries. . . . Developing country elites prefer to rely on regional collective security arrangements to isolate and resolve conflicts or to strengthen their freedom to deal with insurgents.''[13] This strategy represents a rejection of the alternative policies of military action or use of direct assistance from a great-power ally.

ASEAN states have been reluctant to involve a great-power patron in their affairs for a mix of ideological and pragmatic factors. First, the new states are jealous of their new independence and wish to demonstrate self-sufficiency to others and themselves. Also, reliance on the great powers may be difficult to justify in light of protestations of antiimperialism and nonalignment. Pragmatically, these convictions are rooted in the conviction that it is dangerous to become involved in the great powers' rivalries. Then too, the unsuccessful outcome of the war in South Vietnam discredited the value of big-power assistance. Finally, the great powers have encouraged this self-help approach.

ASEAN as a symbol of peace also represents a consensus on the futility of military force to resolve conflicts. Indeed, the foundation of ASEAN followed a contest of force that produced an equilibrium. This consensus has been reinforced because several regimes continue to face preoccupying internal challenges, especially active insurgencies and societal cleavages with violent histories and potential for eruption.

States learned the utilities of accommodation and cooperation, so often referred to as the ''ASEAN spirit,'' bilaterally. They developed a set of shared beliefs, namely that limiting competition has mutual benefits, that the opposite government is better than other regimes likely to arise in that state—and so is worthy of support—and that common problems, like a shared insurgency, could become volatile through what Singapore's Rajaratnam described as ''competitive interference'' by great powers.[14] In this situation, even neutrality can be damaging; a neighbor's inaction in effect allows your insurgents sanctuary. This condition of interdependency fostered a belief that cooperation is the only meaningful way out of mutual destruction.

The other four security-related utilities of cooperation—dispute settlement, prevention of secession, domestic policy coordination, norms of behavior—are also dependent on this deterrence relationship. First, these ASEAN regimes have practiced self-restraint in disputes because they believed that the costs of conflict outweigh the benefits. States have not encouraged secession because they feel vulnerable to this form of destabilization themselves. While smaller states may face conquest and destruction of homeland by the large state, larger neighbors fear the smaller serving as bases for insurgents or terrorists. Costs from wars of attrition and political concerns, such as international reputation or the opponent's invitation of undesirable external aid, also deter larger states. The final dimension of ASEAN cooperation, the organization that institutionalized multilateralism, responds to the anarchical nature of the international system. Since no resolution can be taken as final and conflict is always a possibility, agreements need to be reinforced continually by public evidences of good faith and by interlinking bilateral promises. It is in and through the framework of the organization that these are proffered.

ASEAN Principles

"ASEAN . . . served an immediate political objective of restoring peace between Indonesia, Malaysia and the Philippines in 1967."[15] This common conclusion converges with Nye's derivative utility: ASEAN first served as a face-saving and non-contentious instrument of war-termination diplomacy. The need for such a public and legal instrument is explained by Terry Nardin: "Peace is not merely the absence of war but a social state in which aggression is not feared because peace is guaranteed by a pact creating political institutions to define and enforce the terms of the association."[16] Nardin continues and suggests an etymological link between the words "peace" and "pact." The connection is most explicitly retained in the idea of "a peace," a compact or agreement—typically a solemn agreement—not to fight. ASEAN membership served as such a guarantee and institution.

The use of this organization instead of a precise and formal treaty of peace and nonaggression is explained by the governments' dilemmas. They still had mutual suspicions; yet, they were compelled to promise restraint because competition had proved costly, futile, and foolish. Moreover, the cultural imperative to save face necessitated a formula to allow the aggressive states, Indonesia and the Philippines, to accept failure. The solution, to use the treaty setting up an economic and cultural organization, was a legal means to a modus vivendi and thus peace. ASEAN's symbolic dimension defines these norms by including behavioral expectations and coordination. The organization itself had additional appealing utilities. Inspired by the success and theories of the European Economic Community, regional cooperation was a framework much in use in the 1960s. Its attractiveness was enhanced by optimists' arguments that economic networks of collaboration would spill over and bring about pressures for political accord in the area. If this proved difficult or long-range, others saw cultural exchanges developing a sense of community and regionalism. But most important, the ASEAN organization would provide machinery for reaffirmation of the cooperative process. Substance is reflected in style as commitment to the ASEAN principle of restraint is reaffirmed by the members' adherence to the procedures and machinery of the organization.

The framework reinforces a second principle, respect, wherein states show mutual acceptance by gathering at least annually in a public session. This machinery of the ASEAN organization includes regular and apolitical occasions for meetings. Respect is also shown in communication. States can discuss problems, air grievances, and get explanations through a network of ongoing, multiple-channel consultations. The regular and neutral contexts for meetings are important in preventing distancing; disputants can meet in an ASEAN context knowing that a problem can be compartmentalized or postponed, or discussed in secrecy with or without advocates and mediators. A third principle, responsibility, grew out of this process and the reality of states' interdependence. States practice responsibility by considering effects domestic policies might have on a neighbor. After twenty years, responsibility has also come to mean helping a partner in difficulty. Thus, ASEAN cradles the political process.

The ASEAN Political Process

Describing the participants' desire for peace and the institutions and procedures of their diplomacy does not explain how the ASEAN political process has been sustained for more than twenty years. These procedures and desires are shared and mirrored in other international organizations; but they have not been so successful. Even in the cases where they have, including ASEAN, it is well to remember that "These organizations are little more than governments linked in permanent conclave. They have no power and personality beyond the collective will of governments and no capacity to grow apart from the ability of governments to learn."[17] This caveat about reification is important because usage of ASEAN can be misleading, suggesting at times a new actor or structure of confederation that does not exist. Rather, establishing the imperatives behind accommodation better explains ASEAN's success and demonstrates that ASEAN is neither actor nor confederation, but a consultative process.

The primary motivation behind states' continued participation in this political process—each wishes a secure external environment—shines through the basic norms of behavior: restraint demonstrated by noninterference in other's domestic affairs; respect practiced in consultation; and responsible consideration of others' interests and sensitivities.

The Origins of ASEAN

The salience of ASEAN accommodation and the challenges the states faced is seen in a review of earlier regional cooperation attempts, which show the futility of pursuing regionalistic idealism divorced from shared national and regime interests. Regional cooperation, the commitment of several states to reach common goals by means of joint-policy undertakings, often institutionalized in the form of agencies to fulfill programs, differs from regionalism, which is more a belief that a commonality (if not a community) exists and should be fostered. Regionalism assumes that affinities and shared grievances will promote cohesion; it was important to early Southeast Asian and other Third World movements. States did share a common colonial legacy. Memories of conquest and exploitation enhanced the shared perception that many current problems are or were externally generated by the colonial regime; this served as their bond of bitterness. Such a commonality was observed among ASEAN leaders in Estrella Solidum's work on the formation of an ASEAN community:

It has been mentioned in many speeches and press interviews that colonial experiences have led to disruption of regional exchanges and economic distortions, such as the great gap between the small rich commercial group and the great mass of poor peasants, the plural ethnic societies which breed social and political instabilities; the disturbance of an impersonal administrative system; and an education that further broke the cultural and social continuities.[18]

On the domestic level, this colonial legacy has left a set of obstacles to nation building common to all regimes in developing states. This situational commonality, it is assumed, will produce a sympathy and affinity among leaderships that will provide a basis for collaboration to face challenges from old or new imperialist centers.

On a regional level, it is important to explain further what is meant by the "disruption of regional exchanges." First, there is an ahistorical assumption that precolonial Southeast Asia enjoyed a golden age of peace, prosperity, and unity. This ignores the reality that whether on the mainland or on the archipelagoes, the region was very divided. Second, this grievance blames the end of this golden age on imperialism when European empire building disrupted cultures, leaving the present territorial status quo in the region. Today's nations inherited borders, drawn to suit European interests, which ignored or shattered indigenous economic, religious, linguistic, and social networks. This is especially true across archipelago Southeast Asia, where borders divide several ethnic communities. The Indonesian, Malaysian, and Singaporean area, where the majority of the indigenous people share commonalities of race, religion, and lifestyle, suffered most from this disruption. Consequently, some saw these states and even the Philippines as fragments of a single archipelago proto-state, divided by imperialism, which, even when the tide of European power receded, were not allowed to join together. The fact that the British spheres of Malaya, Singapore, Sabah, and Sarawak did not wish to be absorbed by the larger, former Dutch sphere and chose to perpetuate the division especially irked President Sukarno and his followers, who saw Indonesia as the natural core, a place to which the others could come home.

The imperialist heritage allegedly left another "disruption," the introduction of the Chinese into the Malay world. Small in numbers but powerful in economic reach, the Chinese permeate the archipelago world. Some Malays, perceiving that the Chinese had been imported to satisfy the European need for coolie labor during the nineteenth century, regard them as another negative legacy of the colonial era. Eventually, the largest concentration of Chinese had to be encapsulated and set apart from the Malay world; but this Singapore solution could not be practiced everywhere, nor was the fragmentation and alienation of Malay land seen as desirable. Cultural divisions among Malays from Sumatra to Luzon continue into the postcolonial age, reflecting the residues of the colonial cultures left in each state; these include the different preferences among the elites for social styles, government practices, even religion and language.

The ability to transcend such differences underlies much of the appeal of regionalism, and it occurred at the time of widespread Third World belief that collaboration was the only way to be truly independent and secure from outside powers. Globally, the new states collaborated in macroregional intergovernmental organizations. The lack of progress at this level during the 1950s, however, shifted the focus to more local levels—the region, where the most pressing problems were to be found. Cooperation was inspired by "shared subregional concerns for neutrality, peace, and independent development."[19] In Southeast Asia there were two predecessors to ASEAN, the Association of Southeast Asia (ASA)—comprising Thailand, Malaysia, and the Philippines—founded in July 1961, and Maphilindo, founded in August 1963, whose members were Malaya, Indonesia, and the Philippines. Both associations represent the unsuccessful attempts of newly independent states to deal with the complexities of regional politics by an appeal to regionalism.

ASA is an interesting case because its principles and machinery are much the same as those of ASEAN in its first years. Both were pledged to economic and cultural cooperation and sought to increase consultation through regular foreign ministers' conferences and national secretariats in the respective ministries of foreign affairs. The idea for this regional grouping was first circulated in 1959 by the Philippines and Malaya. The subsequent foundation in 1961 with the membership of Thailand was Southeast Asia's first attempt to regularize consultation and propose coordination of policies when regional issues were at stake. But there were no other takers in Southeast Asia; other countries viewed ASA as a cold-war cluster that would violate their principles, whether socialist, neutralist, or Maoist.

This ideological cleavage does highlight the fact that the pro-West ASA three were sandwiched between left-leaning states and suggests that ASA members may have been motivated by shared policy orientations. The three governments had reason to see a relationship between the cold war and their domestic situations. In the 1950s and early 1960s, each government had been concerned with internal communist insurgencies: The twelve-year antiterrorist "Emergency" was just successfully concluded in Malaya; the Philippines similarly had suppressed the Huks; Thailand's insurgents were still active and were more problematic because they had easy sanctuary in Laos. Significantly, at the time of the formation of ASA, Laos was becoming a flashpoint in the East-West struggle. This Communist threat helped raise a common consciousness among the ASA members, as all were aligned to the West, and bring Thailand into the association. Regionalism, then, served as a nonprovocative facade for a tentative alliance.

When the external environment began to be less threatening due to the Geneva settlements for a neutralized Laos in 1963, ASA began to unravel. The Philippines, which had been one of the most sensitive to cold-war threats, seemed to feel safe enough to break ranks. In mid-1962 it raised a claim to the North Borneo provinces scheduled to be annexed by fellow ASA member Malaya. Apparently, ASA had served its purposes to Manila and could be dismissed at little cost. As for the bond of affinities, the reality is that they were not there. The comment of Indonesia's then foreign minister Subandrio that ASA was "something unreal" because bilateral relations between its members "were unfulfilled" is a useful insight.[20] The Philippines, long isolated from Southeast Asia, felt no commonality with Muslim Malaya. Like strangers after a cloudburst, the ASA allies parted company when the rain stopped.

The Maphilindo plan manifested an even clearer appeal to states to build cooperation based on primordial affinities "among their peoples who are bound together by ties of race and culture." The Manila accord also envisaged "a grouping of the three nations of Malay origin working together in closest harmony." It is more likely, however, that individual national interests and not ethnic magnetism were the reasons behind the membership of the three. Indeed, quite to the contrary, mutual suspicions provide a better explanation for each state's strategy in joining: Each was better able to watch and influence its neighbors. Tunku Abdul Rahman led Malaya into the group to ease the birth of the expanded federation. Indonesia and the Philippines saw Maphilindo as an institution to influence the affairs of this new state by appealing to the organization's spirit. The Philippines also saw this association as a way to deal with and appease Indonesia, which at the time was exhibiting expansionist tendencies. Jakarta was then completing its campaign to wrest West Irian from Dutch control. Ironically, on the other hand, the association could serve to demonstrate local support for this policy. Furthermore, Indonesia used Maphilindo in another way. Even after the initiation of hostilities toward Malaysia, Sukarno continued to support the Maphilindo idea. Seemingly, the organization appealed to him as a framework in which Indonesia could exercise regional leadership (read: hegemony). Sukarno may have been willing to accept Sarawak and Sabah as a new nation or nations within this Maphilindo framework. The acts of aggression during *konfrontasi*, however, destroyed the credibility of both Indonesia and Maphilindo.

While regionalism did not provide a cure, its central grievance that borders do not reflect historical, economic, or social realities serves as a diagnosis of the subregion's problems. To repair this damage, nations first moved in a self-help style to restore lost territories and peoples, complete unification of homelands, or reestablish traditional hierarchical structures. They delayed action until the 1960s because it was only then that the colonial structure was fully dismantled: Malaysia, the state in the center of the region, was the last to become independent. (The other ASEAN members were independent by 1950 and were geographically separated from each other by the British colonies that would become Malaysia and Singapore.) Upon Malayan independence in 1957—or, more importantly, upon the end of British rule in Sabah and Sarawak in the early 1960s—the contending national visions needed to be reconciled. The answer to this challenge was not to be found in ASA's and Maphilindo's affective regionalism, even coupled with consultation machinery. Neither association, ASA or Maphilindo, was able to mute nationalistic interests, and both were destroyed by interstate rivalries that involved irredentism, challenges to others' legitimacy, interference in others' internal affairs, and ultimately Sukarno's war to crush Malaysia. Yet, out of all this came ASEAN "conceived out of the pangs of Konfrontasi, an idea to obviate all future Konfrontasis in the region."[21]

The vitality of the ASEAN process stands in contrast to the other groupings. Unlike them, ASEAN has satisfied the requirement that "cooperative ventures, to succeed, must be related to the prospect of tangible advantage likely to accrue to the principals involved."[22] Ferdinand Marcos's statement that each state's national interest is "almost equivalent to the interests of ASEAN itself"[23] indicates that the ASEAN process does contribute something tangible.

The failures of ASA and Maphilindo illustrate the weakness of a process not built on a convergence of interests. These two cases show that such forms of intergovernmental cooperation cannot be based on altruism or primordial affinities. Rather, using affinities as the foundation for Southeast Asian regionalism is difficult in an area where there is no homogeneity in social structure, political systems, ways of life, or religion.[24] Rather, self-restraint rooted in a fear of consequences lays a more stable foundation. This was not the case with ASA. The defection of the Philippines can be explained by Manila's estimations that the new Malaysia would not be able to protect its integrity or inflict harm. Significantly, Malaysia and Thailand continued cooperation without ASA because their relationship was built on the need to avoid competitive interference along their border. Maphilindo collapsed because the largest power, Indonesia, did not understand the limits of its power. Encouraged by victory over Dutch imperialism both in 1949 and in the 1962 West Irian annexation, and perhaps filled with dreams of a revived-Majapahit empire, Sukarno succumbed to the pressures of the Communist party to use the tactic of military adventurism to bolster his regime.

In the end, however, confrontation among Indonesia, Malaysia, and the Philippines provided the needed object-lesson for the regimes involved. War had been costly and did not change the status quo. Second, several external factors heightened the inclination to restraint. China, engulfed in the most intense period of the Cultural Revolution, was exporting its domestic fanaticism to Communist parties in Southeast Asia, necessitating each government to be on guard. In June 1967 China exploded its first hydrogen bomb, which not only intensified the perception of the Chinese threat but increased the dangers from the Sino-Soviet rivalry. Anxieties were heightened because the United States seemed to be signaling withdrawal from the region. President Lyndon Johnson, on a late 1966 Asian tour, commented that "The key to Asian peace in coming generations is in Asian hands"[25] and he followed up on this theme in his January 1967 state-of-the-union address. In an attempt to unburden itself, Washington was supportive of regional approaches to problem solving. This policy, along with Pakistan's withdrawal from SEATO in June 1967 and the British announcement in August 1967 that it was withdrawing forces from the region, resulted in perceptions that the familiar guarantees to states in the region were weakening.

Third, while governments were concerned with external menaces, they were aware that, as small powers, the most they could do was await the moves of the great powers. On the other hand, they could meet domestic challenges directly. A revival of Huk activity in September 1966 in the Philippines was matched by Thai concerns about its northeast provinces, by Malaysian worries about Communist Party of Malaysia (CPM) bases in southern Thailand, and by Singapore's awareness of its vulnerability to Maoist propaganda during the Cultural Revolution. But perhaps it was Indonesia that faced the largest domestic challenges. The government was still dealing with the aftereffects of the September 30 coup and *konfrontasi*.

The costs of war, domestic imperatives, and external changes inclined the states to restraint, but the twin obstacles to greater collaboration, suspicion, and anxiety, remained. Although Malaysia emerged from *konfrontasi* stronger—it held off the challenges on the battlefield and reaped the benefit of increased nationalism—it viewed Indonesia with uncertainty. Moreover, the birth of an independent Singapore in August 1965 meant the archipelago region was further fragmented into yet another state whose 75 percent Chinese population gave it an orientation different from Malay values. In addition, Singapore was feared by the New Order regime of President Suharto, which felt it had just saved its country from a coup planned by the Chinese-dominated Communist Party of Indonesia (PKI). Singapore was viewed at best as an upstart creation of the overseas Chinese and at worst as a new sanctuary of communism in the region. Malaysian-Philippine relations were negative as a result of Manila's claim on Sabah and its cooperation with Sukarno during *konfrontasi*. Malaysia had just "divorced" Singapore in frustration. Thai-Malaysian relations were the least antagonistic, but they did share a troubled border area: Kuala Lumpur worried about the CPM use of sanctuaries in southern Thailand, and Bangkok was anxious about encouragement to secessionists.

Rapprochement came through Indonesia's lead during 1966 and 1967, and through the good offices of Thailand. Malaysia's deputy premier and representative at the rapprochement negotiations, Tun Abdul Razak, noted that Bangkok "played a very big part in bringing us together, and Thailand is very keen to expand regional cooperation."[26] This broad idea of regional cooperation—easing tensions, limiting competition, even collaborating—fit in with Thai, Malaysian, and Indonesian interests. Singapore would follow for lack of an alternative and the desire to avoid provocation. The Philippines was open to the general principle. The result was a political process to obviate all future *konfrontasi*.

In many ways the new organization that cradled their political process was an expanded ASA; the machinery and principles were not new. The important difference was the membership of the region's largest state and its acceptance of accommodation; the acronym, suggested by the Indonesian foreign minister, Adam Malik, signified a new beginning. And, in reality, ASEAN was new: first, because it confirmed acceptance of the colonial legacy by all five states of the archipelago area, most notably Indonesia; second, because members were well on the way to fulfilling bilateral relationships.

2
The Core of ASEAN:
Malaysia and Indonesia

It all comes down to this. You can imagine Asean without the Philippines, and even without Thailand—though of course the region would be very different. But you cannot imagine Asean without Malaysia and Indonesia, and you cannot have peace in non-Indochinese Southeast Asia without peace between Kuala Lumpur and Jakarta.
—Malaysian official

ASEAN was built on the accommodation between Indonesia and Malaysia. Prior to 1967, during transition from colonialism to independence, Indonesia had challenged and attacked the new nation of Malaysia. With the end of *konfrontasi* came rapprochement and, in the more positive language of Ghazalie Shafie, "a new era of relationship between Indonesia and Malaysia which soon served as the kingpin paving the way for the development of the highly desirable grouping that is Asean."[1]

The following chapters will focus on the bilateral relationships underlying the ASEAN process. The discussion will be divided into two geographical segments: an east flank including Malaysia, Indonesia, the Philippines, and Brunei; and a west flank including Indonesia, Malaysia, Singapore, and Thailand. This chapter will deal with relations between the two states central to the ASEAN process.

Konfrontasi, or the war between Indonesia and Malaysia, began in September 1963 when Jakarta mobs reacted to the establishment of the Federation of Malaysia and lasted until the signing of the

Bangkok Agreement in Jakarta in August 1966. The confrontation included all the Sukarno regime's military, economic, and diplomatic attacks to prevent the union of Malaya with Singapore, Sabah, and Sarawak. Later, after President Sukarno was eclipsed by a new regime in late 1965, the Indonesian leadership moved to rapprochement.

Indonesia's new regime rejected Sukarno's flamboyant, adventurist policies; to them, *konfrontasi* had been futile, costly, and foolish. War had not achieved Sukarno's objective of crushing Malaysia and demonstrating Indonesian primacy: The northern Borneo territories of Sabah and Sarawak remained in union with peninsular Malaya. Moreover, the unsuccessful military attacks increased Malaysian nationalism; Indonesia was held off on the battlefield and the attacks alienated the peoples of Malaysia, including the ethnic Malays. Though the Indonesian trade boycott succeeded in hurting the commercial centers in Malaysia, it cost Indonesia as much. Singapore and Penang, for example, experienced drops in exports and imports; the 8 percent cut in Singapore's economy during the first few months cost thousands of jobs.[2] The same was true for Penang which experienced a drop of 88 percent in exports and 35 percent in imports.[3] But this Indonesian victory was pyrrhic in that the Malay peninsula had been Indonesia's largest trading partner, accounting for one-third of its trade. Moreover, this commerce had been in Indonesia's favor; thus, the boycott meant Indonesia lost significant foreign exchange earnings. These economic strains were seen in Indonesian currency devaluations in April 1964 and shortages of rice. Despite the costs, however, and for whatever reasons— whether he was a victim of his hegemonistic, socialistic, or anti-imperialistic dreams or a prisoner of the increasingly strong PKI[4]—President Sukarno held on to his policy of opposing Malaysia. But others saw the costs and were all the more dismayed by his decision to leave the United Nations in January 1965 and his failure to find international, especially Third World, support for his war strategy.

A watershed came when the PKI attempted to seize power at the end of September 1965. Those who were already critical of *konfrontasi* and the concurrent growing domestic crisis reacted with a counter-coup. After first consolidating power (under General

Suharto, who assumed effective power in March 1966), the new regime started on the road to rapprochement with Malaysia by means of silence on contentious issues. A series of quiet contacts and low-key diplomatic missions followed from June 1966. The unsettled domestic situation in Indonesia demanded that the policy reversal be slow and cautious so that the new regime not lose face and that it avoid a Weimar-like stigmata of defeat. Likewise, the question of relations with the new city-state, Singapore, interfered; Indonesia's announced intention to accord recognition to the city-state before it had done so to Malaysia resulted in a period of "open rancor."[5] This initiative was perhaps necessary to assuage yet-active Sukarno loyalists who could view the birth of Singapore as breaking up Malaysia. Such had been Sukarno's reaction, as heard in his Independence Day Speech of August 1965: "Singapore has separated itself from 'Malaysia.' Yes, 'Malaysia' is beginning to fall apart from the inside! And it will fall apart completely and go to pieces."[6] But Malaysian leaders did not let this slight abort the process; contacts were maintained throughout. By August 1966 the two reached an accommodation in the Bangkok Agreement to Normalize Relations, which provided a de jure means to reconciliation. Having terminated hostilities, the relationship required assurances about the future. Indonesia, the erstwhile aggressor, needed to convince Malaysia of its honorable intentions, especially since domestic politics were not clear to outsiders at this time. Though President Suharto assumed executive powers in March 1966, Sukarno was still a voice with a faction and perhaps a future.

To cement the relationship, the new Indonesian regime made several confidence-building gestures in an area of mutual concern—the control of Communist terrorists in Borneo. Adam Malik touched on this shared problem soon after the Bangkok Accord negotiations.[7] Insurgency was a joint security problem as PKI groups had established networks in Sabah and Sarawak, where large ethnic Chinese populations (Sarawak 32 percent, Sabah 23 percent) could provide support. There was also a large non-Malay indigenous population that did not identify with the Malay/Islamic-dominated Federal government and could be lured into resistance movements. Kuala Lumpur remembered the difficulties of the Emergency—the twelve-year war to suppress the Chinese-supported Communist guerrillas on the Malay peninsula—and knew that controlling and integrating these new provinces, especially the independent-minded Sarawak, into the federation was already a challenging task of nation building. (Emergency rule had to be declared there in 1966.) Having to suppress a Communist insurgency, which was aided by sanctuaries inside Indonesia, along a long border in provinces separated by the South China Sea was a nightmare. The Indonesian initiative was singularly appropriate to healing the wounds of *konfrontasi*. By October, liaison teams for communications were set up and plans for joint controls were suggested.[8] Malaysia and Indonesia moved to root out insurgents who could destabilize either regime.

But Kuala Lumpur still had to be concerned about dealing with Indonesia's more subtle expectations to be a leader in the region. The current Indonesian regime, while not a victim of grandiose expectations, is influenced by what has been called a "sense of entitlement."[9] It is based on pride in revolutionary achievement (they fought for their independence, unlike others who were granted it peacefully), size of population, land and maritime possessions, natural resources, and strategic location, and it includes a leadership role in Southeast Asia. Sukarno's dream was frustrated, as the former British spheres continued ties to London, fueling his charge that imperialism still influenced the region. Ironically, the experiences during *konfrontasi* assisted rapprochement with his successors. Malaysia faced future relations with its large neighbor more confidently because it had acquitted itself well during *konfrontasi*. Not only did the military perform professionally but the population demonstrated loyalty. Subsequently, a more confident Malaysia could afford some deference to Indonesia's "sense of entitlement"; they conducted negotiations in secret and agreed to "ascertain" the wishes of the people of northern Borneo concerning merger into the Malaysian Federation.

The form of this agreement fostered the rapprochement. It followed Ghazalie Shafie's principle for a peaceful settlement: Malaysia's sovereignty should not be questioned, and Indonesia should not lose face.[10] General Suharto's redefinition of *konfrontasi* as the "struggle for the rights of those people [Sabah and Sarawak] for democratic self-determination"[11] allowed Indonesia to accept Malaysia with honor if it could be ascertained if these citizens wanted to remain in the Federation. Furthermore, these negotiations helped to redress the irritation that helped precipitate *konfrontasi*, namely, that Indonesia had not been fully consulted in this regional matter. The 1966 negotiations and agreement satisfied Indonesia's need to be consulted. Meanwhile, the formula of recognizing the northern Borneo peoples' participation in local elections as the means of ascertaining their popular will to be part of Malaysia acknowledged what Malaysia fought to prove—its sovereignty over that area. Finally, the departure of British troops in August appeared to fulfill Indonesia's goal of removing imperialist forces from the area.

These lessons about hierarchy, consultation, and sovereignty learned from the rapprochement process had, in the words of Bernard Gordon, an important by-product: the foundation of the ASEAN organization.[12] Indonesia snatched victory out of the jaws of disaster when it exercised a regional leadership role and proposed the organization for cooperation. And the initiative reaffirmed the Indonesian-Malaysian relationship by further demonstrating Jakarta's acceptance of the Federation. The symbolic function of ASEAN as a nonaggression pact is clear: it was only after the August 7 establishment of the ASEAN organization that Indonesia and Malaysia exchanged diplomatic recognition on August 31, 1967.

Throughout the next few years, the two regularized their collaboration on internal security and created a firm bond. Jakarta's acceptance of elections ended the northern Borneo states problem. The situation so reversed as military cooperation pushed forward that Malaysia helped solve Indonesia's logistic problems along their Borneo border. The Indonesians were "assisted by the Malaysian helicopters which help to fly in supplies and evacuate wounded Indonesians for treatment at Kuching [Sarawak]."[13] Indonesian and Malaysian commanders met each month to pool information. Results were good as the number of rebels seemed to fall. The Malaysian-Indonesian turnabout was so complete that Foreign Minister Malik found it necessary in 1969 to deny that a confederation existed between the two states.[14] Their relationship was even characterized as a "love affair" due to the policies of Malaysia's second prime minister, Razak (1970–76). Since his administration both sides have sought to modify this impression and base the relationship not on romanticism but on specific collaboration.

Management of the Malacca Straits and the 1982 treaty to delimit the South China Sea boundary illustrate more recent accommodation. While Indonesian sovereignty in the South China Sea does cut between East and West Malaysia, Kuala Lumpur enjoys rights of fishing, transit, rescue, and air lanes and takes part in joint police patrols in Indonesian waters.[15] The two countries have also found it advantageous to coordinate their policies toward the Philippines and Brunei. More challenging were the strains during 1979 when Malaysia adopted the policy of pushing the Vietnamese boat people back out to sea, effectively sending them to Indonesia. Fortunately, the creation of temporary refugee camps assuaged this problem. Questions about border demarcation in Sabah and the presence of illegal Indonesian immigrants in Malaysia (an estimated 100,000 in Johore's 1.3 million population[16]) have been generally handled by postponement or silence.[17] An exception that exposed the grievance occurred in 1984 when discussions appeared in the Malaysian press. Unemployment or rising crime associated with the recession of the early 1980s or a Malaysian desire to be a more assertive younger brother occasioned this departure from the rule of silence. A better economic situation later made laborers again desirable, and so the two have tried to complement each other's interest by a 1984 agreement to curtail the entry of illegal workers while still admitting some to help meet the Malaysian labor shortage.[18]

These problems point to the security dimension at the heart of this and most ASEAN relationships. Porous borders, which allow illegal immigration and the influx of Vietnamese boat people, provide both governments a daily reminder that states are not able fully to control entry to their territories. Helping each other control the borders is, on the other hand, a way to compensate for this vulnerability. Interior Minister Ghazalie Shafie of Malaysia captured the essence of this cooperation, and its broader significance, during a meeting of the General Border Committee in 1979: "Let the understanding and cooperation now closely binding [our] two countries serve as a warning to any power that has ill intentions towards us. We will act together to oppose this threat completely and we shall never tolerate any nonsense from anywhere."[19]

Collaboration on joint border patrols strengthens the relationship with a higher common interest; these partners have virtually freed themselves from insurgency supported by third parties in Borneo.

Such is the success that operations are being scaled down, and the 1986 Border Committee moved to concentrate efforts on the Malacca Straits.[20] Likewise, domestic concerns play an important role in the decision of both to continue accommodation. Should the memory of the military's difficulties and the economic costs of *konfrontasi* fade, the tasks of development and consolidation provide a series of regular reminders that both need good neighbors.

Indonesian Domestic Constraints

Malaysia believed in Indonesian sincerity because it realized that the New Order regime faced preoccupying domestic challenges. Adam Malik spoke of this inward focus when he explained Indonesia's slowness in the rapprochement process: "The fact that, for some eight months past, we have had no opportunity to make our attitude manifest . . . has been caused by developments both in our own country and also in the international world which throughout the period have called for the whole attention of the government."[21] The developments included the immediate financial crisis and insurgency resulting from the coup, for the PKI was resisting in pockets throughout the archipelago. Second, the New Order regime had to address basic economic problems that had brought down Sukarno or more turmoil would follow. The costs of war—inflation, fallen exports, and massive debt—served as economic lessons to deter any further resort to adventurism as a solution. In addition, to persuade creditors to reschedule debts, Jakarta needed to demonstrate good behavior. Last, the new regime sought to consolidate power; putting officials of the old order on trial not only removed opposition, it demonstrated a repudiation of its past. Consequently, Malaysia put greater credence in this regime's initiatives for rapprochement. In sum, Malaysian fears of adventurism and hegemonism were assuaged because the new regime faced many internal challenges caused by *konfrontasi*.

The New Order regime of President Suharto has long been preoccupied (some say traumatized) with the internal Communist threat. After the coup attempt, it faced the massive task of suppressing a well-organized political group that had a membership in the millions. Eventually, through military action and detention camps, the opposition was reeducated, intimidated, eliminated, or imprisoned. Yet, though the round-up could be called complete by 1970, the official line feared the "iceberg tactics" of the Communists, who threatened to resurface when conditions would encourage another insurgency. The scenario foresees the Communists regrouping and waiting to capitalize on unfulfilled economic expectations. The regime's counterattack has been the "resilience" strategy, which calls for economic development so as to raise the standard of living and thus foreclose this type of exploitation to the Communists.

Politically, the regime has sought to consolidate its hold through the process of national elections.[22] These are useful to deny the Communists an argument about political freedoms and also to perform the positive function of allowing all a forum to present their views. The elections, or "feasts of democracy" as they are known, serve to give recognition to all interests, drawing them into the approved political process, itself a unifying ritual. This is not without risks: the political process has to be carefully managed or there is a danger of deepening cleavages in the nation. Hence, elections in Indonesia (the first postcoup elections were in 1971; others were in 1977, 1982, and 1987) become a major preoccupation for the regime involving great care in selection of time, months of advance preparation, and anxious watching after the event. *Tempo* commented: "A general election in Indonesia is not a civil war, but the tension is similar."[23] While the outcomes are virtually assured, surprises can happen. For example, the government's defeat in Jakarta in 1977 (since reversed in 1982) "raised the specter of persistent mass urban opposition."[24]

Next on the regime's domestic agenda are three major social cleavages that demand constant vigilance: Chinese-indigenous relations; the rise of fundamentalist Islam; and geographic separatism.[25] The Chinese community has been problematic both in its role in Indonesian society and in relation to the state's foreign policy. Integration of this physically distinct race has been hindered by Chinese attachment to their language and customs, as well as their successful role as middlemen in the local economy. They are viewed as clannish, snobbish exploiters and, perhaps worse, suspected of disloyalty. The perception of the Chinese as disloyal aliens was reinforced after the unsuccessful September 30 coup. Chinese predominance in the PKI confirmed suspicions that all Chinese were a fifth column for the People's Republic of China, then a revolutionary state. Serious riots against Chinese communities in August 1973, November 1980, and September 1984 indicate the continued strength of popular feelings. As for foreign policy, these events and perceptions have blocked normal relations with China and complicate dealings with Singapore also.

The second social cleavage is in the Islamic community. Fundamentalist Muslims have become more politically active, seeking to use state power to advance orthodoxy. External factors complicate this cleavage also. The Islamic revolution in Iran has encouraged some fundamentalists. Regionally, there is an interconnection with Malaysia on this issue. Kuala Lumpur, like Jakarta, faces opposition from religion-based political movements, but they have been controlled by the dominant, moderate-Malay party, the United Malays National Organization (UMNO). Likewise, in Indonesia, the Muslim United Development Party (PPP) has not been able to unseat the government's party (it did garner 28 percent in 1982 but only 16 percent in the last election). Both parties have similar goals and are in communication. The shared challenge to the regimes is summed up in the observation "that a change of fortunes away from [either] of the governments towards its respective opposition is bound to enhance the strength of the rival of its counterpart [government]."[26]

The first major challenge from fundamentalism came in 1973 when the government attempted to secularize marriage laws. Similarly, in 1978, a government initiative to give some legal standing to Javanese mysticism as a religion (the *kepercayan* issue) also was checked by the fundamentalists. In January 1981 the government bowed to pressure and banned gambling and television commercials which were seen to glorify Western lifestyles. The PPP's nomination of a vice-presidential candidate to run against President Suharto's choice in 1988 was another gesture to show dissatisfaction with the state's secular orientation. In response to this cleavage, the regime has tried to separate the political parties from religious affiliation, requiring that parties accept the national ideology of toleration of all religions (*Pancasila*). In return, all are allowed autonomy in their own sphere.

The third cleavage is geographic separatism. A "new nation," the Indonesian state includes many peoples and cultures, separated by distance and time, who were only amalgamated by the Dutch colonizers in the last century. From the start, groups have attempted to secede from the state. The South Moluccan independence group drew international attention when it hijacked a train in the Netherlands and held hostages during 1975. Acheh, on northern Sumatra, and West Irian, at the other end of the archipelago, both flared up in 1977. The West Irian situation has been more volatile and lasting because secessionists see themselves as a different people from the main racial stock of Indonesia; their sanctuaries in the neighboring, ethnically related state on the island, Papua-New Guinea, make suppression more difficult and complicate relations with that state.

The regime's sensitivity to exploitation of its frontier weaknesses was evidenced during the East Timor crisis in 1975. Because the then-Portuguese colony seemed headed for independence under a leftist regime, Jakarta feared that this small state, situated in the eastern archipelago, might serve as a base for Communist and separatist insurgents. These anxieties, rooted in past experiences when it was so used, were increased by the Communist victories in Indochina in April 1975. After a year of diplomatic maneuvering the Indonesian regime decided on a military solution in December 1975. The ensuing "pacification" severely tested the military for at least three years and is not yet completely resolved.

In addition to these items on the national agenda, the regime itself faces the direct challenges of corruption charges and an imminent succession of leadership. The grievance underlying a charge of corruption is not that some have enriched themselves but that they are not using their positions of power to better the nation. This undermines the legitimacy of the ruling class and the flashpoint has most often been student riots. A listing of these—1970 riots over gasoline prices, the 1971 boycott of the elections, 1972 reactions to Mrs. Suharto's mini-Indonesia park, the 1973 riots in response to the student coup in Thailand, 1974 actions centered on the visit of Prime Minister Tanaka of Japan, 1978 when newspapers were closed and Vice-President Sultan Hamengku stepped down, 1987 disruptions when President Mitterand of France was jostled by students protesting a devaluation, and 1989 demonstrations supporting peasants' land rights—shows that this grievance has been regularly and dramatically brought up. Even the president and his wife are called upon to deny such charges. Corruption and competence of the regime were put under a spotlight in 1975 when the state-run oil company went bankrupt. Concerns about succession will more and more preoccupy Indonesia's leadership as President Suharto nears the end of his fifth term in 1992. Indications are that he will not run again, so individuals are already preparing their platforms and power bases.

This overview of crises and problems is presented not to suggest disaster but rather to show that events regularly draw the attention of the leadership to domestic problems. Solving them by creating new jobs, increasing food production, developing energy sources, managing the large national debt, and alleviating the population crush on Java is what ''resilience'' requires, and it is what inclines the government to seek good relations with its neighbors.

Malaysia's Domestic Constraints

Malaysia values good neighbors, especially Indonesia, for collaboration against Communist subversives and the primary security benefits, acceptance and noninterference. Soon after rapprochement the relationship with its large neighbor became more important: In January 1968, the British formalized their intention to withdraw from bases in Southeast Asia. Likewise, a secure relationship with Indonesia was important when the Philippines raised its claim to North Borneo in 1968. This time, unlike the first Philippine challenge, Indonesia was quietly supportive of Malaysia. The two joined in disdain as they saw regional cooperation being thwarted by the apparent cause of Manila's claim, domestic campaign politics.

The real challenges to security, however, come from within and are so preoccupying—Mahathir has described Malaysia as ''a society balanced on a razor's edge''[27]—that an inward focus is inescapable. Good relations with Indonesia became even more important in 1969 when the Malaysian regime faced severely destabilizing internal problems. That regime, known as the Alliance government, was a coalition led by the UMNO, with the Malaysian Chinese Association (MCA) and the Malaysian Indian Congress (MIC). As a coalition it is a Malay commitment to the multiracial model for the Federation. Though it accorded Malay predominance, such a structure was also a confidence-inspiring compromise, as the Malay/UMNO leadership signaled its openness to consultation and the rights of other communities. The elections of May 1969 took away the Alliance's two-thirds majority in the Parliament, significant because this was the quota needed to amend the constitution. Riots between Malays and Chinese followed, and a martial-law government took control until February 1971. Malaysia appeared to be on the brink of civil war, a situation that Sukarno would have been happy to exacerbate during his "crush Malaysia" policy. Yet, during these difficulties, the new regime in Jakarta showed its good faith by pursuing a policy of silence on the events in Malaysia. Moreover, rather than contributing to the problem, President Suharto helped to reestablish normality with a visit to Malaysia in March 1970. In one stroke, he reassured the Malay regime and the Chinese community. Dr. Tan Chee Khoon of the Gerakan party commented:

> In a strange way, President Suharto and the Indonesians have become a source of hope to the Malay Chinese. We know . . . President Suharto has greatly improved his government's policies towards the Indonesian Chinese. We also expect [he] has counselled moderation and conciliation on racial questions during his visit here, just as Foreign Minister Malik has done on previous visits to Malaysia since last May.[28]

This 1969 crisis, like the earlier Emergency (1948–1960), parallel, as political trauma, the 1965 coup attempt in Indonesian thinking. The regimes seemed to draw similar lessons; both perceived the state as extremely vulnerable to disruption by groups that were culturally, economically, or racially alienated and that could be manipulated by outside forces. The antidote to disaffection was the economic reform strategy that planned to involve all groups in a common effort of nation building. More specifically, it assumed that loyalty to the state could be achieved by giving citizens a stake in a rising prosperity. The tactic converges with the Indonesian concept of "resilience."

The Malay regime's anxiety about managing a multiracial society is seen in the policy of "silence." The 1969 experience resulted in

Sedition Laws, which legislated restrictions on personal and political liberties by forbidding any public questioning or discussion of the "special bargain" behind the Malaysian state. This bargain between the two major ethnic groups had its inception in the 1956 preparations for the independence of Malaya. It sought to recognize and reconcile the special rights of the Malays, as first inhabitants, with the economic power of the ethnic Chinese in these ways: In return for the retention of their dominant role in the economy and the citizenship principle of *jus solis*, the Chinese agreed to a state with Malay and Islamic characteristics. Also included in the bargain were special concessions to the Malays (expressed as "natural rights" of the original inhabitants of the land, called *bumiputras*) in the form of land reservations and quotas in the civil service, scholarship, and business licenses.

The consensus had held through the early 1960s, although racial riots in 1964 revealed the growing antagonisms between the communities. When by 1965 it seemed that the *konfrontasi* threat could be weathered, the Malay-Chinese tensions worsened and reached an impasse, only resolved by the ejection of the large Chinese enclave of Singapore. The Malay regime had acted in the hope of restoring a favorable domestic distribution of ethnic power. Yet the Chinese community was still a substantial segment of the population, with a younger generation that either did not know or did not appreciate the circumstances that necessitated the original bargain. Their call for a "Malaysian Malaysia" represented a move to revise the original bargain. This, in turn, raised fears in the Malay community of becoming like American Indians: pushed off to the margins on reservations. Concurrently, the growing sense of Islam strengthened Malay cohesion and will to resist. The electioneering during the 1969 campaign revealed an unraveling of the old accords when both the UMNO leaders and the opposition indulged in open debate on these questions and so violated what had been the unwritten law of Malaysian politics,[29] silence on the original bargain.

Resolving the 1969 crisis involved reasserting a commitment to the original bargain and power sharing in the form of a new coalition, the National Front. It also meant codification of silence. These Amended Sedition Laws are based on the belief that racialism has to be recognized and can be controlled by measures that prevent popular passions and prejudices from being aroused. More recently, the government showed its anxiety by limiting the right of comment to political societies; social or friendly societies were excluded.[30] Recent breaches of the rule of silence demonstrate the continued salience of racialism, most often euphemized as communalism, and the regime's need for vigilance. Public discussion of racial prerogatives and the distribution of power emerged in Parliament and at the 1986 MCA convention, despite its partnership with UMNO in the National Front government. Debate centered on the government's (i.e., UMNO's) New Economic Policy, which has set a goal of increasing Malay prosperity by affirmative-action policies. The NEP was primarily designed to ease the economic and social grievances of the Malays who felt second class, left out of their nation's wealth. In this respect the NEP has been successful as the average Malay has bettered his situation over the years of independence. On the other hand, the Chinese and Indian communities have felt the pain of state-sponsored discrimination. Some MCA members questioned support of this policy because many Chinese voters defected to other parties during the August 1986 elections. Malay dissatisfaction was also made public. A speech by a Malay former minister in September proved inflammatory. He commented: ''Let us make no mistake—the political system in Malaysia is founded on Malay dominance.''[31] Proclaiming this may have been indelicate or insensitive to other groups in Malaysia; but it is an accurate statement of the original bargain and of political reality in the regime. Passions were raised, however, by his addition that Malays, if threatened, ''might even consider a merger with Indonesia.'' Publication of the speech in the Malaysian press, which required top-level approval, added anxiety to the anger. But by year's end there was a return to normal rules. A denouement came in the form of the king's opening address to Parliament, in which he advised all to exercise caution in debating this issue.[32] The rule of silence was further strengthened in other ways. The Secrets Acts were toughened in 1986, including more stringent control of the press,[33] a trend mirrored at the same time in Indonesia and Singapore.

In sum, the specter of the 1969 riots haunts the regime and underlies the perception that Malaysia is a society balanced on a razor's edge. When in late 1987 the MCA joined with the DAP, the other Chinese party, and so broke ranks with its coalition partner over the language question in Chinese schools, UMNO reacted with a sense of emergency. The comment "We moved to the edge of a precipe last week"[34] summarized the government's anxiety about communal cleavages.

As divisive as the racial cleavage and internal politics have become, insurgency threatens national stability, not just regime existence. Admittedly, this could be a convenient pretext for authoritarianism, but events prove the validity of this concern. The September 1975 bombing of the National Monument, in the wake of the fall of Saigon, forced the government to focus on the Communist Party of Malaya once again. New security regulations modeled on procedures used in the Emergency period were instituted, and the regime readied its defenses against Communist subversion. But combating this insurgency is not just an internal matter. The CPM has sanctuaries in southern Thailand, which must be rooted out if the government is to control fully the northern part of peninsular Malaysia. This important internal security concern is dependent on good relations with Thailand (a factor to be discussed in the Malaysian-Thai relationship). Should the Thai government, however, prove uncooperative in combating the insurgents, as it did for a short time in 1976, collaboration with Indonesia would be raised to higher importance. This is recognized in both capitals, and its implications are just as clear: Indonesia's army would not be able to resist a call for intervention to preserve its forward defense line. A de facto security alliance therefore results.[35]

Another concern to the Malaysian regime is the arrival of fundamentalist Islam in the nation. In addition to social disharmony, this has had political impact by strengthening a rival party to the UMNO, the Parti Islam (Pas), which is strong in the northern Malaysian states (and just across the Straits from the stronghold of the Indonesian PPP in Acheh, Sumatra). Viewed as dangerous because its policy to further Islamize Malaysia would polarize the nation, Pas presents a danger to the domestic political accommodation. While UMNO has continued to win in national and state elections, the fear of a broader fundamentalist movement remains. From the late 1970s all ASEAN governments have carefully watched this movement. The September 1978 and June 1979 *dakwah* fundamentalist raids on Hindu temples were important flashpoints of violence that could not be easily dismissed in multireligious Malaysia, especially at the time of the Islamic revolution in Iran. Fortunately, while the events in the

Middle East inspired some fundamentalists, they horrified most Malaysians and reinforced the rationality of tolerance.

Yet, in the north where the population is more traditional and rural, the regime keeps close watch on political activities. Concern about Libyan funding and missionaries was voiced in 1982. Finally, the government had to impose virtual martial law in the northern states in mid-1984. The Kedah state government has been concerned about extremists' movements, which have used leaflets and audio-cassettes to instigate Muslims to rebel.[36] In November 1985 at Memali, Kedah, fighting between security forces and Pas supporters resulted in the death of eighteen, including Ibrahim Mahmood, Pas official and religious leader. Curfews and a ban on religious meetings resulted. The situation, on the whole, seems manageable as long as the majority of Muslims support UMNO, but the concern about ethnic-religious movements, justified by consideration of cases like the Memali or *dakwah* incidents, leads some to fear the worst-case scenario of a Malaysia torn by a racial-religious civil war, exploited by the Communist powers, and resulting in an ideological state or states (either Communist or Islamic) using its territories to serve insurgents attacking all of Malaysia's neighbors, namely, the ASEAN region.

Last in this series of national challenges is the influx of refugees from southern Indochina since 1978. Economically, the cost of maintaining the refugees threatens the resilience strategy. Socially, the refugees upset the racial balance; the initial arrivals were ethnic Chinese. Finally, on a national security level, the easy arrival of the refugees served to remind Malaysia that it was not so far from the front line with Communist Vietnam, even though the border is not contiguous. This new geographic consciousness has since resulted in a new military base being built in the Northeast.

Domestic constraints explain both Malaysian and Indonesian regimes' valuing of secure borders and subsequent commitment to mutual restraint. This convergence of interest has induced both to collaborate in rooting out an interdependent security threat, the insurgency in their border areas. Their successes have added more areas of common interest, which bolster the original relationship to the extent that each identifies its neighbor's stability with its own.

3
Completing the Core: Singapore

We must take care of each other's heart and feelings as we are neighbors.

—Deputy Foreign Minister Abdul Kadir

DIPLOMACY between Malaysia and Singapore reverses roles, for Malaysia is the larger state and Singapore is, at first glance, more vulnerable. This relationship moved from verbal confrontation through a rapprochement to a collaborative plateau; these two have managed suspicions and practiced restraint, respect, and responsibility because both realize that their external security and internal stability are interdependent.

Malaysia and Singapore

The most antagonistic period between Malaysia and Singapore spanned the years of Singapore's union with Malaysia and reached into the early ASEAN era. Separation from Malaysia had been emotional and dangerous: The remark of Dr. Mahathir in 1965, then a young UMNO backbencher, that Lee Kwan Yew was a good example of the "insular, selfish and arrogant type of Chinese" represented the Malay perception of Lee's assertive policies.[1] Acrid exchanges on this point were common in the months before the August 1965 separation. The UMNO responded to Chinese assertiveness with "If Malays were 'hard-pressed' and their interests unprotected they would be forced to merge their country with Indonesia," coupled with Deputy Prime Minister Razak's suggestion that Singapore replace Lee.[2] Lee responded by publicly attacking the "natural rights" of Malays.[3] When Lee labeled Malaysia a "medieval feudal society," Tunku Abdul Rahman compared the charge to the ranting of a mad and frustrated man.[4]

Separation, or, as it was called, "the divorce," did not end these Malay-Chinese problems; it only made them less direct and less immediately pressing. Moreover, Malaysia, not yet out of the *konfrontasi*, was preoccupied with the war with Indonesia. Soon, however, the tensions between the two "divorcees" heightened as Kuala Lumpur joined in the rapprochement with Jakarta. Viewing this as a possible Malay coalition, Singapore began a program of putting its independence on a surer foundation. Some of these policies, however, produced negative reactions in a spiral of increasing hostility between Singapore and the two larger Malay states, Malaysia and Indonesia.

Aggressiveness and seeming insensitivity marked the diplomacy of these early years. Though a member of ASEAN, Singapore did not place great confidence in the pledge of nonaggression, nor did it have realistic expectations or desires about the group's economic and cultural goals. In fact, Singapore was viewed as a "dampener" of early ASEAN activities, sending only low-level officials to meetings in those years.[5] Singapore inclined more to self-help and felt compelled to demonstrate its sovereignty and ability to survive. This "Singapore-centric" policy, as it was then criticized, was reflected and resented in a series of minor irritating interactions. For example, in March 1968 Singapore announced that it would send home the Malaysians left unemployed when the British bases closed. This involved about 45,000 workers. A stand-off was reached when Kuala Lumpur threatened to deport 60,000 Singaporeans working in Malaysia.[6] Later, tensions were renewed when Singapore authorities inflamed Malaysian public opinion by forceably cutting the hair of some Malaysian youths. This seemingly minor incident was to keep the two from comparing notes at the Non-Aligned Conference at Lusaka.[7]

National security policies resulted in additional examples of provocation, best summarized by a 1969 caption: "Singapore—Asia's

Little Israel.''[8] The comparison was suggested by Singapore's use of Israeli advisers to the armed forces and by reference to an intention to follow the Israeli model and achieve prosperity and security even though surrounded by hostile, backward, Muslim neighbors. A later model was less acrid but equally demeaning. This referred to Singapore as Venice: a city-state of advanced civilization shining out from a world in the Dark Ages. Today's model of Switzerland avoids such confrontational imagery.[9]

Besides verbal insensitivities, the defense preparations of the city-state added to tensions. By fortifying itself to raise the cost of conquest, in what has been called the "poison shrimp" strategy, Singapore hoped to dissuade an invader. This strategy's offensive tactics, including tanks and air base facilities around the region, sought to restrict conflict to an area outside the city-state, thus turning the table on the aggressor by bringing the battle to its homeland. But offensive capabilities unnerve one's closest neighbors. Kuala Lumpur questioned the move to acquire tanks in August 1971 in light of the fact that Malaysia had none. Similar misgivings about Singapore's F16 aircraft and Awac still exist, but, because of the matured ASEAN process, they are muted. Nevertheless, continued denial of access to the Johore training center (with only a symbolic exception, illustrating a concession to the ASEAN image[10]) remind that confidence between the two is limited, if not at the leadership level, then at the popular level. Kuala Lumpur gives concern for its citizens' anxieties as reason for exclusion: it is reluctant to have Singaporean (read: Chinese) troops on its land. The 1989 decision to build another causeway may signal greater reciprocal trust as both are willing to chance increased vulnerability as they set up a second bridge over their protective moat.

Another set of tensions in the early years related to Singapore's potential choice of allies. Due to its size, negative Malaysian attitudes, and the Malaysian-Indonesian collaboration, the most realistic evaluation of the city-state's situation was that Singapore "is capable of self-protection for a period of time sufficient to bring political pressure on the aggressor."[11] Accordingly, to bolster its political position, Singapore could offer itself as a base to a great power; but the choice of patron had different implications to Malaysia. China would give the CPM and the PKI sanctuary; the USSR, then making its debut in the Indian Ocean, might support new forms of Communist subversion or intensify great-power competition in the region. Surprisingly now, at one point Malaysia had even feared an Indonesian base in Singapore.[12]

The best option for Singapore was the United States. At first, however, the city-state hesitated to become too closely involved with the United States. As part of a diplomatic strategy to bolster independence by gaining global and especially Third World and Indonesian recognition, Singapore voiced policies of nonalignment.[13] Malaysians perceived these as confirmation that Singapore was leaning more to the left, and so these moves added to the local tension. Such fears faded when Singapore, with an assured international status, looked more to the United States. Several reasons account for this policy change, including departure of the traditional guarantor, Britain. The United States could serve as a guarantor of, but not be in, Singapore. Conveniently, the U.S. military was already in the Philippines, Thailand, and South Vietnam. Singapore also saw the important economic benefits from good relations with the developed world, especially access to the large U.S. market. Last, U.S. ideology and tactics were not as disturbing to Singapore's neighbors as those of China or the USSR. Indeed, Indonesia was quietly pursuing the same path.

Singapore's Domestic Constraints

Singapore's preoccupation with domestic development explains both its move toward the United States and the antagonisms that challenged an accommodation with Malaysia. Access to markets was a major consideration because Singapore's leaders were concerned about the destabilizing effects of unemployment. Having endured riots as late as 1966, the regime hoped economic growth would satisfy the population and prevent leftists from taking advantage. Therefore, this strategy of seeking tranquillity through prosperity (the resilience model) became more important than a defense buildup, especially since Singapore's leaders really did not expect an invasion. (They reasoned that neither neighbor wanted the additional Chinese population in its state; Malaysia itself had only just decided to eject them.) The dangers were to come from internal dissent; the solution was to give all a stake in the status quo.

By the time Singapore neared its twenty-fifth anniversary of self-rule in 1984, such dangers would seem long overcome. Singapore achieved an enviable prosperity and tranquillity. One observer commented that Singapore's was "*the* world's most successful economy" (author's emphasis).[14] More important to domestic stability, there was "full employment, rising real incomes and constant if not declining income inequality."[15] Prosperity worked to bolster the regime for these twenty-five years; its party, the People's Action Party (PAP), enjoyed nearly unanimous hold on the Parliament during the boom years. But with prosperity came a sophisticated populace and demands for political liberties. This has unsettled Prime Minister Lee, who views discord from the perspective of the troubled 1950s, and has made him preoccupied with the threat from within. A recession, the economic irony for this anniversary period, meant the regime would not have largesse to assuage demands. Despite all of Singapore's achievements, then, the fear, Singapore senior statesman S. Rajaratnam said, is that "all this can break up and disappear totally. All might be totally lost."[16] Perhaps not surprisingly, the 1984 elections, which reduced the PAP's seats by one, bringing the opposition up to two seats in Parliament, severely unsettled Prime Minister Lee. In 1985 Lee announced he would postpone his retirement until 1990 to avoid a transition in these times. The regime has begun to silence the foreign press, having reined in the domestic press years earlier. So far it has moved against the *Asian Wall Street Journal*, *Time*, and the *Far Eastern Economic Review*. It attempted to curtail criticism from the Law Society by parliamentary means but faced opposition from the lawyers. In the spring of 1987 twenty-two were detained without trial, released, and some rearrested. These incidents show a new type of opposition—not insurgency, but democratic challenge from Singapore's well-educated population, which is well aware of liberal democracy in other developed countries.

Singapore's regional foreign policy objectives are also determined by the regime's perceptions of the prosperity-stability linkage and of the strategic vulnerability of the city-state. Singapore had first tried to promote its prosperity in spite of its neighbors' hostilities and internal problems by looking beyond the region for materials and markets. The Malaysian racial riots of 1969 not only produced a Singaporean defense buildup but also helped create the global-city concept whereby Singapore sought a worldwide hinterland to insulate it from regional problems.[17] But even this distancing caused suspicions. Malaysia and Indonesia saw this attempt to move away from the region as overdone, self-centered, and arrogant behavior.

The charge of arrogance—sloganized as ''the Singapore superiority complex''—has been the most enduring antagonism in the region. These are not new perceptions but are part of the historical continuum. Rivalries derive from the colonial era when Kuala Lumpur and Singapore competed from political and economic positions of importance in the British colonial regime. The 1963–65 compromise, which used the metaphor that Kuala Lumpur played the role of Washington and Singapore the role of New York in the Federation of Malaysia, was an attempt to balance political and economic power and might have been an acceptable division of labor but for the ethnic cleavage between the two cities. The parallel reveals another strain: the ''New York'' actor, which can threaten the political center with its economic clout, pays a price of suspicion, disapproval, and perhaps envy on the part of the rest of the country. With separation, this cleavage deepened as Singaporeans could be regarded as interfering aliens. With economic advancement, they were seen as rich exploiters. Economic grievances between Singapore and Malaysia (as well as Indonesia), in effect, parallel the North-South debate with an agenda calling for a new regional economic order.

In sum, economic well-being took on a security dimension for Singapore and Malaysia. The twelve-year Emergency had taught both the connection between prosperity and internal stability. Whether it is land reform or encouraging the purchase of flats, the regimes hope to coopt their citizens by offering them a stake in the good life. With this perspective, security seemed to be ruled by the economic law of scarcity, and economic competition took on a national security dimension. Because of this perception, each state moved to gain independence of the other. Plans for new entrepot ports were drawn up in Malaysia (and Indonesia); Singapore retaliated with greater economies, efficiencies, and facilities. Competition between airlines touched national sensitivities. Yet despite these anxieties, collaboration on security issues continued.

Security Interdependency

Despite the emotionalism of separation and the later economic rivalries, Malaysia and Singapore have collaborated in an area where they are unavoidably interdependent, in intelligence and security. External events during the late 1960s promoted accommodation. Singapore and Malaysia both valued the security guarantees from Britain, Australia, and New Zealand and joined a Five-Power Defense Pact that worked to the benefit of the two Southeast Asian members. The July 1967 British announcement that their forces would be withdrawn by 1971, coupled with a lack of clear commitment from Australia, provided a joint challenge to Kuala Lumpur and Singapore. If the three larger powers were to remain committed, Singapore and Malaysia had to present a united, cooperative front. Uncertainties about U.S. policies in 1968 also increased the importance of the guarantee to both countries. The strength of public demonstrations surrounding the U.S. election and the demoralizing February 1968 Viet Cong Tet offensive seemed likely to speed U.S. disengagement from Southeast Asia. The new U.S. policy termed ''Vietnamization'' confirmed this expectation. Malaysian-Singaporean collaboration required transcending emotions and suspicions and agreeing on the source of external threats. Here, too, was another obstacle. Malaysia had been most concerned about China and local Communism, while Singapore worried more about Indonesia, especially in 1968 when the Chinese community there was raided. Yet, by 1969 Malaysia and Singapore learned to coexist on a correct if not cordial level because domestic turmoil forced both to understand their mutual interests. They presented a common front by focusing on ASEAN joint economic plans and on ASEAN organization issues. As for areas of contention, they followed the rule of silence; namely, if one doesn't agree, one doesn't comment.

Malaysia's racial troubles in 1969–1971 both taught and tested the commitment to accommodation. Singapore, like Indonesia, made no comment about the riots or martial law but watched anxiously as the events across the causeway played out, knowing that it could too easily be drawn into the upheaval because of the interconnectedness of the two societies. (Indeed, one might argue that at this time there was still only one society on the peninsula.) Should Malaysia become a Malay military dictatorship, as some feared during this martial-law period, then the Chinese resistance would look for ethnic support in Singapore to obtain supplies and sanctuary. Besides drawing the ire of Malaysia, this would have repercussions within Singapore as the communal war would enter the city-state. Another worst-case scenario attributed to a top-level official foresees regional escalation:

> What worries us most is the possibility that if the [Communist] threat to Malaysia becomes very serious, Kuala Lumpur as a last resort will ask the Indonesians for help. The Indonesians will almost certainly respond, since they don't want to have a Communist state bordering Sumatra. Then you will have real racial war, with Vietnam coming in on the side of the MCP [CPM].[18]

The immediate reaction to this dilemma was to fortify Singapore and diversify friends, but later, when Malaysia stabilized and was restored to a compromise polity, Singapore developed more confidence in its northern neighbor. The prospect of losing the moderate Malay regime created a Singaporean commitment to it.

To complement the Malay regime's fair and balanced policy toward the Chinese during and after the martial law period, Singapore turned in on itself and pursued a policy of creating a Singapore identity. This has ultimately served to reassure Kuala Lumpur, because Singapore's educating its ethnic Chinese to have an identity besides race makes them less apt to meddle in their neighbor's domestic affairs. In effect, building a perceptual fence separating transnational communal groups has helped make for good neighbors. Furthermore, on another level, Singapore increased its participation in ASEAN; this mollified Malaysia, which saw Singapore moving more in line with the policy orientations of its neighbors.

Across the causeway, Kuala Lumpur also inclined more to accommodation because domestic political concerns influenced policy toward Singapore. Relations with the city-state became a weather vane of the Malay regime's policy toward the Malaysian Chinese community in that quarrels with Singapore disturbed them and made them wonder how they could expect to fare better than their Chinese cousins who were in a separate country. On the other hand, good relations with Singapore assuaged apprehensions of the Chinese communities. Both governments shared the anxiety about dealing with the local Chinese in the late 1960s when the Cultural Revolution was at its peak and the Maoists called for revolution in overseas-Chinese communities. The riots of 1969 seemed to portend a worst-case fulfilled. Singapore serves the interest of the Malay government in another way: the city-state offers the Chinese in Malaysia a political and economic outlet, serving as an escape valve for the discontented.[19]

Recognition of interconnections moved the relationship to its second watershed. Prime Minister Razak's visit to Lee Kwan Yew in January 1971 opened the door to collaboration on shared problems; Lee visited Razak in January 1972, accepting rapprochement. This was not a visit filled with cordiality as disputes over the splitting of airlines and currency systems were in progress. It began, however, a consultation process of annual summits and eventually meetings on the ministerial and officials levels, a process that has come to be the most extensive of any ASEAN pair. The comment of Prime Minister Razak on his 1973 visit that both would take into account each other's perceptions when they made policy summarizes accommodation in action.

More recent incidents have validated this prescription. First, it was a seemingly mundane issue of water that restated the importance of consultations at all levels. Singapore obtains over half its fresh water from the adjacent Malaysian state, Johore. A 1961 pact guarantees Singapore's supply for ninety-nine years, but the pact is subject to review every twenty-five years. Concurrent with the lead-up to the 1987 revision, Johore suffered drought and rationing in 1983 while Singapore's supply was uninterrupted. Aware of Singapore's rising annual need for water (6 percent) some Malaysians in 1985 voiced the concern that ''Malaysia will always face a military threat if ever the supply has to be cut for one reason or another.''[20] Negotiations dragged on into September 1986 when Lee visited Mahathir in a summit to give impetus to the stalled talks. Symbolically, the meeting of national heads restated the priority of national over provincial interests. Indeed, problems can be first traced to allowing summits to lapse, indicating the importance of this procedure to the ASEAN process. During the mid-1980s, despite increased contacts between national and local officials, leaders failed to meet for four years. Singapore's agreement to buy supplies of natural gas from Malaysia also helped to resolve this issue.

Discretion, consultation, and attention to detail were again important elements in the second case of mismanagement, the visit to Singapore of Israel's President Herzog in November 1986. Government protests, cancellation of sports events, and demonstrations resulted, with UMNO youth calling for Singapore to be expelled from ASEAN, and even Singaporean Muslim MPs expressing concern about the action. Malay suspicions about Singapore's intentions or lack of sensitivity were matched by Singaporean observations that the episode showed the enormous hostility still harbored against Singapore. Singapore senior minister Rajaratnam made the "un-ASEAN" comment that the crisis reminds Singapore that it must stand on its own.[21] The incident created a breakdown in the normal ASEAN process, rending the important facade of "good neighborliness."

Resolution began with the resumption of the rules of silence. When the Singapore government did not officially respond, its restraint in public diplomacy helped prevent a spiral of increasing hostility. Prime Minister Mahathir also avoided public diplomacy and chose other channels to remind Singapore that it cannot ignore the concerns of its Muslim partners. He also actively intervened on November 28 to restrain public protest after a demonstration of three thousand had taken place in Johore Baru. The lesson learned was not that Singapore must compromise its sovereignty to placate Muslim sensitivities, but that Singapore, for its own well-being, must not ignore the effects of its policies on neighboring societies. In this case, the event plunged its own hinterland into threatening chaos. A second lesson is that negative public opinion can prevent a regime from pursuing accommodation despite the ASEAN image.

Foreign policy coordination has also been problematic for this pair; the Singapore-Malaysia relationship has not moved into joint foreign policy ventures. From their first bilateral summit in 1971 through to the present, the two regularly express different foreign policies. Singapore has never been confident in Malaysia's 1971 Zopfan plan, and they continue to diverge on the source of threats to the region. Nonetheless, the Singapore-Malaysian relationship persists in the face of conflicting perspectives and policies in this area. Since 1973 relations have been most strained over responses to the new order in Indochina. Kuala Lumpur and Singapore disagree about the dangers as a whole but share a common apprehension about the effects events will have on their common security problem, the CPM.

Their interests, then, converge in national security; collaboration rests on the consensus that they must work together to prevent a mutually destructive destabilization from occurring in any quarter, especially from within themselves. Much like the Communist terrorists, the two regimes realize that communal/racial warfare can drag them both down almost simultaneously. Managing this interdependency of internal security for decades reinforces the logic behind cooperation. Accordingly, both fear the consequences of an alternative regime in its neighbor. Singapore dreads either a Malay dictatorship or an ethnic Chinese Communist regime arising in Malaysia. The CPM has never accepted the "divorce," and a chauvinist Malay regime could see the city as irredenta. An even worse case would be a long civil war, or strong insurgency; a lawless peninsula would open opportunities to terrorists and handicap Singapore, which depends on the peninsular hinterland for water and food. Such a war would also drive foreign investment away from Singapore.

Kuala Lumpur has long feared a leftist or pro-Chinese regime in Singapore. Labor disturbances in the early 1960s created a strong impression that a leftist government was probable in Singapore. This led Kuala Lumpur to demand the city's inclusion into the projected Federation in order to control it. After separation, Singaporeans "adopted defiant positions to prove they could survive and stand on their own," explained Lee.[22] Leftist political stands, taken in its search of Third World support, kept fear alive in the conservative government of Tunku Abdul Rahman. But this concern was soon muted as Singapore moved more to the center. The important virtue of the Singaporean regime has since been its commitment to noninterference in Malaysia.

Since 1979, with increased instability in the region, relations between the two governments have seemed in many ways cordial. Their commonalities in policies and beliefs account for much of the cordiality. The Mahathir administration has extolled the virtues of efficiency and pragmatism, and in line with looking east to Japan,

Malaysia can look south to the achievements of Singapore. The present tone was set by Prime Minister Mahathir on his visit in 1981 when he paid tribute to Singaporean economics and diplomacy: ''I view the Singapore leadership as pragmatic. They have been able to adapt themselves to the neighboring countries in the region.''[23] For its part, Singapore is more positive in its evaluation of Malaysia, recognizing not only the problems and differences in political style across the causeway, but also the achievements made despite them.

Even foreign policy disagreements appeared to decrease in the early 1980s. Singapore was quieter in its denunciation of Vietnam and championing of China. Apparently, Singapore did not feel the need to be the town crier of Communist threats while the United States was headed by Ronald Reagan. Furthermore, the disaster in Beirut highlighted the importance of a stable hinterland to a city's prosperity. Fear of a Lebanon-like peninsula moved the Singaporean leadership to contribute more to the regional political process.[24]

To borrow one observer's model, the two regimes have lived in a ''need-suspicion'' relationship.[25] Each has a stake in the continued existence of the other, and this pragmatism overrides suspicions and distastes to the extent that institutionalized accommodation is being promoted. Moreover, the regimes share perceptions of interdependency in national security, with Singapore seeing its line of defense on the Malaysian-Thai border, and Malaysia relying on the city-state's denial of bases to Communists who would use them against southern Malaysia.[26]

Indonesia and Singapore

The relationship between Indonesia and Singapore completes the triangular core of the ASEAN process. Both regimes have managed racial, economic, ideological, and historical suspicions, parallel to those outlined in the Malaysia-Singapore case. Once again, the leaderships have recognized that their well-being rests on managing shared vulnerabilities derived from the economic and social network that transcends these states on the archipelago; the benefits come largely in the form of acceptance and security. Accommodation began with the minimal promises of restraint at the foundation of ASEAN, reached a plateau of positive relations in 1973 when Lee visited Suharto, and has since 1986 ripened to the extent that the Singaporean military will be using air and land facilities on Sumatra. Acceptance of Singapore through the ASEAN symbol in 1967 meant only that Indonesia was willing to tolerate an upstart overseas Chinese creation,[27] filled with ''rapacious businessmen'' who live off Indonesia.[28] Yet, in an extension of the accord with Malaysia, Indonesia offered the same coexistence arrangement to Singapore. The reasons are the same: Indonesia needed to protect its northern borders while it attended to domestic matters. Singapore, for its part, accepted the accord because of economic dependence on Indonesia, the new regime's good faith shown to Malaysia and to the rest of the region in the broad ASEAN package, Indonesia's demonstrated usefulness as mediator in Singapore's relations with Malaysia, and the moderating influence of the United States on an anti-Communist Indonesian regime.

In the first phase of relations in the ASEAN era, national interests clashed in an unusual test of resolve. This case presents an insight into the complexity of the states' accommodation. In October 1968 Singapore executed Indonesian marines captured during *konfrontasi*, a bold act in light of the feelings and repercussions that could be engendered. Indonesian leadership might have reacted aggressively for reasons of regime survival and personal honor: execution meant refusing newly installed President Suharto's request for leniency. Moreover, the times were unsettled and added to the risk; the whole ASEAN concept of accommodation was endangered by the Philippines' revived claim on Sabah. Nevertheless, Singapore pushed through, apparently feeling that it had to demonstrate its independence and sovereignty.

The Indonesian reaction was restrained. Despite mob violence in Jakarta, the government accepted the Singapore move. In reality, its options were limited: Force was not seen to be either diplomatically or militarily possible for such a minor provocation. Perhaps, restraint is better understood as reflecting Indonesia's new policy of regional responsibility. In that same month Indonesian officials were trying to heal the Malaysia-Philippines rift over Sabah. Quite probably, President Suharto tolerated indignity for his larger interests in the ASEAN project, cooperation and a cordon sanitaire.

The incident helps mark the beginning of a more cooperative era in 1973. When Lee made his first visit to Suharto, he placed flowers on the tomb of those same marines that his government had executed. With this dramatic event, Singapore made amends in deference to Indonesian sensitivities and Indonesia offered full acceptance of Singapore. Annual summit meetings since then have ritually reminded them that they cannot escape their relationship as neighbors.

This awareness is necessary as several different interests and perceptions continue to require accommodation. From Singapore's foundation in 1819 when it displaced Jakarta as regional entrepot, Indonesia has viewed Singapore as a rival and spoiler. By 1972 Singapore had taken on a new role, becoming a significant investor in Indonesia. Some Indonesians saw this positively, but others viewed it as a new form of exploitation. Indonesians have long suspected that Singapore has aided smuggling, thus depriving Jakarta of revenue; only in 1980 did Singapore agree to allow Indonesian officials a private viewing of trade figures. Another contention has been the desire of Indonesia to establish its own entrepot center and so reap the benefits of the middleman. Although Singapore has tried to move into industrial, high technology, and service areas, the establishment of another entrepot still threatens the security of the trading state. The 1976 proposal by Suharto to make the designated Indonesian site at Batam a joint venture with Singapore illustrates an economic accommodation that limits competition and attempts to mitigate suspicions by sharing benefits. A pact was signed in 1980.

Malaysian and Indonesian development has brought other conflicts of interest. For example, Singapore has lost business as the two reach self-sufficiency in oil refining and open direct trade links with China;[29] this has caused the city-state to look elsewhere, especially to China, to fill the gap. But it remains to be seen how this Sino-Singapore relationship will be viewed by the city-state's neighbors. In the past, because of Indonesian perceptions about its "Chineseness," Singapore has always downplayed connections with China, even to the point of putting off diplomatic relations with China until Indonesia opened them. There is reason for concern because past policies, such as promoting a global-city orientation or the use of Mandarin and English, were seen as arrogant and selfish attempts to move out of the Malay mainstream of the region. Singapore has been aware of this perception: its national anthem is sung in Malay, and, on a personal level, Prime Minister Lee's fortunate fluency in Bahasa has on occasion assuaged such sensitivities.

Aside from economic and racial strains, Singapore, dwarfed by Indonesia, understandably needs security reassurance. While the expansionistic policies of Sukarno seemed to have been rejected by the Suharto government's years of good behavior, one ominous event clearly hit the security-sensitive nerve in Singapore. In December 1975 Indonesia ended its anxieties about the imminent independence of East Timor by annexing the territory. Singapore, disturbed at this dangerous precedent, shattered ASEAN solidarity by not immediately supporting Indonesia when its action was challenged by resolutions at the United Nations. Two years passed before Singapore voted in Indonesia's favor on this issue. Nonetheless, while the Indonesian conquest strained the relationship, disapproval never went so far as to break the rule of silence, and Singapore only abstained on these votes. It was in the interest of both to preserve the relationship and the image of ASEAN solidarity in that unsettled year, which saw the end of the Vietnam war, the independence of Papua-New Guinea, and Portugal's announcement that its decolonization of Timor would be accelerated to a date later that year. Consultations also helped assuage anxieties: Lee met with Suharto in Bali and was given an informal briefing on the Timor situation in September 1975. The leaders reached compromise on their shared suspicions about Marxist Fretilin, the predominant group in East Timor.[30] To show continued mutual commitment, the two states also held their second set of joint naval exercises in that month.

Finally, foreign policy toward Indochina has been particularly divisive, especially in the aftermath of the Vietnamese occupation of Cambodia in December 1978, the influx of boat people during 1979, and the Soviet invasion of Afghanistan in December 1979. On one level, both Singapore and Indonesia appeared to put aside differences. In the early months of 1979, there seemed to be a strengthening of an ASEAN consensus and Singaporean-Indonesian solidarity as Indonesia moved away from its accommodating stand toward Vietnam. Indeed, Indonesia announced a military buildup—a move seen positively by ASEAN partners Thailand and Malaysia. Surprisingly, this action exposed the intramural security anxiety again; army chief-of-staff General Widodo assured Singapore in May 1979 that there was no need to worry about this buildup, and that Indonesia would not attack.[31]

Concurrently, Singapore demonstrated ASEAN solidarity in October 1979 by speaking out for the first time in favor of the integration of East Timor into Indonesia. Support for Indonesia followed a Suharto visit in September during which Cambodia was the main topic. Similarly, in the 1980 bilateral summit, the Vietnamese incursions into Thailand were one of their major talking points. This meeting and the Singaporean-Indonesian joint air exercises demonstrated mutual commitment.

In sum, the September 1982 visit of Prime Minister Lee to Jakarta can be used to review the rationale of the Singapore-Indonesia relationship. Lee brought along about twenty younger ministers to foster links among the next generation[32] and to teach younger leaders the lessons of the earlier era: in regional politics, competition means disaster. His concern was to pass on an appreciation of accommodation to those who did not live through the original learning experiences; he also hoped that frequent contacts would help mitigate suspicions that are bred in isolation. Both Lee and Suharto, in office since the decision to practice restraint was made, have had time to get to know and understand each other through the process of consultations.

In addition the leaders are trying to pass on an appreciation for the positive aspects of the interdependence. Singapore is moving away from competition in labor-intensive industries toward the role of a services center for the region.[33] One expression of this is found in an Indonesian editorial, reprinted in Singapore, that commented that Singapore's progress is related to Indonesia's constant overall economic growth, that Indonesia recognizes Singapore as the center of commerce, banking, and technology, and that "it is this spirit of cooperation and interrelated economic system that makes ASEAN grow in strength."[34] This conceptualization of ASEAN as a higher common interest provides a means to secure popular support for policies of accommodation. Moreover, the Indonesian elite is more inclined to respect Singaporean achievements and to attribute any Singaporean economic advantages over Indonesia as Indonesia's own fault. Indonesian feelings are also buoyed by the satisfaction of having done well. Hard decisions taken by President Suharto—devaluation, cutting of food subsidies, deregulating banks, reaffirming a personal income tax—evidence such confidence.[35]

On the other hand, no amount of beneficial complementarity can stand against insensitivity. Singaporeans have learned to practice more discretion in commentaries on their neighbors and thus mute their image of arrogance. Realizing that their less developed neighbor is important to them and that they must live with it, some practice verbal restraint out of expediency. Others have come to clearer awareness of the challenges faced by the leaders in Jakarta. Finally, some have come to a greater appreciation of Indonesia's, and especially President Suharto's, contribution to the creation and management of the oasis of stability that is ASEAN. Recently, this was dramatized by Suharto's effort to soothe Malaysian-Singaporean relations after the Herzog incident. Playing the role of elder statesman visiting his neighbors to prepare for the upcoming ASEAN summit, Suharto warned both of the dangers of defection. Symbolically, as is his style, Suharto reminded both of their interdependence by traveling for the first time from Malaysia to Singapore over the causeway. Suharto managed in this way to point out clearly the diplomatic, economic, and security imperatives of accommodation.

In summary, each of these three relationships in the core of the ASEAN process overcame economic, ideological, and racial suspicions in a spirit of expediency. Management is assisted by a consultation process and a tradition of trust, but commitment to the process is grounded in the pragmatism of a "specific bargaining situation."

> Each would refrain from supporting the rebel group across the border in the expectation that this would be reciprocated by the other government, and because competitive externalization of civil strife appeared more costly than a mutual agreement to avoid interference or even to cooperate in restraining the rebels.[36]

This summary statement, applied to the core-relationships of the ASEAN process, is taken from an analysis of Thai-Malaysian relations to show the parallels in motivations behind ASEAN relationships.

4

The Western Flank: Thailand and the Lower Peninsula

> Thailand has been a buffer state for many decades. But we have
> been an independent buffer state all along and we want to help our
> neighbors.
>
> —Prime Minister Kukrit Pramoj

THE bilateral relationships between Thailand and ASEAN members
to the south bind the western flank together. Thailand and Malaysia,
who have long understood their security interconnection, are central
to this collaboration; their cooperation predates ASEAN. Furthermore, this relationship, besides being the oldest in the region, underlies relations between Thailand and Singapore and Indonesia; both
value Thailand's contributions to the well-being of Malaysia, their
buffer zone.

Thailand and Malaysia

From the time of Malayan independence (1957), Kuala Lumpur and
Bangkok recognized a shared security vulnerability to insurgent
groups who operate across their common border, made porous by its
hilly and jungle terrain. Insurgency has persisted over decades because
the populations involved—Malays, Thais, and Chinese—were to
varying degrees alienated from each other and their governments. This
can be traced to "historical heritage, local unfamiliarity with the
administrative system and resentment of bureaucratic attitudes and

behavior, absence of meaningful social intercourse between Muslim and Buddhist communities, concentration of wealth in the hands of non-Muslims, deteriorating economic conditions, and failure of authorities to provide protection for the local people.''[1]

Moreover, the insurgents were supported at times by outside Communist states, such as Vietnam or China. Both governments share a sensitivity to the dangers of insurgency because they face similar problems elsewhere in their states, and such experiences have taught an appreciation of cooperation with a neighbor.

Malaysia's lesson was learned in the traumatic experience of the Emergency. Remnants of the defeated Communist Party of Malaya (CPM) were able to find sanctuary in the jungles and mountains of southern Thailand at the end of the 1950s. Although they still remain there and at times cross into Malaysia to terrorize the population, Kuala Lumpur has been able to keep them in check through Thai cooperation in coordinated or joint military campaigns. For its part, Thailand needs the Malaysian government to help control a separatist problem in its four southern provinces. This area is 75 percent Malay Muslim and one of Thailand's lowest income regions. The desire of these provinces to separate from Buddhist Thailand has sometimes focused on the restoration of an independent state, once named "Patani," or on joining Malaysia since it is seen as *Tenah Malaya*, the land of Malay customs and Islamic law.

These conditions provide the basis of another "need-suspicion" relationship. Thailand must worry that a Malaysian regime might be tempted to aid secessionists in order to incorporate more Malays into the Federation and so better the racial balance in the Malay favor. Some in Malaysia suspect that Thailand tacitly tolerates the CPM in southern Thailand so that a bargaining chip remains to exert influence on Kuala Lumpur. A less Machiavellian interpretation is that Bangkok has not been concerned about the south due to its problems elsewhere: it views the Chinese/CPM not as seriously threatening but as a useful local balance to the separatist forces within southern Thailand. Nevertheless, since the result is the same—the CPM is not eliminated—Malaysia is frustrated and left questioning Thailand's sincerity.

From the early 1960s, demonstrations of good will and consultations have been used to contain suspicions derived from this interdependent problem. An important result of Prime Minister Abdul Rahman's visit to Bangkok after Malayan independence was "the promise to review cooperation . . . in the capture—or at least containment—of the Communist terrorist remnant."[2] This move may have been facilitated by the first prime minister's familial links to the Thai elite, but the need to control the porous border presents a sound national-interest motivation. Later, Thailand's invitation to the Malaysian king for a state visit, a gesture of support to the newly enlarged Federation, also bolstered the young relationship. All were reassuring gestures to the Malay leadership facing *konfrontasi* with Indonesia. Kuala Lumpur also found a friend in Thailand's Thanat Khoman, whose good offices facilitated peace talks in this troubled period.

A bench mark for Thai-Malaysian accommodation that predates ASEAN and stands as the precursor to ASEAN bilateral cooperation is the agreement on border patrols in 1965, which institutionalized consultation and collaboration against insurgency operating between these two states. The subsequent establishment of ASEAN in 1967, therefore, was not a new direction in their relations, but a continuation of their shared hopes for cooperation. This commitment enabled both to ride out times of anxiety and suspicion.

During the 1969–1971 ethnic instability in Malaysia, the relationship was tested. In view of Malay martial law, Thailand had to consider the repercussions of a worst-case outcome. Should the Malays attempt to rule by dictatorship, the consequences—a civil war to Thailand's south—could be very destabilizing. At a minimum, such a war would strengthen the CPM or Malay insurgency as Kuala Lumpur would have to concentrate on other fronts. Even worse, a more militant Malay regime might actually exacerbate Thailand's problem if it supported its "lost brothers" in southern Thailand in a covert or open war of irredenta.

The reestablishment of the racial compromise in the Malaysian government in February 1971 assuaged Thai fears, but the journey to the brink highlighted the stake that Bangkok has in the National Front coalition regime. Yet, a problem still exists because UMNO does not represent all Malay views; active minority groups have different policy preferences. In 1970, during the troubled period of martial law when moderation and quiet were imperative, Datuk

Mohammed Asri of Kelantan called for struggle against Thailand as a holy war.[3] Since his party, Parti Islam (Pas), controlled the local government of the Malaysian states that bordered on southern Thailand, Bangkok was justifiably concerned during this uncertain time in Malaysia. In 1973 the Pas was incorporated into the National Front. Again Thai reactions were mixed; some wondered if this signaled a shift in Kuala Lumpur's policy, necessitated by a need to appease the extremists. Events were to prove that incorporation was more a technique for the moderate Malay regime to reign in and watch the Pas.

More serious suspicions and anxieties emerged in the mid-1970s as the Vietnam war ended. By 1973 Thailand had begun to alter its foreign policy from one of exclusive reliance on the United States to one with more security options. Signs of Thai interest in Chinese support gave much concern to Kuala Lumpur, which had its historical reasons for distrusting the People's Republic of China as well as a concurrent revival of insurgent activity, inaugurated by a radio broadcast from southern China. The conclusion of the Vietnam war, which meant U.S. withdrawal and the emergence of a militarily powerful Vietnam, heightened regional states' security concerns in 1975, especially frontline Thailand. The Kukrit government's order to close U.S. bases—whether motivated by leftist student pressure or deference to Vietnam, or in conjunction with U.S. desires—gave the appearance to some that Thailand was distancing itself from the United States and perhaps moving closer to China. This did not remain purely a Thai national security matter; Bangkok soon initiated a new policy in its border cooperation with Malaysia, calling upon Malaysia to withdraw military and intelligence facilities from its territory. The new government of Prime Minister Seni adopted this policy to counter domestic charges of not defending Thai sovereignty. Similarly, it had recently speeded the timetable for U.S. withdrawal from bases in Thailand to defend itself from such charges. Now the government moved to defuse demonstrators' accusations about Malaysian violation of Thai sovereignty and integrity.

These changes in Thai policies were all the more worrisome because they were in response to CPM tactics. The May 1976 demonstrations took place in Betong, the capital of the southern Thailand district that was almost totally under the control of the CPM. Kuala Lumpur saw this as a clever CPM propaganda tactic designed to force the removal of Malaysian forces, clearing away the only effective check on their operations in the area. The *New Straits Times*, a quasi-official voice of the Kuala Lumpur government, signaled concern that "We must not play into the hands of the Communists whose objective . . . is to drive a wedge between Bangkok and Kuala Lumpur."[4] Yet, Thailand did ask Malaysia to pull out in May 1976.

This break might have signaled the devolution of the relationship, but accommodation was sustained by continued consultations and Malaysian patience. Malaysia complied with Thailand's wishes, taking only a promise that the Thais would control the Communists. Kuala Lumpur felt a particularly great loss in the breakdown of collaboration in light of recent encouraging events. In January 1976, only a few months earlier, a joint operation involved Malaysian troops for the first time in a sweep through southern Thailand that rounded up over one hundred guerrillas. This was followed in February by an especially warm summit at Chiengmai, which seemed to confirm the new close collaboration. Prime Minister Kukrit of Thailand had said that the two countries enjoy "more than a close relationship, it is brotherly."[5] Much of this was diplomatic rhetoric to set the stage for the upcoming ASEAN summit, but the military operation had been a concrete, reassuring action in a time of change.

Loss of the border-patrol agreement and access to CPM sanctuaries on Thai territory was ominous, for they had served as the symbol and substance of Thai commitment. Fortunately, consultation provided some bridging reassurances. In July 1976, two months after the breakdown, Prime Minister Seni visited Prime Minister Hussein of Malaysia for an exchange of concerns. This Penang summit accepted the present situation as necessary but announced a new symbolic bond—there would be yearly meetings of the two prime ministers.

This diplomatic bandage had to hold only a short time as a new administration came to power in Bangkok. With Prime Minister Thanin and the return of military rule in October, the old policy of border patrols was restored. The CPM tactic of demonstrations may even have backfired because the military, surprised at the CPM's ability to raise such rallies, wanted to whittle down its strength. Thus, in September 1976 the border agreement was revised, and in November this third new prime minister of the year visited Prime Minister Hussein.

A new border agreement negotiated in March 1977 finally buried any uncertainties about Thailand's position. Malaysian intelligence again had a base in Thailand, and Malaysian troops were granted unlimited rights of hot pursuit. Moreover, the public signing ceremony for this agreement during Hussein's visit to Bangkok included Malaysia's concession to Thailand. Hussein pledged that "as far as security is concerned, most of us [ASEAN members] are indivisible."[6] He stated: "If there should be a time—which I pray to God will not happen—when Thailand requires assistance from Malaysia, Malaysia will do her best to cooperate and be of assistance to Thailand."[7] Both regimes wanted to reaffirm what they came close to losing, so they raised the level of their commitment by articulating the rationale of the relationship in high-level agreements and promulgating them in a highly visible act of public diplomacy, the summit.

The government of Thailand changed in November 1977, but the new prime minister, Kriangsak, gave no immediate concern to Kuala Lumpur since his past service as cochair of the joint-border security and boundary committees assured his awareness of the Thai-Malaysian connection. Beyond this personal predisposition, the Thai leader had other reasons to see security issues from a Malaysian point of view. First, in February 1977 it was reported that the Communist Party of Thailand (CPT), strengthened by students who joined to resist the return of military rule, was cooperating with the CPM.[8] The Thais now had a greater stake in the control of the CPM; those who may have toyed with the idea of using the party as a local balance had to view this as a more dangerous option.

Besides a shared stake in the interconnected Communist threat, the two regimes faced a new joint problem, increased fundamentalist Islamic activities. In late 1977, incidents of violence began to increase in south Thailand. The September 1977 explosion of a bomb only 110 meters from the king and queen during a royal visit to Pondok Yala was the first of what one observer has called the Big Four violent acts, including a casino bombing at Yala in December 1977, a bomb at the

Yala railroad station in October 1979, and a shooting at Bannang Star in February 1981.[9] Moreover, these acts were seen as especially dangerous because of the worldwide eruption of Islamic fanaticism whose epicenter was Iran and whose shocks reached from Lebanon to the southern Philippines. Libyan Muslim preachers in Malaysia were another source of concern.[10]

The times demanded great coordination of national policies to avoid internal destabilization. Restraint by the neighboring Muslim regime was more important to Thailand at the same time that Kuala Lumpur faced greater pressures to provide sanctuaries for the Muslim movement in Thailand. Likewise, Bangkok's policies toward the secessionists could have impact on the Kuala Lumpur regime—Bangkok must go gently in its suppression so as not to inflame public opinion within Malaysia. Kuala Lumpur's claims of anxiety over domestic Malay reactions were real; fundamentalist violence was also occurring in Malaysia. Conservative Muslims, known as the *dakwah*, made headlines first in 1978 with their attack on Hindu temples. Political instability and challenges to the moderate Malay regime have been most frequent in the northern provinces where the government has had to resort to martial law. These provinces, which border Thailand, form a sociogeographical interdependency between the two states.

In effect, the two face a joint challenge of dealing with Islamic sensitivities. This transnational Islamic problem reached a flashpoint in 1981 when many of Thailand's Malays moved into Malaysia to escape the Thai crackdowns. Malaysia's response, gathering them into refugee camps, horrified Thailand because the camps would draw international attention. Such a development would be a tremendous publicity victory for the Patani United Liberation Organization (PULO), the major resistance group. Yet the crisis was mitigated when Kuala Lumpur settled refugees with relatives who live in northern Malaysia.

But difficulties persisted in 1981 when joint border operations were not held. Thailand explained the suspension as necessary to assuage inflamed public opinion in the south,[11] but Malaysia feared that this would increase CPM influence. This rupture in Thai-Malaysian collaboration occurred against the backdrop of increased separatist violence and activity. PULO was becoming more dangerous as it circulated an appeal at the Islamic Conference in January 1981 and published a plea in the *Journal of the Muslim World League* in April.[12] Then too, regional events were making matters more complex. The Vietnamese Army had arrived on Thailand's border in January 1979, and the June 1980 Vietnamese incursions increased Bangkok's anxiety and its search for security guarantees from the United States, ASEAN members, and China. Malaysia, ever suspicious of China, saw Thailand's suspension of the joint patrols as a dangerous move toward Beijing; the most suspicious believed Thailand had reciprocated for Chinese help by the suspension.

Again, patience, consultation, and restraint were important, but the rationale behind this accommodation, the special bargain, explains the commitment. Unlike the access that Thailand allows Malaysia in pursuing the CPM, the help that Kuala Lumpur can give Bangkok is limited, even verbally. Consequently at this local level, Bangkok must live with an uneven quid pro quo. Their compromise reads that the CPM is a common enemy, but the separatists are a Thai domestic problem, that is, not of concern to Kuala Lumpur. It is understandable that rights of hot pursuit into Malaysia cannot be granted—the effect on the Malays would be volatile. But Malaysia refuses even verbal alignment with the Bangkok government, in the form of an affirmation of Bangkok's legitimacy as ruler. Border agreements say nothing about the separatists and, judging by a 1982 disagreement, the issue does not even make the informal agenda of the border talks. The official Malaysian reasoning behind this policy of detachment is that the border committee's speaking to the issue "would be giving [the separatists] political recognition and . . . would be getting Malaysia to give them political recognition."[13] Furthermore, Kuala Lumpur argues that it must retain credibility as an Islamic government, both to retain domestic power and to speak for Thailand in the Muslim world. Finally, Malaysia explains that it cannot call PULO a common enemy since the organization has not attacked Malaysia.

These arguments, however, despite their rationality or persuasiveness, do not assuage feelings of ingratitude, exploitation, and suspicion in some Thai quarters. Suspicion that the Malaysian government harbors sympathy for the separatists is the most disruptive. Kuala Lumpur has attempted to reassure the Thai government with public statements that it is not supporting the separatists, and these have been accepted by Bangkok[14] as credible and useful policy stands. Yet Bangkok is sure that private aid is going across the border. In the interest of quiet diplomacy, this is expressed in coded language, like the following: "The root cause of separatism in the South is foreign-inspired. But for the purpose of preserving good relations with our neighbors, we cannot elaborate on that."[15] While Bangkok accepts that Kuala Lumpur cannot help with the secessionist problem, it must deal with the fear that the present regime might capitulate to the demands of militant Islam. These anxieties also extend to Kuala Lumpur's future ability to defend Thailand before the Muslim world. In this regard, Thailand's establishment of information services in the Middle East are a preparation for the day when Malaysia no longer speaks up for Thailand.[16]

A compromise and a crisis followed in the next year. The joint air-force raids in March 1982 allowed both to work together against the common enemy while not inflaming public opinion with the use of ground troops. Much like joint naval exercises, this form of cooperation is hidden from public view and so allows governments to circumvent domestic restraints. The crisis centered on the public questioning of the diplomatic compromise. At the close of the annual border talks, the local Thai commander, Lieutenant General Harn Leenanond, spoke out publicly, contradicting the official line of satisfaction voiced by Interior Minister General Sitthi and General Saiyud. Harn asked: "Where was the appreciation for our [recent] effort to crush the communist movement? This is what Malaysia is like. We have been trying to save their face in all the past meetings. But we will do it no more."[17] Harn, who was reportedly behind the Thai offensive to assert control over the South,[18] was referring to Malaysia's lack of assistance in controlling the Muslim separatist insurgency. His frustration was all the greater because the talks did not even discuss the separatists.[19]

Repairing the relationship began by rebuilding the image of solidarity; since damage had occurred by violation of the rule of silence, the reaffirmation needed to be public. During a December visit, Prime Minister Mahathir candidly answered the dissatisfaction of the Harn faction. He declared that "the Malaysian government is not supporting the insurgency in south Thailand, but that some other people in

Malaysia might be. My government is not going to tolerate anything that would sour relations between Thailand and Malaysia.''[20] Bangkok accepted this and disclaimed the statements of Lieutenant General Harn as not reflecting official thinking.

Harn's ''Peaceful South'' campaign, which weakened the Muslim separatist movement, also took a toll on the CPM. Success against the Muslim separatists has not produced hubris in the area of insurgency. The Thais have signaled Kuala Lumpur that they will continue the joint struggle against the CPM; for example, a later southern commander declared that ''a sovereign state like Thailand cannot allow the presence of foreign [and illegal] armed force.''[21]

But current successes or past crises still highlight a significant question about these states' accommodation. Thailand faces its insurgency, aided only by Malaysian restraint. The formal Thai-Malaysian agreement actually works to control the insurgency problem of only one partner, Malaysia. The Thai problem is not handled positively by joint or coordinated patrols; it is not even an effective noninterference solution because Thailand accepts Malaysian inability to move against the separatist sympathizers in Kelantan. What, then, is the quid pro quo in this relationship?

Malaysia has reciprocated for Thailand's border help in these ways: it controls the separatist sympathizers' public activities and, more important, stands by Thailand in its Indochina problems. In the early days of regional uncertainty, Home Minister Ghazalie spoke the usual diplomatic phrases to signal solidarity: ''Our future and fate are interwoven, and nobody will ever succeed in separating us.''[22] When reassurance was needed during the border cooperation suspension of 1976, Prime Minister Hussein used images of brotherhood and references to indivisible security. In the aftermath of the occupation of Cambodia, clearer reassurances were given. After a visit from Thailand's defense minister, General Prem, Ghazalie stated simply, ''What hurts the Thais will hurt us.''[23] In October 1979, in the context of signing a treaty delimiting the territorial sea, Prime Minister Hussein declared: ''Malaysia reaffirms our support and solidarity with the government and people of Thailand in the preservation of its independence, national sovereignty, and territory.''[24] In the next month, Deputy Prime Minister Mahathir said even more clearly, ''Malaysia will come to the aid of Thailand should its own security be threatened by the situation in that country."[25]

These statements amount to a virtual, albeit ambiguous, mutual defense arrangement. The forthright style of Dr. Mahathir gives insight into Malaysia's apprehensions and reasons behind this commitment. Shortly after the quotation above, he indirectly laid out the Malaysian anxiety for the public. He said he was "very confident that Thailand would not let Vietnam have free use of its territory to invade Malaysia." Some saw this as a possibility because of "what happened during the Japanese invasion in World War II." This would not recur, he argued, because "the Thais' attitude toward the Vietnamese was different from their attitude toward the Japanese during the war."[26] In other words, fears of a fallen or compliant Thailand motivate Malaysian strategic support and patience. Similarly, Thailand's fears of an Islamic, chaotic, or neutral Malaysia complemented by its appreciation of diplomatic support from the present regime motivate continued collaboration and patience with Malaysian domestic politics, especially in the northern Malaysian states.

Besides relying on the history of good faith and the rationality for cooperation, both are working to assuage disruptions caused by domestic opinion. The two regimes have adopted several prudent approaches. The military assaults are coordinated so that there is no question of violations of sovereignty by foreign troops. (Coordinated operations, meaning troops patrol on their own territory within a synchronized plan, are the present tactic, adopted to avoid objections about violations of sovereignty raised by joint patrols that had allowed Malaysian security patrols to pursue and search out terrorists' sanctuaries in southern Thailand during the 1970s.) A push by Thai troops in December 1983 with Malaysians waiting on the border illustrate this tactic.[27] Politically, the governments are attempting to draw more lower-level officials into the bilateral consultative process. Exchange programs, extended to lower-ranking officers and bureaucrats, will produce an empathy for the other's challenges and a similarity of perspectives (an ASEAN approach) on security. Thus, through personal contacts and teaching the official "interwoven" message, it is hoped that suspicions can be assuaged.

The regimes have also tried to solve the border problem by

applying the "resilience" economic strategy, that is, a commitment to a socioeconomic development of the troubled areas. It is hoped that this "more permanent cure" will remove the grievances of those who support the CPM or the separatists.[28] Development has not been a quick fix, however; implementation has even caused some ironic irritations. Kuala Lumpur would prefer that Bangkok's investment priority would not be in the Malay areas but in the Chinese CPM areas near Betong. The Thais, of course, are hoping to coopt the most alienated who have greater resources to cause them troubles,[29] much as the Malaysians are hoping to build the economy of the Chinese areas near Betong. The two have also differed over an amnesty program that Malaysia rejects as too trusting of the CPM.

Irritations will be a persistent challenge to this relationship because the states appear to benefit unequally depending on the focus, either at the local or regional levels. Malaysian support of Thailand seems to be a one-sided foreign policy concession, but Thailand appears to make greater concessions to Malaysia on the border issue. The challenge has been managed by focusing on mutual advantages and converging interests. Each realizes that it plays a role in the other's domestic stability, and both value collaboration with a government that has never been hostile to it. The ASEAN dimension also helps by providing a neutral rationale for cooperation. Malaysia can say "ASEAN" when it means Thailand and so avoid domestic repercussions from supporters of the separatists. Likewise, ASEAN provides a linkage in Thai thinking between the strategic benefits gained from Malaysia's support vis-à-vis Indochina and the concessions Thailand makes on its southern frontier. In sum, the benefits of accommodation, positively articulated in "ASEAN" language as the benefits of "having good neighbors," underlie commitment to the relationship. These benefits have been important enough to have influenced the policies of both states for over thirty years including a dozen Thai and four Malaysian administrations.

Thailand and Singapore

Cooperation between Singapore and Thailand has been most evident in their diplomatic activities. Often they are paired as the two ASEAN members with the same threat perception, and this convergence of beliefs and images underlies their coordinated policy toward Vietnam's domination over the Indochinese peninsula. Domestic factors also bolster this foreign policy coordination. Unlike Malaysia and Indonesia, Singapore seems to have put aside the memories of Chinese interference and accepted Thai reliance on Chinese support. Perhaps the ethnic makeup of Singaporean society, or a belief that the present regime in Beijing is different from its Maoist predecessor, or confidence arising out of prosperity, accounts for this perspective.

Aside from perceptions and policy commonalities, Singapore and Thailand are "intertwined" in a way not immediately obvious: Singapore's defense against invasion or insurgency depends in large part on Malaysia and the perpetuation of a moderate regime in Kuala Lumpur. Strategically, Singapore remembers the lesson of the Japanese invasion and knows that Malaysia is indispensable to its defense. More to the point, Singapore wants the CPM controlled because it is also a declared enemy of the city-state; the CPM does not recognize the independence of Singapore. Thus, Singapore benefits from Thai aid to Malaysia in the war on the CPM. Through this commonality with Malaysia, and because of historical, familial and personal, and economic interconnections, Singapore has a virtual border with Thailand. Consequently, most of Malaysia's thinking about the necessity of collaboration with Thailand is mirrored in Singapore. Early in 1971 Lee Kwan Yew, sounding much like Dr. Mahathir, discussed the critical and uncertain role of Thailand:

> If there is a precipitate collapse of the non-communist regime in Vietnam, and the whole of Laos and Cambodia become appendages of a communist Vietnam, and the Thais fall or bend even before the wind blows and, instead of a buffer, act as a conduit for the supply of materials, arms and ammunitions down the (Malay) peninsula, then a very awkward and uncomfortable situation can arise within five years ... it may even be less if things go wrong.[30]

When something went wrong, that is, after the October 1973 student uprisings and subsequent fall of the military government, a Singaporean commentator expressed similar thoughts about the new civilian, and suspected-leftist, government: "Will the new government do more to satisfy the students' demands for more independent policy?'' she asked. The reports of Communists in the student movements raised hackles and posed the dilemma: Will this mean the end of ''having Thailand as the last frontier between communist and non-communist states''?[31]

Anxiety about Thailand's policy had begun before the October change of regimes. The U.S. peace pact with Vietnam in January 1973 and gradual withdrawal centered attention on how Thailand would deal with abandonment by its great-power patron. Then, after the fall of Saigon in April 1975, sensing the heightened Thai anxiety, Singapore moved to support Thailand's China option; Prime Minister Lee said it was necessary for the salvation of Thailand and all Southeast Asia.[32] In July, Prime Minister Kukrit made a visit to Singapore, the first for a Thai prime minister, and talked of friendship and the need for an ASEAN summit. Lee concurred with the comment that ''We have never been more conscious that the future of ASEAN countries is so interwoven.''[33] The great fear of the moment was that Vietnam would begin distribution of abandoned U.S. arms to subversives throughout the region. Specifically, Singapore was concerned that the CPM on the Thai-Malaysian border might receive them. The question of the post-Vietnam era, begun as early as 1970, was asked by the Singapore *Herald*: Would Thailand be a ''conduit or a stopper''?[34] With the restoration of the military regime in October 1976 under Thanin, Singapore and the other ASEAN members were less anxious about the possibility of Thai defection. Nonetheless, Singapore still followed a policy of actively supporting Thailand. Consultations at the ministerial level were frequent, and the prime ministers have met annually since 1975.

Small though it is, Singapore has attempted to keep Thailand in the ASEAN process by fulfilling Thai expectations of collective political defense. Singapore's loud warnings about Soviet-Vietnamese advances were important for drawing attention to the region and so allowed Thailand to reap the benefits. The Singapore involvement and support of the resistance forces in Cambodia, including its role in the formation of the Coalition Government of Democratic Kampuchea, are additional examples of the Singapore policy of being diplomatically useful. Thus, the city-state demonstrates that cooperation with the lower peninsula, that is, with ASEAN, brings benefits. Singapore, for one, is willing to reciprocate to the Thais for serving as the "front line."

Finally, besides this accommodation, which mirrors and complements the interests of Kuala Lumpur, Singapore and Thailand share a common interest in dealing with the state between them. Singaporean diplomacy on behalf of Thailand may be viewed as an investment against the rainy day of a hostile Malaysia, most likely in the form of a radical, Islamic state. The relationship involves more than diplomatic burden-sharing; there is military cooperation in what might be termed a proto-alliance. Thailand has (as have the Philippines, New Zealand, Taiwan, and Australia—other once-removed neighbors) allowed Singapore access to military training camps and air force facilities, enabling Singapore to keep its eggs in many different baskets.[35] In turn, Singapore maintains a first-rate, compatible air force including an Awac to patrol the skies of the region.

Thailand and Indonesia

Much like Singapore, Thai-Indonesian relations are mediated by Malaysia. Jakarta recognizes Thailand's "front-line" role, buffering Malaysia from the Indochina war. Though Indonesia's stake in the stability of Malaysia is not as great as Singapore's, security interdependencies do motivate Indonesia's accommodation with Thailand. A destabilized or Communist Malaysia would not pull down Indonesia like a domino, but Jakarta would no longer enjoy secure and comparatively trouble-free northern borders. In effect, the twenty-year-old cordon sanitaire would be lost, adding a large defense burden to past and current difficulties on other fronts in Timor, the Moluccas, Sumatra, and with Papua-New Guinea. A Malaysian civil war would also present Indonesia with secession in East Malaysia along north Kalimantan. Regionally, supporting Thailand and keeping it from drifting toward Beijing helps keep China out of the region. Thailand's dependence on China might, it is feared, result in Chinese access to the CPM as payment for assistance.

Geography also presents an immediate security interdependency in the Straits of Malacca between southern Thailand and northern Sumatra, the home of troublesome separatist and fundamentalist

Islamic movements. A revival in 1977 reminded Jakarta and Bangkok of this interdependency. Working from bases in a compliant Thailand, communists could exacerbate provincial and religious cleavages within this part of Indonesia. Dramatically, in April 1977, Prime Minister Hussein of Malaysia and President Suharto signaled their concern by meeting in and discussing this troubled area.[36] This Penang summit came shortly after Thailand and Malaysia revived and strengthened their border cooperation. Completing the triangle in a more direct and clearer statement of intent, General Panggabean, at the Indonesian-Malaysian border committee meeting the previous month, spoke of their collaboration as a prototype that could improve security within ASEAN.[37] An indication that the Indonesian interest was shared in Thailand was the subtle comment in the *Bangkok Post*: "The visit of President Suharto and the launching of operations by Thai-Malaysian forces on communist terrorists in the jungle hideouts of Betong salient in south Thailand on Monday were, indeed, a rare coincidence." It went on to endorse this policy: "We feel that similar security actions between Thailand and other Asean partners like Indonesia would help tremendously in safeguarding our freedom and preserving our countries from being troubled by terrorist activities."[38]

Such reciprocally reassuring signals were important in the uncertain era after the Vietnam war, but consultations also assuaged anxieties about Thailand's attempts to cope with the new balance on the mainland. The Kriangsak government's announced willingness to deal with Vietnam again raised the specter of appeasement, giving Communists access to the border guerrillas. In a move to reassure ASEAN partners, Prime Minister Kriangsak visited President Suharto in February 1978 (and also Prime Minister Hussein) with the successful outcome that Indonesia endorsed Thai normalization with Indochina.[39] Reportedly, Kriangsak removed the impression that Thailand would sooner or later fall to the Communists.[40] His policy of "pragmatic accommodation," based on supporting contending forces in Indochina, seemed to demonstrate a sense of Thai confidence and gain the support of ASEAN members.[41]

A year passed and saw conditions change when Vietnam occupied Cambodia in January 1979. Jakarta had seen Bangkok's unease with Vietnamese troops on its border and moved to support Thailand, both militarily and diplomatically. By meeting where they are most contiguous at Medan, northern Sumatra, the Kriangsak-Suharto consultation was again a situational signal of Thai-Indonesian interdependency and solidarity. General Panggabean, also during this time, said Indonesia would help Thailand.[42]

Since this high water mark of solidarity, consultations have dealt with coordinating divergent foreign-policy approaches on the Vietnamese occupation of Cambodia. Accommodation has not been easy because of different geographical and historical experiences, as well as the less compelling nature of their security relationship. Yet, while some feel that Indonesia is independently secure, safeguarded by insular isolation or size, events have pointed to vulnerabilities. The persistence of piracy, the floods of boat people, the smuggling to and from Singapore, the traffic of illegal workers across borders, the Chinese seizure of the Paracels in 1974 from South Vietnam, and Vietnam's challenge to Indonesia's claim to the sea-bed border north of the Natunas islands remind Indonesia that its borders are porous, that insularity is not an absolute guarantee, and that its continued security against insurgency is interwoven with the good relations achieved with its ASEAN neighbors.

While both have publicly disagreed and gone separate ways in regional politics, they have remained in the ASEAN process to conserve the benefits it provides. Thailand has continued to serve Indonesia's interests by not allowing terrorists to flourish and by serving as a buffer to the lower peninsula. In turn, Indonesia has stood by Thailand in the ASEAN-sponsored collective political defense of Thailand; and, at the Vietnamese occupation of Cambodia, Indonesia demonstrated bilateral support in the form of promises of aid to defend Thailand along with actual secret flights of military cargo during the 1979 crisis period.[43] In addition, the two have used bilateral military exercises as reassurance signals. Last, Indonesia has also accepted Thai sovereignty over the Malay provinces and has shown restraint in this matter; but the body of an Indonesian army officer found in south Thailand in 1973[44] served as a useful reminder that the Malays of southern Thailand do have another potential patron and that, in this area at least, the states are directly interwoven. (Jakarta denied involvement, suggesting he was a refugee after the 1965 coup.) In sum, the relationship stands on empathy

for the problems the frontline endures, other participants' understanding Thai historical and geographical sensitivities to the
Vietnamese, and Thai appreciation of other states' apprehensions
about China. Pragmatically, Thailand must limit the amount of aid
it accepts from China in return for continued support from other
ASEAN members.

The western flank of ASEAN is built on the asymmetrical exchange
between the lower peninsula and Thailand. Singapore, Malaysia, and
Indonesia join in a strategic concession—diplomatic support—to
Thailand's national security in return for Thai cooperation in tactical
control of Malaysia's insurgency problem. The next chapter will
discuss the manner in which accommodation of national interests
plays a role in widening the western flank to include the Philippines,
Brunei, and Papua-New Guinea.

5

The Eastern Flank:
The Philippines and Brunei

The danger which we face is common to both countries. Our only
hope of saving ourselves from destruction, be it in Malaysia or in
the Philippines, is to work closely together to minimise the risks.
                                                    —Tunku Abdul Rahman

THE ties between the states on the eastern flank of ASEAN—Malaysia,
Indonesia, the Philippines, and Brunei—form another set of interlock-
ing relationships. Indonesian-Malaysian collaboration, discussed in
the context of western-flank politics, carries over to the eastern flank,
serving again as the core of the larger ASEAN phenomenon. Malaysia's
security relationships with the Philippines and Brunei are the most
immediate and central to this eastern flank; Indonesia's interests with
these two are less direct but still important to its desire for a stable
border with Malaysia. Jakarta and Papua-New Guinea, the unofficial
seventh member of the ASEAN process, have also developed a security
accommodation.

Malaysia and the Philippines

Malaysia and the Philippines illustrate an accommodation at the
lowest level of intensity, that is, both states merely honor a pledge
of self-restraint without undertaking more positive forms of cooperation. In this case, not only have there been no bilateral ventures,
military exercises, or even high-level public consultations;

Malaysia's prime ministers also refuse to visit the Philippines. This is a high suspicion relationship which was destructive in the past (when it froze ASA and ASEAN) and still tarnishes the ASEAN solidarity image. This rift illustrates, however, that accommodation can transcend such obstacles.

Hostilities between Malaysia and the Philippines derive from the Philippine claim to Sabah, described by Prime Minister Mahathir as a bone "stuck in the throat, painful to swallow and difficult to remove."[1] Manila has claimed that all lands on northeastern Borneo once subject to the Sultanate of Sulu, now part of the Philippine republic, belong to the government of the republic, which has absorbed the sovereignty of Sulu. Malaysia responds that the sultan transferred part of his territory in northern Borneo to a British trading company, which then passed the territory to the British crown, which created the Federation of Malaysia. The Philippines has challenged the legality of these transfers.[2]

Several motivations can explain this Philippine action, which risks provoking both its neighbors and its patron, the United States (which had recognized a border that excluded Sabah from its colony). First, Sabah, a resource-rich, underpopulated land, is a tempting piece of real estate. Second, the claim has served to promote the fortunes of Philippine presidents and presidential candidates. Third, the claim is part of a national security policy.

The first instance of the claim serving domestic political ends was in the early 1960s when the British were withdrawing. Had President Macapagal succeeded in increasing the national territory, he would have had an easy reelection. The 1968 revival of the Sabah claim was similarly seen at the time to be part of President Marcos's reelection campaign. Though an agreement to resume relations was announced in December 1968, the Malaysia-Philippines rapprochement came only in December 1969, one month after the Philippine elections, lending credence to this evaluation: "Whenever there is some big internal crisis brewing in the Philippines," analyzed one Malaysian official, "you find Manila reviving its claim on Sabah."[3] Perhaps holding this perspective mitigates the sense of danger and explains why Kuala Lumpur has been able to put up with Philippine intransigence and the irritation. Realizing that campaign pledges can follow a politician for his career, Malaysia may have grudgingly accepted the status quo. From September 1972, when the Marcos regime entered the internal crisis of martial law, through his 1986 departure, the Philippine leader found it difficult to back away from his advocacy of his country's claim on Sabah.

A third dimension of the Philippine claim relates to the security interdependency between Mindanao, the large southern island of the Philippine archipelago, and Sabah. The Philippines suspects that the rebels are supplied and even trained in the Malaysian state. Countermeasures to the failure by Kuala Lumpur to control this subversion include intervention in a form of hot pursuit. Philippine columnist Valencia discussed the claim to sovereignty as a lever held to legitimize a Philippine invasion made in self-defense.[4] The 1969–1971 crisis period in Malaysia confirmed Philippine fears that Malaysia was inherently unstable; the breakup of Pakistan shortly thereafter gave rise to speculations about a "Bangladesh effect" in Malaysia. But Malaysia's general stability since that period has removed this apprehension. Admittedly, evaluating official perceptions of another's cohesion is difficult because diplomatic sensitivity and prudence proscribe public discussion of another state's viability; but unofficial observers have been freer to make comments along the lines that Malaysian union is at least "not a foregone conclusion."[5] So the specter of instability can still stand as the third element in the explanation of the ongoing Philippine claim.

The claim and the accompanying suspicions have been managed through restraint, diplomacy, and trade-offs. The ASEAN rules of silence and official noninterference have been practiced: contrast the comment of Deputy Prime Minister Razak in 1969 that "It is a fact President Marcos did not look after the welfare of the people in the southern islands and this is worrying him. If the President cannot look after his people he has to answer for it,"[6] with today's "ASEAN spirit," which would rule out such interference and lack of discretion. Soon after Razak's comment, the 1969 riots occurred, reminding Malaysian leaders of their own glass house. But this accommodation is fragile and volatile, as the claim still exists and as such is regarded as a hostile act by Malaysia. When the Philippines attempted to wind down the controversy quietly in 1969, Malaysia demanded a public and legal renunciation. Manila then complained that Malaysia did not leave a face-saving way out of the problem. Malaysia walked out of the talks, frustrated with this Philippine expectation that it help the Marcos regime out of a foreign policy embarrassment of its own making. Pressure from other ASEAN states, concern about regional events, and the domestic crises in both countries finally forced a resolution.

A move for the better was possible after 1975 because of several factors. First, the Philippines seemed reassured when Tun Mustapha was removed as chief minister of Sabah. He headed the provincial government that was suspected of aiding the Philippine Muslim rebels, and, indeed, with his departure came the decrease in arms shipments.[7] Second, by this time the Malaysian regime had weathered the racial upheaval and proved its staying power. Third, regional instability, as the Vietnam war reached its end in 1975, raised the incentives to accommodate.

By 1977 a qualified resolution of the problem evolved. In July, the chief minister of Sabah visited Manila, and President Marcos visited Prime Minister Hussein in the context of an ASEAN summit. He also went on to visit Labuan Island, part of the Sabah state. The significance of these visits was made clearer at the preliminaries to the second ASEAN summit held in Kuala Lumpur in August 1977. There, President Marcos announced that the Philippines was going to take steps to drop the claim. This Philippine positivism lasted through the next three years and was probably due to Manila's problems with increased guerrilla war in the south and its concern about the reactions of the Islamic Conference. Manila needed Kuala Lumpur's cooperation both in controlling supplies to rebels and in countering the rebels' influence with adventurist Islamic states like Libya. In October 1978, another Philippine indirect resolution was offered in the form of a border-crossing agreement and joint patrol. The essence of this circumvention is laid out by Prime Minister Virata of the Philippines: ''a border agreement is already in their favor, because if you recognize that is the border, then south of the border is Malaysian.''[8] This solution was not accepted and Prime Minister Mahathir stands firm on his position that this claim is not a matter for negotiation; first the Philippines must formally renounce its claim.[9]

A controversy in late 1981 resulted when some in the Philippine National Assembly called for resurrecting the claim. The occasion for this was the report of Mindanao National Liberation Front

(MNLF) bases in Sabah; the late opposition leader Benigno Aquino had even made a visit to one of them.[10] The Sabah government escalated the crisis by calling for a break in relations with the Philippines. Prime Minister Mahathir rejected this, saying Malaysia would not allow any matter "to rupture the spirit of ASEAN that we have nurtured for so long."[11] Six months later the Philippine worry was rekindled when an Australian television news team visited these bases and reported that mercenaries were training the MNLF troops in camps financed by Libya with the support of the Palestine Liberation Organization (PLO).[12]

Besides the actual insurgency problem, resolution is still blocked by Malaysia's insistence on a definite renunciation and the Philippines' need for a face-saving way out. Kuala Lumpur's insistence on a straightforward and clear renunciation is based on its desire to counter any revival of the Philippine legal-historical argument. Malaysia suggested that this resolution could take the form of an amendment to the Philippine constitution. As could be expected, the Marcos regime saw this as a humiliating concession and an unnecessary action as there was no specific reference to Sabah in that document. (It was reported, however, that Marcos told Prime Minister Hussein in July 1976 that the constitution did keep him from giving up Sabah.[13])

A compromise was also floated suggesting that the Philippine National Assembly might change section 2 of the Philippine Baseline Act of 1968, which reads: "The territorial sea of the Philippines as provided in this act is without prejudice to the delineation of the baseline of the territorial sea and the territory of Sabah situated in North Borneo, over which the Republic of the Philippines has acquired dominion and sovereignty."[14]

In 1983 Foreign Minister Romulo of the Philippines said this was in process of change. A parallel tactic centered on using the mechanism to be set up by the Law of the Sea convention and treaty. But to date the Philippine law stands.

Other approaches included "no-issue" or "already settled" responses to Malaysian demands for a legal conclusion. Emmanuel Palaez's 1982 statement that "You cannot drop something you've never had" was the first.[15] Then Philippine foreign minister Tolentino offered another approach in comments at the time of the

ASEAN Annual Ministerial Meeting in July 1984. He noted that the claim has already been dropped, apparently in reference to President Marcos's remarks in 1977, and alluded to this consistent policy of the Marcos regime.[16] In dealing with the Aquino government, Malaysia has continued to demand a legislature-ratified renunciation to end ambiguity. This is even more urgent in the post-Marcos era because a new government might dismiss the Marcos promise and other diplomatic bandages as the invalid or illegal acts of a martial-law dictator.

Because the southern rebellion is currently under control and because domestic issues are preoccupying, the Aquino government in Manila seems to be holding to the no-issue stance until its house is in order. Secret negotiations have been conducted, but progress is slow; the Philippines is reported to be attempting to link the claim with other issues.[17] More optimistically, the new Philippine constitution drops reference to a Sabah claim.[18] Moreover, the removal of Marcos may dissolve personal obstacles, such as his desire to avoid the embarrassment of retraction or history's judgment as the man who lost Sabah.[19]

The issue persists into the Aquino era because a larger bargaining factor—the security situation in Mindanao—dominates. Before leaving for Kuala Lumpur to discuss the matter with Prime Minister Mahathir, Vice-President and then Foreign Minister Laurel of the Philippines stated, "The Philippines has not abandoned its claim to Sabah. We will not give up our claim just like that. We want a package deal."[20] The deal refers to cooperation in border patrols to stop weapons smuggling. The Malaysian demand for renunciation before negotiation requires the Philippines to give up its best card before the play begins. But the stakes are also high for Kuala Lumpur: before it takes the costly step of even discussing actions against Muslim insurgents, risking negative Muslim reactions at home and globally, it wants to receive its compensation.

While this parallels the interdependency between Malaysia and Thailand, other factors account for the stalemate over Sabah. Kuala Lumpur helps Thailand control Muslim insurgency, and in return gains the favor of hot pursuit or coordinated action, a favor that Thailand can withdraw at any time. The Philippines holds a favor that it can grant only once—the surrender of its claim. Then, too, the card is less valuable; Manila's claim is only seen as irritating, while the CPM problem is seen as lethal. Third, the Malaysian relationship with Thailand has developed a positive perception derived from the benefits that years of cooperation have yielded to both partners. So, while Thailand is seen as part of a solution, the Philippines is viewed as the cause of the problem, because it brought up the claim. Moreover, Thailand accepts Malaysian inability to control support given to separatists because Malaysia renders its support in demonstrations of solidarity vis-à-vis Vietnam, bilaterally and through the ASEAN process. The Philippines does not face such external threats or need such favors from Kuala Lumpur (other than help in the control of adventurist Islamic states, like Libya, an interest shared by both).

These considerations explain the lack of improvement, but it is fear of outside interference and ASEAN good offices that have preserved the modus vivendi. The two countries have mediated their relationship through ASEAN, using membership as an indirect, bilateral nonaggression pact. It was at the first Annual Ministerial Meeting (AMM) that they agreed to a cooling-off period; at the second AMM in December 1969 they restored relations. Since the Marcos regime found full renunciation an embarrassment, it fell back on the ASEAN Declaration to pledge respect for others' territory and, albeit indirectly, to recognize Malaysia as the government of Sabah. The price Manila paid for linking this issue to ASEAN is its future in the region. Should Manila revive the claim, alienated ASEAN partners could be expected, at least, to pelt Manila with condemnations and isolate it from the region.

Likewise, Kuala Lumpur has its own domestic and regional constraints parallel to its dilemma with Thailand; the regime cannot move against Muslim insurgents for political and ideological reasons. Pragmatically, the dilemma is compounded by the difficulties the government faces in controlling this activity in an area so far from the centers of federal power. So it, too, offers only a partial pledge, with implied qualifications about how much it can do. For its part, the Philippines accepts Malaysian commitment to accommodation first because of the record of good faith. Not since 1968 has Kuala Lumpur sent aid to the MNLF and that was a response to a perceived plot of interference by the Philippines (the "Corregidor

Affair''[21]). Second, ethnic links between the Kuala Lumpur regime and the Moro separatists are weak, weaker than those that tie Kuala Lumpur to the groups in southern Thailand.[22] Malaysia's restraint there strengthens the credibility of its commitment to resist interference in the southern Philippines. Furthermore, Malaysia has shown good faith and concern for the ASEAN image and so can be expected to honor the principles of noninterference.

Finally, Kuala Lumpur fears destabilization and external interference in Sabah also. The problematic Tun Mustapha Harun, Sabah's chief minister until 1975, apparently had dreams of forming his own new state carved out of the southern Philippines and a secessionist Sabah.[23] Currently, the concern is more ironic. The 1985 election of a Christian chief minister in Sabah is symptomatic of the increasing politicization of the non-Malay, indigenous peoples in both Sabah and Sarawak.[24] These peoples have responded to Christianity as an identifying institution to differentiate themselves from the ruling Malay Muslims. Should the Muslim Malays feel threatened and move to suppress this challenge, Christians might look to their coreligionists in the Philippines for support. In such a scenario, Kuala Lumpur may have as much or more to lose than Manila.

In sum, this relationship is truly grounded in an ASEAN context: both partners' policies have ramifications for all their other ASEAN relationships. Malaysia must demonstrate consistency in noninterference or its commitment to its other neighbors would be suspect. Exposure of a Libyan-PLO base in Malaysia alarms not only Manila but also Jakarta, Bangkok, and Brunei and their reactions move Kuala Lumpur to control the problem. Like other ASEAN states, the Philippines' restraint is based on preference for the status quo in Kuala Lumpur— this regime has shown good will and is better than the alternatives of a crusading Islamic state or chaos on northern Borneo. Meanwhile, Philippine restraint, intrinsic to its membership in ASEAN, is guaranteed by security interdependency with Malaysia and its desire for good relations with Indonesia, as well as the collectivity that ASEAN represents.

Indonesia and the Philippines

Indonesia and the Philippines are not so intertwined, but there are security interdependencies and anxieties about the role the larger state will play. Philippine suspicions center on Indonesia's aspirations in the region, more acutely perceived and publicly articulated in the pre-ASEAN era as the danger of the *Indonesian Raya*, a pan-archipelago empire. This heightened distrust grew out of President Sukarno's alignment with Maoist China and his flamboyant talk of a revived Majahapit empire. Fueling the suspicions in 1965, Senator Gauzon of the Philippines spoke of a map in Indonesian government offices that included parts of Mindanao.[25] While Manila has not expected an invasion, it has been anxious that Jakarta might support the insurgency of coreligionists in order to gain influence over a potential secessionist state.

The ASEAN process has lessened this concern. The New Order regime has opted for a *kleinstat* policy and has denied the validity of ethnic self-determination as a general principle.[26] In addition, the regime has kept to a secularism that eschews a specific role for Islam in the structure and policies of the state. This commitment to control politicized Islam reassures the Philippines as it reduces the likelihood that Indonesia would become involved in a liberation *jihad.*

Diplomacy at the foundation of ASEAN marks a milestone but also illustrates some opposing national interests and perspectives. The strongly pro–United States Philippines resisted Indonesian desires to remove the bases of that great power from the region. President Marcos had held out for the U.S. bases because he was as fearful of Indonesian domination as he was of Communism and Japan. Such suspicions made Philippine participation in ASEAN uncertain; Marcos had been advocating an alternative to ASEAN, the Asian Forum, a wider group that would dilute Indonesian influence.[27] Yet when his initiative fell on deaf ears he moved to take up the next best alternative, the offer of nonaggression by Indonesia to its neighbors. As for the bases, the final compromise in the ASEAN Declaration accepted the foreign bases but referred to them as temporary.

Indonesian anxieties about the Philippines have not been so concrete. In the Sukarno era, the nations were divided by cold-war ideologies, but since the ASEAN era, this cleavage has been removed. On the whole, the tensions between the two have never been overt; they even appeared as collaborators during *konfrontasi.* That alignment was due to expedience and opportunism: in addition to territorial ambitions on Malaysia's Sabah, Manila had some dreams of replacing Malaysia's Singapore as Indonesia's entrepot.[28] But once Jakarta, Kuala Lumpur, and Singapore began rapprochement, Manila backed away under the security of the U.S. umbrella as earlier suspicions about the regional giant, Indonesia, reasserted themselves. To Indonesia, Mindanao remains an irritating interdependency, primarily related to repercussions from domestic policies. While the Philippines' policies toward its Muslim citizens concern in theory only that sovereign state, these policies, if oppressive, can embarrass Jakarta and Kuala Lumpur, Manila's ASEAN partners, in front of their own Muslim citizenry and the Islamic world.

Transcending suspicions, the two states have engaged in joint operations dealing with their most direct security interdependencies, which are centered in the seas between Mindanao and the Sulawesi islands. Here, for centuries families have straddled borders where movement has been both customary and easy in the calm seas. In recent years eighty thousand Indonesian workers have moved north to work in the Philippines. In the early 1970s, the governments began to assert control over this frontier; border talks culminated in a Suharto-Marcos summit in the area in May 1974. Marcos traveled, significantly by sea, to Menando on Sulawesi and spoke of his government's efforts to better the situation of Muslims in the Philippines. This unusual apologia of domestic policy included mention of protections in the legal system, the more symbolic building of a mosque in Manila, and establishment of an Institute of Islamic Studies at the University of the Philippines.[29] Suharto's choice of the predominantly Christian city in Sulawesi was a more subtle response, showcasing how well the Christian minority fares in his Muslim-majority state.

The Indonesian-Philippine relationship evidenced more cooperation in the late 1970s when the Mindanao insurgency threatened to escalate. The Philippine government faced the broader challenge of the rebels' securing aid from the international Muslim community. Largely because Indonesia and Malaysia intervened at the Islamic Conference in May 1977, Manila was able to block this aid. The call by Foreign Minister Malik of Indonesia for a resolution of the question within Philippine sovereignty was much appreciated. As for the rebels, Manila gratefully acknowledged that Malaysia and Indonesia were "actively involved" in moderating the demands of the MNLF to the extent that its head, Nur Misuari, agreed to drop his demand for total independence in the face of "friendly pressures from our friends."[30] Foreign Minister Romulo commented that "Indonesia is a very courageous and loyal friend . . . same goes with Malaysia."[31] By July 1977, this good feeling between Indonesia and the Philippines resulted in a border agreement allowing hot pursuit and a system for families to cross the borders.[32]

These policies not only worked to favor the Philippines, they benefited Indonesia by stabilizing the eastern flank. Jakarta, too, feared an uncontrollable Muslim movement in Mindanao and the intervention of rich, activist Muslim states, which would destabilize not only the Philippines but also Malaysia and that sector of the Indonesian archipelago. The Philippines also supported the ASEAN process; Manila had faithfully complied with basic ASEAN principles intramurally and, significantly because it is not an immediate interest, joined in the rallies to defend Thailand and the western flank. Last, Indonesia once appreciated the Philippines on another level: it served for a time in the 1970s as a successful model of Malay development in contrast to the Singapore (read: Chinese) model. Indonesians felt more at ease with the personalities and style of their ethnic cousins and wanted to foster this alternative form of modernization.

From 1980 through the end of the Marcos era (1986), Manila and Jakarta evidenced a curiously mixed relationship. Border cooperation continued, yet Marcos remained suspicious of Indonesian aspirations or pretensions in the region. From January 1982 until April 1984 there was no Indonesian ambassador in Manila after the Philippines objected to the Indonesian ambassador's comments in a Philippine newspaper, namely, that the Philippines and Malaysia should hold talks and settle the Sabah claim, and that the Philippine National Assembly should pass a formal resolution on the issue because, while "there are many denials, . . . Malaysia is not convinced." Foreign Minister Romulo expressed his government's "extreme displeasure" about the "undue interference" to Ambasssador Lopulisa, who was recalled later in the year.[33] In April 1984, Rear Admiral Mudjono Purbonegor was appointed the new ambassador to Manila. This clash was troublesome because it damaged the image of ASEAN solidarity at the very time when ASEAN members were having difficulties coordinating their policies on Cambodia. It also reveals the concern for sovereignty; states will accept outside involvement only on their own terms. The spirit of ASEAN is at times not so much unity and community but more ''mind your own business.''

Bridging the Flanks

Because the Philippines has the smallest number of security inter-dependencies with other ASEAN states and the greatest security on its own, more needs to be said about its commitment to the ASEAN-sponsored collective political defense of Thailand. Security benefits from cooperation with Malaysia and Indonesia acting under the ASEAN umbrella underlie Manila's involvement in ASEAN diplomacy. Insurance against isolation is another motivation; the ASEAN process widens one's circle of friends. Just as Thailand can count on the support of five states even though it is intertwined with only three, so, too, the Philippines seems linked with five even though its security interests are interconnected with only two. Intramurally, within the subregion a convergence of interests with Singapore and Thailand is also important. The Philippines values ASEAN association with these states as a means of diluting Muslim or Malay predominance, a concern shared by all these states. Last, as a whole and individually, the other members of ASEAN have prudently given Manila other reasons to stay in the process, such as endorsements of the regime, in both the Marcos and Aquino eras, and acceptance as a Third World, Asian nation.

Control of the southern Muslims, Manila's primary boon, is also contingent on ASEAN involvement. Manila's insurgency has become a regional political issue, in addition to a military issue, because these Philippine Muslims have looked to Indonesia and Malaysia ''for orientation. Instead of regarding themselves as a minority, they have argued that they form the majority in the region.''[34] Indonesia and Malaysia have acted responsibly; their intervention to outside Muslim states and reassurances to the Philippine Muslims helped secure acceptance of the autonomy plan as an alternative to independence. Consequently, as popular opinion feels that ''ASEAN had made a significant impact in the development of the autonomous [Muslim] region,"[35] defection from ASEAN could begin the devolution of the Manila-Moro accords.

Membership in ASEAN is key to this intramural diplomacy; all realize that the success of the whole process depends on the commitments to noninterference. Because the Philippines is viewed as a partner, Indonesia and Malaysia can support Manila's sovereignty over Muslims. Equally important, ASEAN membership allowed the Philippines to ask for and expect to get help in managing this sensitive internal affair. Alternatives to the ASEAN approach explain its value. Without the euphemism of "ASEAN," Indonesian and Malaysian collaboration on an internal matter would be much more difficult for the Philippines to accept and for them to offer. An even more dangerous situation, worsening the Mindanao insurgency, would follow Philippine defection from ASEAN process; the pivotal Philippine-Malaysian promise of restraint, as well as the relationship with Indonesia, would lose its guarantee. Finally, Manila would be seen as a destroyer of yet another regional organization and would risk future ostracism and face grave obstacles to creating good faith in the future with its erstwhile partners.

Along with these national security interests, concern about national identity ties the Philippines to the ASEAN process. Filipinos are "insecure about their identity and unsure that their brand of nationalism can pass inspection before the other nations of the Third World. . . . [They feel that they were traumatized by the Second World War, and that they have been] traitors to the high cause of the colored races in the East."[36] This insecurity provided the motivation for earlier Philippine moves to regionalism. The apologia of Diosdada Macapagal, the president behind ASA, illustrates this mentality: "The accretions, additions and embellishments from without have not altered the innate qualities of the heart and soul nor the fundamental mould of temperament and character that make the Filipinos an indubitably Asian nation."[37]

Membership in ASEAN signifies acceptance as an Asian country, which is especially important to Philippine nationalists who wish to distance themselves from their colonial past. Psychologically, the ASEAN focus and identity serves to cure the "colonial mentality."

The Marcos regime was quick to use ASEAN to reject the charge that it was a U.S. puppet. Membership in ASEAN signified the regime's Asian, nonaligned, independent policy. In an interesting political drama, Marcos used ASEAN membership to counter the opposition's call for the removal of U.S. bases. After he first agreed to removal, he then yielded to U.S. demands, claiming that the Philippines must sacrifice some sovereignty to help ASEAN partners. The opposition then had to choose between the bases and regional cooperation (ASEAN). Turning to ASEAN partners, the card is played again; Manila often reminds that it has sacrificed sovereignty in the name of ASEAN. Since the ASEAN partners are glad not to have bases in their countries, for domestic and international reasons, but do want them in the neighborhood, they are indebted to Manila for its regional security contribution. More problematic is the Aquino government's stand. Calls by the nationalist Foreign Minister Monglapus for ASEAN states to publicly support the bases have been so far resisted—ASEAN partners instead followed the past pattern of offering other inducements, like the series of regime endorsements that occurred at the Manila summit.

Marcos also used ASEAN membership to enhance his regime and consolidate his power. Acceptance by the other leaders—in visits and at conferences—added to his legitimacy. For years, Marcos ruled without a legislature or regular elections (it was only in 1978 that elections for a puppet National Assembly, the interim *Batasang Pambansa*, were held), and these endorsements were important. Subsequent elections were suspect, and after the 1983 assassination of Benigno Aquino outside support became even more important. Marcos looked for the ultimate ASEAN endorsement, a summit, knowing that precedent required it be held in Manila. In addition to public diplomacy, the Marcos regime used membership in ASEAN to justify martial law, arguing that strong government is the norm in developing countries. For example, an editorial from the *Times Journal* stated:

> This is perhaps why almost all of the member states of ASEAN have included in their Constitutions or laws express authority to their respective heads of state to act immediately for the safety and security of the state. Singapore and Malaysia have "internal security acts" which empower their leaders to crack down on dissidence and take in

tow those seeking to overthrow the government. Thailand and Indonesia are carefully governed by military men who hold in their hands powerful laws which many would consider contrary to western mores.[38]

Initially, other ASEAN members with authoritarian systems were in agreement with the Marcos style. Prime Minister Lee was a welcome guest to Manila.

[In 1974, he commented that there is] not much difference in the martial law situation here in comparison with other countries undergoing similar experiences.[39]

[In 1977, he] expressed confidence that under the leadership of President Marcos, the Philippines will meet the challenge before the Filipino nation with wisdom, with vigor, and with foresight.[40]

With the downturn of the regime's fortunes in the 1980s such endorsements ceased; and ASEAN partners practiced discreet silence on the Philippine situation.

The Aquino government presents a new factor in ASEAN politics. Security interconnections and national identity motives remain important, and the 1987 Manila summit—held despite difficulties to bolster President Aquino's government—shows that ASEAN endorsements may still be a valued contribution from neighbors. In accord with ASEAN custom for a new head of government, Aquino visited ASEAN partners, signaling that Philippine commitment has transcended the change of government in Manila.

Brunei and ASEAN

Brunei's 1984 admission to the ASEAN organization confirms another set of accommodations between this small state and its two large neighbors, Indonesia and Malaysia. In so doing, it illustrates the continuing utility of the ASEAN symbol and the bridging function of these core ASEAN states.

Suspicions between Malaysia and Brunei are rooted in past interactions and geographic factors. The small state is surrounded and divided by the territory of Malaysia. Brunei, small in territory and population (only 200,000), but extremely rich in oil reserves, has reason to fear the policies of any neighbor. Specifically, Malaysia and Brunei had to overcome a series of negative incidents, reaching back to confrontations during the planning for the Federation of Malaysia. Disagreements over the sharing of oil revenues and the monarchical succession led to Brunei's refusal to join Malaysia. A greater security danger occurred in 1962 when a resistance group was given refuge in Malaysia. The rebels were leftovers from the Party Rakyat Brunei (PRB) who had unsuccessfully attempted to seize power after gaining half the elective seats in parliament. Afterward, they escaped to sanctuaries in adjacent Malaysia and to a headquarters in Jakarta.[41] Brunei responded by raising a claim to the sanctuary area in Malaysian territory, Limbang. Strategically, Brunei reaffirmed its connections with Britain, extending its term as a protectorate and facilitating this by funding the British forces on duty in Brunei. The oil-rich state also kept its reserves in British banks as another inducement to London. However, all this only put off the inevitable; the Anglophile sultan faced ultimate British withdrawal and the challenge of coexistence with Malaysia and Indonesia.

The question of Brunei independence was affected by the apprehensive months of 1975; Hanoi was on the road to victory, and Indonesia resolved a Brunei-like dilemma in East Timor when it eventually annexed the Portuguese colony in December 1975. Malaysia had strong reasons to consider annexation as the answer to its concerns about Brunei. Small though it is, Brunei threatened Malaysia with a destabilized East; it had claimed Malaysian territory in the Limbang salient, and an independent Brunei might encourage and fund separatist movements in Sabah and Sarawak. Brunei's territory might become a base for subversion if the sultanate should be replaced by a radical regime.[42] Since Indonesia shared the last two concerns, which paralleled its motives for acting in the Timor case, it was sympathetic to Malaysia's dilemma. A military solution seems to have been considered; in the third quarter of 1975, Malaysia "successfully tested its offensive capability in a combined operation which involved a seaborne landing of a full infantry brigade of about 3,000 men with supporting arms." This included naval and air support near Mersing on the east coast, where the terrain is similar to Brunei and is "not usually part of the array of methods available to planners of an anti-insurgency strategy."[43]

But Timor did not provide the prototype solution because there were different domestic and regional factors in this case. Internally unlike Timor, Brunei had potential to assume the role as a viable international actor. Its government had historical and religious legitimacy; it could expect popular support to grow out of the largesse it had been bestowing, unlike Timor's poverty and lack of development, which had served Marxists as exploitable discontent. There was no reason to expect a civil war as was the actuality in Timor. Moreover, Brunei had the funds to develop its security forces and committed itself to self-defense. From 1978 to 1980 Brunei spent nearly U.S. $1 billion, and substantial yearly outlays have followed; the country spent U.S. $216 million in 1985.[44] Helicopters, guided missiles, and additional battalions signaled Brunei's staying power to Kuala Lumpur and Jakarta.

Regional politics in the aftermath of Hanoi's victories in Cambodia added a sense of urgency, uncertainty, and caution. The costs of a war of attrition and the possibility that an endangered Brunei might offer its good harbor, centrally located in the South China Sea, to any number of dangerous powers deterred aggressive action. Finally, the Malaysian government came to view the Brunei question differently out of its own changed domestic situation. Luckily, Malaysia discovered its own oil reserves, thus removing the temptation to acquire the Brunei fields. As for grievances rooted in the contentious period of refusal to join Malaysia, time passed, healing memories and removing personalities who had been directly involved.

Singapore entered the diplomacy supporting Brunei to defend their common interests. Singapore and Brunei developed a relationship on the commonality of size. The small city-state disliked the precedent of the Timor solution and acted as an advocate for Brunei. It argued that Timor's troubles do not prove the inviability of small states, because Singapore itself demonstrates the ability of small states to be stable and prosperous. Singapore also actively helped Brunei; throughout the 1970s Singaporean technology and personnel flowed to Brunei. In return for its expertise and training, Singapore gained access to jungle training facilities—long denied to it by

Malaysia. Singapore's advocacy of Brunei linked its treatment to the future of the ASEAN process and so raised the costs of a Timor-type solution.

These considerations, then, separated Brunei from the Timor situation. Brunei was domestically stable and prosperous, was capable of self-defense, had regional allies, and even had diplomatic leverage through its claim on the Limbang salient. Malaysia was not worried about an imminent leftist government in Brunei as Indonesia had been, and Malaysia was not now tempted by the oil of Brunei. Last, Malaysia did not follow the military option because conquest of East Timor has been a moderating experience for the Indonesians. The military sent in 30,000 men in 1975, and almost ten years later some 15,000 remained in the territory, fighting an estimated 500–800 guerrillas.[45] Estimates of 100,000 deaths from famine since 1975 are given.[46] Diplomatic repercussions, though perhaps only an annoyance, have lingered long after the conquest. Indonesia has faced criticism at each session of the UN General Assembly. Foreign Minister Mochtar found it necessary to tour the South Pacific in July 1983 to rally support on this question.[47] And Timor has plagued relations with Australia. Reports from groups like Amnesty International continuously raise concern in Australia and put pressure on Canberra to intervene on behalf of the Timorese. The inquiries of journalists, human rights groups, and the foreign governments, however, are viewed by the Indonesians as "meddling."[48] The possibility of the guerrillas having a representative office in Canberra has on occasion severely strained relations between the two neighboring states.[49] The diplomatic battle over Timor has other fronts; even the former colonial power, Portugal, claims as the internationally recognized administering power that settlement has yet to be found. In 1984, it announced its "resolve to achieve self-determination for its former colony"[50] and followed through with reminders.[51] Secretary of State George Shultz brought up the Timor situation on his July 1984 visit, and the Vatican has rebuked the Indonesian ambassador. The diplomatic and military costs of the conquest inclined Malaysia and Indonesia to work with the emerging state of Brunei.

By early 1976 Prime Minister Hussein began a more cooperative approach to Brunei. The May 1978 Suharto-Hussein conference at

Labuan, a site close to Brunei, sealed the decision to arrive at an ASEAN accommodation with Brunei. They acknowledged the state's sovereignty, saying the form of independence was "solely the affair of Brunei, which the people of Brunei have to decide." However, they hoped Brunei would join ASEAN when it became independent.[52]

Tengku Rithauddeen visited Brunei in February 1979 and acknowledged need for "a common understanding,"[53] acts of good will, and cooperation; the relationship now began to take public forms. Acting Foreign Minister Taib Mahmud reassured Britain's Lord Carrington that Kuala Lumpur considers "the security of Brunei of prime importance, primarily to ASEAN."[54] In March 1980 the king of Malaysia visited Brunei, and in September 1981 the sultan of Brunei visited Kuala Lumpur. Deputy Prime Minister Musa announced when he visited Brunei in March 1982 that Malaysia would sponsor Brunei for membership in the Islamic Conference and in ASEAN. During a visit of Prime Minister Mahathir in March 1983, Malaysia began a program of training officials. Most significantly, the two recognized their security interconnectedness by setting up a communication link between border police, filling a last security gap in the ASEAN area.[55]

To complement this bilateral diplomacy, Brunei was invited in June 1980 to be an observer in the ASEAN process even before independence. Brunei accepted the arrangement because it converged with its interests: "The significance of Asean to Brunei is not so much in the joining as in what must come before it . . . the unequivocal acknowledgment of the state's international legitimacy by Asean members."[56] Though the visits and promises of Malaysian leaders in the years since the Labuan summit had addressed this need, the ASEAN organization enhanced the promises. Malaysia gave Brunei recognition and the pledge of noninterference with ASEAN as collateral. In return, Brunei pledged local cooperation and diplomatic solidarity. In sum, accommodation gave Malaysia a stable and peaceful neighbor committed to controlling insurgency and gave Brunei "a kind of security guarantee."[57]

Papua-New Guinea and Indonesia

By way of summarizing the importance and linkages of security accommodations to the ASEAN process, one more pairing under the ASEAN umbrella is offered: Indonesia's relationship with Papua-New Guinea (PNG). Here again, states are attempting to avoid a mutually destructive situation by controlling border insurgency. The nexus of security interdependency is the border between the Indonesian province of Irian Jaya (West Irian) and Papua-New Guinea, which occupies the other half of the island of New Guinea. The West Irian inhabitants are ethnically related to some of the Melanesian Papuan peoples in the nation of Papua-New Guinea. Problems have been arising out of Jakarta's development strategy, which relocates farmers from Java and other islands and settles them on West Irian. The indigenous Melanesian response to this ''Javanization'' has been a guerrilla resistance called the Free Papua Movement, which has links and support on the other side of the jungle border. International frictions develop when reports circulate that the Indonesian Army has violated PNG territory in pursuit.[58]

A 1979 border agreement articulated the states' commitment to continue friendly relations and deal with their security interdependency by denying sanctuary to insurgents.[59] Restraint is the only practical policy because a military option on this scale is unthinkable: ''Irian Jaya and Timor have already caused them more than enough [worry and expense] already.''[60] Concurrently, the cooperative policy of Port Moresby has reassured Jakarta; it has joined in a joint-border committee that supervises border crossings.[61] For its part, Papua-New Guinea has practiced restraint by resisting the ethno-nationalistic calls to unite the island. In return, it has gained the benefits of acceptance and coexistence with its larger neighbor. From the start this has been a positive relationship; the independence of Papua-New Guinea in 1975 was not marked by confrontation but, rather, by consultation—a relationship much like those Jakarta pursues with its other neighbors.

Bilaterally built on the principle of restraint, this relationship has been strengthened by the ASEAN process: Papua-New Guinea is an associate member of the Association and has acceded to the Treaty of Amity and Cooperation. So far, though it has been invited, Papua-New Guinea has declined to become the seventh member on the grounds that such an action might dilute its voice in the South Pacific Forum.[62] Nevertheless, its attendance at annual meetings allows both Papua-New Guinea and Indonesia to reaffirm their mutual commitment under the ASEAN symbol. As with the other bilateral relationships, the ASEAN context enhances Indonesia's promise by linking it to other ASEAN promises of restraint. This was made explicit at the signing of an October 1986 Indonesian-PNG friendship treaty, one which contains a nonaggression clause. (The treaty, a formal and legal pledge to the principles of sovereignty and noninterference, was a surrogate for the ASEAN treaty.) Foreign Minister Mochtar used the history of ASEAN to underline the good intentions of Indonesia toward Papua-New Guinea in this statement: "If we can live in peace and harmony with our neighbors in the region we can live in peace with you."[63]

Papua-New Guinea acknowledges this ASEAN reality, working with Indonesia bilaterally on the border problem, and supporting the ASEAN process—both by attendance at annual foreign ministers meetings and by joining in common policy stands, such as on Cambodia. But even on this issue, Foreign Minister Namaliu can be heard expressing his state's basic interest in condemning the occupation: "We have a strong and obvious commitment to the right of small countries to be free from external interference or coercion."[64] This statement highlights the value all ASEAN states place on noninterference. As this far-removed state joins in defense of Thailand, the price of belonging to ASEAN, it skillfully includes a reminder to the larger state that participation depends on the latter's commitment to restraint. This complements the way Indonesia earlier used its history of good behavior in ASEAN to assuage the fears of the small state. The statement also illustrates the complexity of ASEAN diplomatic activity; at times states will concert their foreign policy stands to support the intramural process. This understanding of ASEAN solidarity explains much of the joint diplomacy that will be discussed in the next chapters.

6

ASEAN Diplomacy: Talking to Each Other

> This empathy, this rapport is a very important intangible in our bilateral relations.
>
> —Prime Minister Lee Kuan Yew

STRONG bilateral ties among many of the ASEAN six provide the sure foundation for their multilateral cooperation while ASEAN procedures and institutions strengthen their ability to remain within the political process. Annual visits between most heads of government have become customary and are described as *empat mata* (four eyes), a Bahasa expression meaning a direct one-on-one meeting between leaders, without agenda or interpreters, if possible.[1] Visits serve, in the words of the *Straits Times* on the occasion of Prime Minister Lee's visit to Manila, "to further Asean regionalism and to promote closer bilateral ties. . . . [I]n international terms, of course, the activity is a sign of continuing Asean solidarity, or at least an interest to work towards this objective."[2] Talking points, such as fishing rights, water supplies, porous borders, and insurgents, as well as regional politics, reflect the interdependence of contiguous neighbors and the convergence of interests that bind them in a policy of accommodation. Moreover, leaders bring an entourage, hoping that familiarizing counterparts, notably intelligence and security officials, will facilitate communication. Cooperation has also included joint military exercises and intelligence cooperation.

But there are limits to bilateralism within the ASEAN process. While the four states of the western flank have almost unbroken records of annual visitations, the record is not so good on the eastern flank where the Sabah dilemma prevents the fullest show of solidarity. Domestic problems within the Philippines also inclined other states to distance themselves from the Marcos regime (but with President Aquino, summit visits have resumed). Despite summit lapses, consultations continued for officials at lower levels, demonstrating the importance of institutions and established procedures to multilateralism. In this case, the ASEAN organization's schedule provided regular, apolitical occasions for gathering.

The ASEAN organization itself has fostered rapport and addressed a cause of past frictions. In the pre-ASEAN era, leaders did not know each other and had no institution for consultation and negotiation. Since its founding, ASEAN members have fostered their cooperation through several instruments of public and quiet diplomacy. The annual meeting of foreign ministers, known as AMM for Annual Ministerial Meeting, is the Association's oldest institution and most salient to an analysis of political development. Though the first listed aim of ASEAN was "to accelerate the economic growth, social progress, and cultural development in the region through joint endeavor" (Bangkok Declaration, 1967), the organization was created by, and has since been directed by, a meeting of the states' foreign ministers. (Not until 1975 did economic ministers have their first meeting.) From the start, states realized that they must lay a political foundation for future economic cooperation.

This Annual Ministerial Meeting has served several functions: it is a yearly reminder and demonstration of mutual intramural commitment to ASEAN ideals and principles. The ministers regularly issue joint stands on what is defined as ASEAN business, namely, economics. The forum is an acculturating process; new representatives are brought into the regional ethos. Called a "meat grinder" by one observer, it represents a process of continuous consultation and repeated deliberations, putting proposals and policies to the test of open debate, criticism, and peer pressure.[3] This prevents a distancing or remoteness from obscuring the ASEAN obligations. In effect, the "meat grinder" has introduced an accountability mechanism into the consultation process. States can discuss problems, air grievances, and get explanations through a process of ongoing, multiple-channel consultations.

States have accepted this infringement on their sovereignty because the demands of the process—its frequency, expectations, and regularization—have been incremental and did not require an immediate, large concession. Gradually ASEAN members developed the habits of consultation. The members also accepted the procedure of discussion, debate, and defense of their actions to each other because it is done in secret and is built on the reservoir of good faith created since the beginning of the ASEAN era. Time has also developed the identification dynamic wherein understanding, credibility, and empathy have increased among ASEAN diplomats. This all ameliorates accountability, as explanations are accepted on the word of the member. Most important, the consultation-accountability procedure is accepted because it is seen as the price and guarantee for ASEAN peace and stability. Accountability now works to influence national policies at the time of formation. The ''spirit of ASEAN'' is present in each capital as foreign policies are being discussed, reminding leaders that they will have to face the ''meat grinder,'' that is, justify their actions at the next ASEAN session. Responsibility, that important element of accommodation that requires one to consider the effect one's actions will have on others, is thus bolstered by both positive and negative ASEAN inducements.

Between annual meetings, other ASEAN institutions carry on consultation and accountability. A Standing Committee, chaired by the foreign minister of the host country for the next AMM and comprising the ambassadors accredited to that capital, meets regularly. Its chairman can, when necessary and after notification, speak for all members of the process. (This function does not fall to the secretary-general of the ASEAN organization, highlighting the compartmentalization of political activities from organization business.) Because this gives great voice to one foreign minister, and because some misunderstandings have arisen, such statements are infrequent. Nine additional committees (Budget; Culture and Information; Finance and Banking; Food, Agriculture and Forestry; Industry, Minerals and Energy; Science and Technology; Social Development; Trade and Tourism; Transportation and Communications) serve to promote cooperation at functional economic and social levels. A secretary-general and secretariat are located in Jakarta.

Finally, another institution has evolved outside the organization's structure. Substantive negotiations are now conducted at a Senior Officials Meeting (SOM). Originally created to prepare ASEAN's first collective policy in 1971, it most recently worked on the agenda for the summit in Manila. Consultations on the end of the Vietnam war in 1975 and 1976 matured this institution, and it has since become "a continuing feature of ASEAN cooperation in the political field."[4] In other words, it has become the de facto political coordinating committee of the ASEAN process. Though its members are referred to as ASEAN senior officials, this committee is not an ASEAN organization body. Because its meetings take place quietly to avoid the pressures and expectations of publicity, it is not itself used as a symbol of ASEAN solidarity. Rather, the SOM facilitates consultations on such divisive questions as Cambodia by taking care to stay out of the public view. Calls for formalization of this body have gone unanswered, including the recommendation of the 1984 ASEAN Task Force report commissioned to study the structure of ASEAN. ASEAN has been reluctant to acknowledge its political functions, preferring instead to cultivate an apolitical economic image.

Codewords

In addition to machinery, ASEAN states have developed several instruments and approaches to aid their consultative process. These include codewords, collective political stands, special foreign ministers meetings, summits, and meetings with great-power partners. Foremost among these aids are codewords, that is, the language of their empathy and rapport. Codewords articulate harsh realities, threats, or understandings in acceptable common language. As conceptualizations of ASEAN members' consensus, they provide insight into the calculations and compromises made during the consultation process. Moreover, a codeword serves as a "signal for coordination, so unmistakenly comprehensible and so potent in its suggestion for action that everyone can be sure everyone else reads the same signal with enough confidence to act on it, thus providing one another with the immunity that goes with action in large numbers."[5]

The first set of codewords—"ASEAN," "interdependence," "Balkanization," "Zopfan," and "resilience"—reveals the rationality and strategy behind ASEAN "solidarity," itself a codeword. The first codeword is the acronym "ASEAN," which aggregates all uses of the term and characterizes today's cooperation, in contrast to the *konfrontasi* era before 1967. The expression "before ASEAN" recalls that the subregion was competitive, while "ASEAN" represents the prosperity and stability. "ASEAN" crystallizes a mood of relief and gratitude.

In turn, there is a price, tolerance, which means the automatic acceptance of each other's domestic systems. This was expressed most directly by Prime Minister Kukrit of Thailand on a visit to Malaysia in 1975: "What choice have we but to learn to live together and to adjust to one another in the spirit of tolerance."[6] This awareness, of course, results from the states' futile, foolish, and costly attempts at interference during *konfrontasi*. Reciprocal acceptance was the first step in creating the ASEAN process.

Konfrontasi taught the lesson of tolerance, but it is reinforced by a commonality in leaders' beliefs, evidenced in their similar responses to domestic pluralism. All have chosen to manage religious and racial antagonisms through tolerant authoritarianism. This "live-and-let-live" principle parallels the ASEAN spirit of noninterference to the extent that ASEAN has been called "a replication of the domestic circumstances."[7]

Indonesia, whose approach to pluralism is well articulated in the national slogan "Unity in Diversity," has been said to include seventeen old nations[8] and has been called "almost itself a regional organization."[9] It works because the government enforces tolerance and acceptance. Centrist leaders have balanced conservative and moderate forces while suppressing those of more radical persuasions.[10] Meanwhile, they have tried to build an appealing higher common interest, the modernizing state. To bolster regional cooperation, the New Order regime applied the same tactic, holding up the common interest of a stable, secure environment.

Likewise, Malaysia has had to organize three races into one state. The ruling party coalition allows each race its own representative institution (its own party) within the broader structure. Dr. Mahathir explains:

> Problems cannot be wished away or legislated away. Problems have to be faced squarely and tackled in a rational manner. In Malaysia the

face of race is recognized. Hence, the parties are racially based. But because the need for cooperation between races is also recognized, the racially based parties are prepared to work together in a coalition. Nevertheless it is recognized that a coalition of absolute equals is not durable. For a coalition to work, it must have a strong party to form the backbone, and that party must recognize that its interest is best served by give and take within a coalition.[11]

While this means Malay leadership within Malaysia, extending these principles to the ASEAN process implies the need for a regional leader, Indonesia.

"ASEAN" has a human dimension also. Personal familiarity and years of good faith in their dealings have reinforced the image of ASEAN. "Human nature being what it is, the mere process of contact with foreign rulers breeds desire to be helpful, to see those we know personally succeed . . . nowhere [is this] more true than in Southeast Asia where personal charm is endemic and hospitality has been developed to a fine art."[12] While optimistic, the actions and articulations of local statesmen do seem to subscribe to this dynamic. A founding father of ASEAN, Ali Moertopo, explained that consultations are successful because leaders have been old friends "who know one another so well."[13] Many speak of the ease of telephone contacts as facilitating their relationships. Ghazalie Shafie has described ASEAN as an "almost telepathic community."[14] A more restrained view of this familiarity dynamic takes into account that all-too-human reality that some ASEAN leaders, having met, have found that they do not like each other. In such cases, contact can create a more limited bond of obligations or just a facility to negotiate with those who are well known, if not well liked. Prime Minister Lee, a believer in the socializing process, has described the function of understanding personalities as a "safety net": "Thus, when an official spoke loudly, his counterpart would have known from long association that he was one to speak loudly anyway, whether happy or angry, and thus, knowing that there was no significance in it, would not get unduly excited."[15]

The organization's cultural activities have benefited the ASEAN image. Its international prestige, its meetings and programs (such as film festivals and exchange programs), the wide-and-loose use of the acronym to label events like professionals' conventions, the wide coverage given to individual achievements of ASEAN partners, and the programs of member governments to promote "ASEAN consciousness" ("to think ASEAN") all suggest that ASEAN is a vibrant entity. Sometimes these suggestions are grounded in only the thinnest reality. For example, an *Asiaweek* headline, "ASEAN Pulls It All Together," referred to the laying of a submarine telecommunications cable.[16] In reality the cable linked only two members of ASEAN, but the reader at first glance is left with the impression that ASEAN did the work, owns the cable, and is benefiting the societies involved. An ASEAN personality emerges. "ASEAN consciousness" has also resulted from an identification factor found in the thinking of foreign-policy makers. They see their interests converging with the group's well-being; they take pride in group successes and recognition; their ASEAN divisions within the foreign ministries are constant reminders of the ASEAN bond. ASEAN consciousness has been so embellished that it has been aptly called "a myth," namely, the significance of the story is seen in its application, not in its content. At times, ASEAN's success record has appeared to seduce statesmen into more cooperation. At other times, the popular image has allowed governments to assuage domestic opposition, misgivings, or apathy and act on behalf of other states by couching policy in terms of ASEAN.

The motivation behind restraint and cooperation and that which is the reality behind ASEAN consciousness is preserved in codewords like "intertwined" and "interdependent." These are used in statements such as "Our future and fate are interwoven and nobody will ever succeed in separating us,"[17] or "We have never been more conscious that the future of ASEAN countries is so interwoven."[18] Malaysia and Singapore cannot alter the fact of being "interdependent."[19] The "destiny and future of Malaysia and Thailand are intertwined."[20] This awareness works at the multilateral level also; consider another codeword, "regional resilience," defined as a common security resulting from the "ability of each state in the region to be fully committed to their organized interrelatedness and interdependence as the first principle of foreign policy."[21]

Interdependence means that borders do not insulate states from neighbors' political destabilization, nor do they deter secessionists or insurgents. Memories of *konfrontasi* and ongoing insurgencies that straddle borders teach states that they must not fall into disastrous interference. Those in the vulnerable area of the Malacca Straits feel this threat most intensely, and they have been most active in collaboration. In sum, "interdependence" reminds that subversives might be enjoying support and sanctuary camps across the border line if not for the cooperation practiced in the name of ASEAN. On the other hand, "interwovenness" makes joint stands of solidarity and unity real and not just convenient diplomatic posturing. Finally, the codeword recalls some states' use of ASEAN as collateral in their bilateral relationships. It implies that no state is isolated, and that a single violation of restraint against one will affect relations with all the others.

"Balkanization," another codeword, also plays on the fear of destructive rivalry that existed before the ASEAN era; it alludes to the situation that prevailed in southeastern Europe before and through the two world wars. For instance, Ali Moertopo reminds ASEAN members that regional rivalries "will weaken all sides, as was the case in the Balkans."[22] Rivalries give great powers the opportunity for involvement, perhaps resulting in a destructive war fought in the small states' territories (the fear of this eventuality, having already occurred during World War II, is heard in the ASEAN warning about becoming "the cockpit of the powers"). Finally, "Balkanization" results in loss of independence when the small states fall into the sphere of a great power.

Loss of independence resulting from intramural rivalries is also the lesson drawn from local history when these states were colonized. Both "imperialism" and the less controversial term "colonialism" recall the value of solidarity. For example, "The lack of unity or a larger federation among these little kingdoms was the major factor that led to their collapse before the invading *conquistador* or commercial company of a colonizing power."[23] Thus, "Balkanization" or "colonialism" warn of the alternatives to ASEAN solidarity.

In addition to codewords that describe dangers, the ASEAN lexicon contains two words that address solutions. The acronym "Zopfan" (Zone of Peace, Freedom, and Neutrality) is based on the 1971 initiative that attempted to gain great-power cooperation in the neutralization of the region. While the ASEAN consensus does not consider Zopfan a realistic formula to achieve the goal in the immediate future, the codeword nonetheless expresses the general wish to be free of outside interference. As such, it provides another way to underline dangers without appearing alarmist. "Zopfan" also demonstrates ASEAN members' commitment to nonalignment, a useful credential in Third World forums and an arguing point in attempts to reassure Vietnam that the grouping is not an alliance.

"National resilience" is perhaps the most noted ASEAN codeword; it stresses the need to guard against outside interference and includes a forestalling formula that is indicative of the individualism intrinsic to the process. ASEAN ministers first jointly explained in 1972 the necessity "for member countries to develop national resilience which would enable them to face present changes and challenges of the future with greater confidence"(Joint Communique, April 13–14, 1972). "Resilience" accepts the diagnosis of Peter Lyons that insurgency is preeminently a symptom of political instability, of government weakness and the absence of a stable statewide system of law and order.[24] As has clearly been the state policy in Singapore, Indonesia, Malaysia, Brunei, and Thailand, "resilience" first means raising standards of living to gain the support of the populace. Bolstered by this sort of legitimacy, the government will be able to check subversive movements because the satisfied populace will not support them. As for regional resilience, it is a sum of the parts: Prosperity and stability are achieved by each individual nation, not from joint actions; none is promised despite ASEAN's facade of economic cooperation. This bottom-up process explains the low level of ASEAN joint economic activity. When all are politically stable and prosperous, neighbors will benefit because they need not fear destabilization next door. If all states are resilient, then the cumulative "regional resilience" results. In sum, the 1987 Manila Declaration restates, "Member states shall strengthen national and regional resilience to ensure security, stability and growth in the ASEAN region."

The codewords "front-line" and "solidarity" deal with a specific foreign policy problem, the security of Thailand. "Front-line," a term that speaks to the military background of so many in ASEAN governments, signifies that Thailand provides a first line of defense and consequently bears the brunt of conflict. Calling Thailand the "front-line state" acknowledges this service and the obligation to repay this debt. Complications about actual responses arise, however, because members' divergent threat perceptions and interests keep them from forming an alliance against Vietnam. Therefore, "front-line" is a measured reaction to the war in Indochina; it does not imply common expectation of Vietnamese invasion—these are not quaking dominoes, and some, like Malaysia and Indonesia, have a sympathy for Vietnam. "Front-line," in many ways, is a great concession for these two. They wonder how Thailand can accept a Vietnamese-dominated Laos but not Cambodia. Some, like the editorialist in *Sinar Harapan*, suspect that they are being used by Thailand to maximize "its traditional ambition in the 'Trans-Mekong' region (meaning Kampuchea) through the Kampuchean conflict and in the ASEAN political framework."[25]

Yet they accept "front-line," acknowledging the reality that Thailand stands as a buffer separating the lower peninsular states (Malaysia, Singapore, and Indonesia) from incursions and refugees. Even the remote Philippines has shown appreciation for the front-line function, as President Marcos explained: "We depend on the strength of the Thai government and the will of the Thai people to maintain a peaceful stalemate. This would allow countries in the region a breathing spell wherein to develop."[26]

"Front-line" expresses the relief and gratitude felt by those states that are distanced from the troubles in Cambodia; it expresses their support not in military terms, but rather in what Adam Malik described as help "in the form of ideas, prayers, and diplomatic steps."[27] This support, described earlier as "collective political defense," is played out in displays of unity and common political articulations, all of which are grouped under the codeword "solidarity."

Mufakat and *mushawarah* are terms that express the ASEAN art of accommodation. Together, *mufakat* (consensus) and *mushawarah* (consultation) ground ASEAN diplomacy in village decision making. The salience of asking others' advice and opinions, and recognizing others' interests and stature, becomes clear by looking back to the origins of the *konfrontasi*. Though Malaysia had agreed to *mushawarah* to settle the northern Borneo dispute in June 1963, Tunku Abdul Rahman signed the declaration forming Malaysia before such consultations were completed. Sukarno regarded this as a breach of faith, if not an insult, and used this as justification for the outbreak of violence.[28] The criticisms that *mushawarah* produces broad, lowest common denominators and thus weak positions are not justified. States have avoided destructive competition and strengthened sovereignty and independence; these successes explain that *mushawarah* is a prudent approach to accommodation.

ASEAN consensus has handled difficult choices by postponing difficult decisions to the future, leaving and living with the unsettled issue for the present.[29] This tactic also reflects indigenous culture. Prime Minister Razak, at the time of signing of the 1966 Malaysian-Indonesian treaty to end *konfrontasi*, compared the event to a *kenduri*, a village feast held before a decision-making council.[30] The treaty was important not for its articles, but because it was the start of a relationship. Given a positive and happy start, the details will follow. In practice, this means that to diffuse tensions or to strengthen the image of solidarity, states have announced decisions without creating all the machinery necessary for implementation. Thus, if a general principle is agreeable, or if another issue might be prejudiced by bickering, or if agreement itself is seen as desirable, a decision is declared; getting the job done is left to later. Postponement and broad decisions prevent haggling from destroying a positive mood.

Quiet diplomacy is also important to sustaining ASEAN decision making—"We should not hang out our washing in public."[31] Contentious issues are not discussed in public, certainly not in the press. They may not be discussed at all if silence and postponement are seen as a useful cooling-off device. Since this is an unwritten rule and a nonevent, it is only possible to observe it in a breach. But at the first Singapore-Malaysia Inter-Governmental Committee meeting, Minister Dhanabalan was clear: "The less we talk [in public] about the problems we discuss, the better." Tungku Rithauddeen explained that issues become problems when the press blows them out of proportion.[32] Foreign Minister Mochtar's response to charges that Indonesia did not fully appreciate Thailand's front-line position in 1979 was: "Let's have quiet diplomacy."[33] In 1982, Indonesia reacted to foreign troops (the Malaysians were never identified as such) on Sipadan: "We don't want this to come out in a glare of publicity.''[34] Also in that year, reactions to attacks on Prime Minister Lee by the Indonesian newspaper *Merdeka* made it clear that criticizing the head of a friendly state was considered unusual and improper.[35]

Quiet diplomacy and consensus are practiced in the "no one leads" approach. Ghazalie Shafie has linked this to the overall process: "Asean has become a very solid group that one doesn't think one [country] is doing more or less or doing more or less important work."[36] Sovereignty and self-images challenge accommodation, while a policy of eschewing the spotlight assuages such basic divisions—most notably the Indonesian sense of leadership entitlement and the Singaporean superiority complex. For example, the Singapore *Monitor* responded to Jusuf Wanandi's comment that Indonesia was on the threshold of a new foreign policy era with the counterpoint: "in ASEAN nobody leads and nobody follows."[37] Members generally agree that unilateral initiatives damage cooperation because they give the impression that some merely follow or that the process is run by one member. Experience has shown the futility of circumventing consensus and attempting to use public diplomacy to move things along. Past instances, such as the 1980 Malaysian-Indonesian Kuantan initiative, the 1981 Singapore initiative on the Khmer resistance, the 1983 "five-plus-two" initiative, the 1984 Indonesian plan for Cambodia, and the 1987 cocktail party announcement, proved disruptive and required demonstrations of solidarity. "No one leads" requires individuals to forgo credit and to clothe initiatives in ASEAN garb.

The ASEAN process has utilized compartmentalization to control disputes. Like the British monarch, the ASEAN organization is kept separate from politics. From its foundation, its members tried to erect an apolitical image, concentrating on economics and culture. Even when they are at odds bilaterally, members can rally to the ASEAN organization and the cooperative ideals it promotes; bilateral problems are kept out of the ASEAN context. Such problems do not appear on an ASEAN agenda, nor are they handled by the ASEAN divisions within the governments' foreign ministries. Second, the political coordination committee of the ASEAN process, the SOM, is not part of the ASEAN organization. Compartmentalization also assures that ASEAN organizational meetings remain noncontentious forums that will not impinge on any state's sovereignty or pride. The best illustration remains the attendance by Prime Minister Mahathir of Malaysia at the Manila ASEAN summit—even though the Philippine claim on Sabah was still outstanding and he continued the policy of previous administrations, refusing to visit the Philippines until Manila rejects the claim.

As suggested earlier, ASEAN members have maintained this success image by not having any failures. To use the words of critics, ASEAN works because it isn't asked to do anything. While seemingly true of the intramural economic agenda, the ASEAN process has, on the other hand, proved useful in defending economic interests in multilateral forums.[38] But a happier appreciation of the process comes from adopting the perspective of the members themselves. One local observer commented that avoidance of violence on the intramural level can be considered the ASEAN process's greatest success;[39] sometimes, inaction is necessary to avoid disruptions over secondary interests.

The terms "nuances" and "interlocutor" help bridge the gap between sovereignty and solidarity in practice. Not surprisingly, there are independent policy stands; members face different security problems and have adopted different foreign policies toward other powers, most notably China and Vietnam, but also Japan, the United States, and the Soviet Union. But since solidarity has required periodic joint statements of support for Thailand, individuality has been accommodated in the terms "nuances" and "interlocutor." Both grew out of the need to reconcile apparent contradictions between what is said in an ASEAN context and what is done unilaterally.

While tensions are sometimes mitigated through adoption of broad policy stands, individual members have their own interpretations of these stands, called "nuances" or "trends within ASEAN." For example, rejecting "foreign interference" covers a spectrum from making comments about another leader to an invasion. In the case of Cambodia, calling for the withdrawal of "foreign forces" can refer to Vietnam's army or China's supplying the Khmer Rouge. Such ambiguity, however, has led to confusion and challenges. Singapore's Rajaratnam explains: "The Vietnamese think the nuances in our approach constitute a fundamental difference. So they

go around trying to divide ASEAN. . . . You must never confuse
nuances with basic positions."[40] Unlike the previous codewords,
these terms have not been publicized (why draw attention to the
chink in the armor?). Rather, they have been used to defend ASEAN
solidarity when outsiders have inquired about policy cleavages.
Indeed, before 1979 and the increased importance of solidarity to
Thailand, the divergences of policy were explained as a fact of
sovereignty not requiring an apologia. Only after the occupation of
Cambodia and Thailand's greater anxiety was members' outspoken-
ness addressed and reconciled.

"Interlocutor" is also used to ratify the reality of divergent threat
perceptions and foreign policies. To resolve the Cambodian question, Indonesia had pursued contacts with Vietnam while Thailand
developed a closer relationship with China. Singapore, careful not
to offend Indonesia and Malaysia by dealing with China, followed
a middle path of strong anti-Vietnam stands. All trends dismayed
the other states and created the impression to friend and foe that the
ASEAN process was in disarray. At first, these unilateral policy
moves were rationalized through a functional approach. Prime Minister Lee spoke of Malaysia's and Indonesia's dialogue with Vietnam as an advantage so "we know what Vietnam wants ASEAN to
know."[41] Indonesia commented that Singapore's actions were useful because "we need a toughie" in ASEAN[42] or that the different
attitudes are an asset, "like a lion tamer presenting a stool with
several legs to a lion."[43] As the question persisted, resolution began
to take form. Prime Minister Mahathir's acts of reassurance to
Thailand in 1981 included a soothing recognition of the ASEAN
process's pluralism. "We feel," he said, "Thailand's ability to
contact China would be as useful as Malaysia's ability to contact
Hanoi. . . . It is probably a good thing because, in order to solve
problems in the region, we should have contacts with different
parties of influence."[44]

By 1984, as the Cambodian question dragged on and Thailand
faced border challenges from Laos, increased contacts with Vietnam
and China gave the appearance of an ASEAN rift. In response came
a masterful public-relations stroke to bolster the image of solidarity:
the ASEAN foreign ministers bestowed their joint blessing on these
individual diplomatic activities, designating each state as the ASEAN

"interlocutor" to the party that it was already contacting. Yet the move counteracted centrifugal forces; "interlocutors" do not have plenipotentiary functions. The obligation for consultation remains: as Foreign Minister Mochtar explained, an interlocutor does not have a full mandate but has to refer back to his colleagues.[45] While this might be criticized as only a cosmetic or temporary bandage for the solidarity image, it is better viewed as adept political realism: members bolstered the group image, transformed a perception of cleavages to one of division of labor, and still preserved their own rights to individual policies.

Ambiguity

Codewords reveal how ASEAN diplomats achieve accommodation through ambiguity, as they reach back into their traditions of "veiled politics." To illustrate further, one observer notes that the Javanese have the "ability to indicate something without saying it, to identify the boundaries of acceptable political activity without committing themselves to uphold them. The technique is to infer rather than state, cautiously spiraling inwards to the crux of an idea, but leaving room for flexibility by keeping definitions murky and interpretations variable."[46] Veiled politics were present from the beginning; the founding five used the economic and cultural organization as an indirect pledge of nonaggression and good faith. Subsequent demonstrations of solidarity have been made in the name and context of the ASEAN organization.

Economic development goals make for an apolitical image, and ASEAN members have sometimes used this activity to indicate unity. Agreement to give each other priorities on sales of rice and oil was an important low-cost expression of solidarity during the 1979 oil crisis (sales were to be made at prevailing world market prices).[47] The first summit in 1976 took action mainly in the economic sphere, though it was commonly assumed to be a political response to events in Indochina.

Using the veil of economics, however, is not without problems; divisive economic issues threaten to rend this curtain. Indeed, some ASEAN states were hesitant to have that first summit because they feared that Singapore would use the occasion to push for more movement toward a free-trade zone (by enlarging the preferential tariff lists). The same hesitations were heard before the 1987 summit. Ironically, concern that divergences in economic policies and levels of development might damage the image of solidarity partly explains why ASEAN has not taken on more projects or begun movement toward economic integration. Even when used as a bargaining coalition against developed states, economic interests have divided members. For example, in 1979 Singapore resisted Australia's new airline stopover policy by making Canberra deal with ASEAN as a whole. Other members had been happy with earlier Australian offers, but Singapore kept the group in line by stressing the need for consistent ASEAN unity. As these negotiations were conducted against the backdrop of the recent occupation of Cambodia, members responded to this call. Fortunately, the subsequent victory over Australia muted intramural strains over Singapore's aggressiveness.[48] Similarly, Singapore attempted to use ASEAN in its individual problem with New Zealand, which wanted to remove the developed city-state from its GSP list. Singapore countered with a plan to use an aggregate figure for all ASEAN and with a threat of retaliation by ASEAN.[49]

Another price for using the economic veil to cover political realities is confusion and disappointment. For instance, consider one Philippine comment in light of that country's economic difficulties: "If ASEAN cannot come to the rescue of a member-state that is economically hobbled, what's the organization for? A great debating society?"[50] ASEAN is seen as "flawed" because it has no provision in its charter to help member states when their economies are in trouble; here the economic screen obscured the basic and more essential achievement of the ASEAN process.

Ambiguity is not always practiced with the economic veil; mixed signals have often been used, though perhaps not entirely purposely, to keep outsiders off guard and members placated. The Treaty of Amity, which was open to all Southeast Asian states, including Vietnam, is only one example of carefully constructed articulations. The institutionalization of "nuances" as individual interpretations of these articulations, "interlocutor" status allowing independent policy approaches, and the informal use of the expression "ASEAN official" to describe any diplomat from a member of ASEAN also illustrate how ambiguity arises about "ASEAN positions."

Cooperation among ASEAN members in the area of military exercises provides another example of ambiguity. If ASEAN members have been anxious to appear apolitical, they have been even more careful not to act as a military group. Yet, in crises, members have been quick to pledge support. Adam Malik explained: "If Singapore or Malaysia is attacked, and they ask Indonesia for help, we certainly cannot remain idle as we are morally bound to help them."[51] But the when and how of support must be left undefined; for example, in late 1976 Prime Minister Thanin of Thailand commented in Jakarta that "if the time comes we [implying ASEAN states] will join hands and fight to the last." Quickly an Indonesian official attempted to diffuse the message: "If we turned ASEAN into a military pact we would be creating the very situation that Vietnam says exists right now."[52] Publicly, ASEAN policy rejects the idea of a military pact. President Marcos brought up such a plan in 1968,[53] and it received no response on his tour of the region. The members' defense policy statements and diplomatic actions do, however, suggest support in murky signals, open to interpretations. More recently, Minister Mochtar rejected a Singaporean call for an ASEAN defense pact, saying he did not believe the time had come "but we don't exclude the possibility of stepping up military cooperation on a bilateral basis."[54] Almost all ASEAN members hold joint military exercises on a bilateral basis, a practice reaching back to the mid-1970s. These are always described as outside ASEAN, but may be under its umbrella. Former Thai supreme commander General Saiyud Kardphol also rejected the Singapore-sponsored pact as impractical but added that he favored the joint military exercises. Moreover, he spoke of a "war reserve contingency pool in ASEAN" that the military leaders of all member countries have agreed to.[55] Such references to support or plans, like those during the Bali foreign ministers meeting in 1979,[56] are not specified and often are leaked from unofficial or unidentified sources.

Military exercises are, in light of Vietnamese military predominance and some states' leanings toward Vietnam, intended not as a convincing deterrent but rather as a demonstration of cohesion. Exercises among ASEAN members along with coordinated purchase of matériel and aircraft suggest resolve and so play a political role in bolstering the image of ASEAN solidarity. Ambiguity involves signaling something without saying it; yet danger arises if the intended receiver interprets the signal in another way. So, because military arrangements are both strong and volatile signals, caution is practiced through more ambiguity. Exercises are kept on a non-ASEAN basis, so that regional polarization does not intensify. Even within bilateral arrangements, states have attempted to obfuscate their military activities. For example, a Malaysian discussion of joint arms production and purchase revealed that this would be done by the private sector under license from the Ministry of Trade and Industry, not Defense. The policy rationale was "This distinction should be emphasized lest other non-ASEAN countries interpret this to mean we are moving towards an ASEAN military pact."[57] At times, ambiguity requires assurances about signals not indicated.

Finally, the tactic of ambiguity has been useful to member governments' management of their domestic politics. A government can act on behalf of ASEAN when it could not do so in the name of another state. This allows governments that understand the strategic rationale for cooperation to act in spite of suspicions still held by the general populace. States with Muslims can speak in defense of ASEAN easier than Thailand or the Philippines. Ambiguity is both ASEAN's strength and weakness. While it has facilitated intramural cohesion, it has confused outsiders who have had to ask what the grouping was. Yet ambiguity, through consensus and codewords, is essential to accommodation. It speaks of the imperative to restrain competition in positive terms—"good neighborliness" and "noninterference" and allows individual states to perceive the ASEAN process as serving its particular interests. Membership enhances the Philippines' Asian identity, Indonesia's leadership role, Singapore's bargaining clout, and Malaysia's diplomatic voice, and reduces Thailand's sense of isolation. Moreover, ambiguity applied to foreign policy, through broad articulations and displays of unity, keeps down the cost of solidarity.

7

ASEAN Diplomacy: Speaking with One Voice

> We are all agreed on the concept [of neutralization/Zopfan] itself.
> To be quite frank, we have different approaches to this goal.
> —Foreign Minister Rajaratnam

ASEAN members have demonstrated solidarity in coordinated foreign policy stands and actions. These activities, which have contributed to their notoriety, are interesting on two levels: the founders saw the organization not "as a mechanism for formal dealings with the outside world,"[1] but for intramural reassurance. Common policy resulted, however, when regional instability threatened their subregion; namely, they acted to reassure Thailand. Nonetheless, common stands have been contradicted by members' subsequent, if not simultaneous, reservations and independent initiatives. To manage this tension states have developed a language of solidarity that compensates for and assuages the real divisions in perceptions and policy.

Collective political stands first took the form of a declaration; ASEAN was established with the Bangkok Declaration of 1967. That declaration expressed hope that ASEAN members could achieve among themselves "regional peace and stability through abiding respect for justice and the rule of law in the relationship among the countries of the region and adherence to the principles of the United Nations charter." When U.S. withdrawal from Southeast Asia seemed imminent, the members addressed the external environment with the 1971 Kuala Lumpur Declaration calling for recognition and respect of Southeast Asia as a Zone of Peace, Freedom, and Neutrality (Zopfan).

U.S. Withdrawal

Over three years had passed before this first external collective stand because states were preoccupied with domestic and intramural politics. Management of the internal Malaysian crisis and the Sabah claim dispute in 1969 were quiet but important victories for ASEAN members: peace and stability were maintained in the subregion. ASEAN states paid little public attention to external events because dangers and outcomes were not uniformly perceived; nor was there consensus about reaction. Not that they were not anxious about China, victorious Vietnam, and ambiguous U.S. policies. But President Marcos's initiative on creating an ASEAN defense pact during a tour in 1968[2] was hardly acknowledged; states saw this as confrontational, and among themselves they still faced the challenge of insufficient trust and understanding. It is also ironic that the proposal for closer cooperation came from the state whose Sabah claim had frozen ASEAN consultative machinery in the first half of the year; Filipinos were called "Sabahteurs" of ASEAN. Also, because ASEAN members perceived that they could not influence a great-power contest, they waited to deal with the outcome of the war.

Zopfan, the first declaration since the establishment of ASEAN, responded in general to the changing regional order at the end of the U.S.-Vietnam war, and in particular to Thailand's anxiety about a power vacuum in the region should the United States withdraw. The November 1971 Kuala Lumpur Declaration expressed determination "(1) . . . to secure the recognition of, and respect for, South-East Asia as a Zone of Peace, Freedom, and Neutrality, free from any form or manner of interference by outside Powers" and stated, by way of implementation, in point (2) of the resolution, "that South-East Asian countries should make concerted efforts to broaden the areas of cooperation which would contribute to their strength, solidarity, and closer relationship."

Concern about U.S. resolve to remain in the region had been building since the Viet Cong's psychological victories during the 1968 Tet offensive. Though U.S. forces had repulsed the attacks, the ability of guerrilla forces to seize several objectives from the United States, including part of its embassy compound, hearkened a turning point in the war. Some, like Adam Malik and Ferdinand Marcos, saw a rapid change coming, involving the North taking South Vietnam in two years and then targeting on Thailand.[3]

Political signals also indicated a new direction for U.S. policy and increased expectations of a power vacuum. Richard Nixon, the Republican presidential candidate during 1968, was on record in a 1967 *Foreign Affairs* article calling for states to take care of their own problems by means of "collective effort." His advice was: "To ensure that a U.S. response will be forthcoming if needed, machinery must be created that is capable of meeting two conditions: (a) a collective effort by the nations of the region to contain the threat by themselves; and, if that effort fails, (b) a collective request to the United States for assistance."[4] With his election in November and formalization of this policy on Guam in July 1969, Nixon's advice took on new strength. His trip to the rim of Asia had been meant to build confidence, but the speech, since known as the Nixon Doctrine, seemed to declare that Asia was on its own. This perception was reinforced by U.S. troop withdrawals; Foreign Minister Thanat Khoman of Thailand, a fervent backer of collective activity, probably said it for all when he observed that this "was a major turning point and challenge that is thrust upon us which we have to accept with courage and lucidity."[5]

More signals leading ASEAN states to see the United States as a paralyzed giant emanated from the entire body politic, namely, the assassinations of Senator Robert Kennedy and the Reverend Martin Luther King, political and racial demonstrations turned riots in the late 1960s, and popular demonstrations against the war in Vietnam which brought down the administration of Lyndon Johnson. In Washington, the U.S. Congress was beginning its campaign to establish controls on foreign policy making. The Church amendment of December 1969 barred commitment of U.S. ground combat troops in Laos or Thailand. In June 1970 the Senate repealed the Gulf of Tonkin resolution, the authorization and legislative support for U.S. involvement in Vietnam. Despite White House attempts to reassure Washington's Asian allies with two separate tours of the region by Vice-President Agnew in 1970, Asian statesmen wondered about the ability of the U.S. government to achieve a unified policy and follow it through.

Meanwhile, as the United States seemed to recede, China loomed larger; moreover, this China, embroiled in the Cultural Revolution, appeared ready to spread revolution through local Communist parties in the region. Malaysia was especially sensitive at this time. The CPM observed the twentieth anniversary of the Emergency with a June 1968 radio broadcast, originating from Yunnan, that announced the party had decided to follow the path of revolutionary violence.[6]

But by 1970 it was front-line Thailand that adopted a new foreign policy strategy to counter the Chinese menace. Bangkok knew that China maintained a training school for Thai subversives in Yunnan, and that from this same southern China province roads across Laos to the Thai border were nearing completion. To counter this threat Bangkok sought détente with Hanoi. The initiative began with withdrawal of Thai troops helping the Saigon government and further accommodated North Vietnam by not forming a defense pact with the new, pro-U.S. Lon Nol government of Cambodia (installed in 1970). Hanoi valued these concessions and, in the words of a delegation to Bangkok, ''friendly relations between the two peoples of Vietnam and Thailand.'' Vietnam was at this time recovering from losses incurred when U.S. forces raided Viet Cong sanctuaries in Cambodia. The Hanoi-Bangkok accord took on more substance when negotiations for repatriation of forty thousand Vietnamese in Thailand were begun.[7]

Thailand hoped for an accommodation with Vietnam because it was no longer protected by the Cambodian buffer after the war escalated in May 1970; Indonesia attempted to deal with the problem diplomatically and so reassure Thailand. Attempting mediation, Jakarta sponsored a conference on Cambodia in May 1970 but, as the Communist states did not attend, the conference resulted in only a wish for the neutrality of Cambodia. The conference did serve as a platform, however, from which President Suharto warned the world of the dangers of escalation.[8]

Other ASEAN members made no significant move. Domestic preoccupations were particularly strong as both Malaysia and Singapore were anxiously observing the first anniversary of the 1969 racial riots; Malaysia was still under martial law at the time. The Philippines was also preoccupied with domestic politics, namely, the presidential campaign season, which lasted through the election in November 1969. Then, with the reelection of Ferdinand Marcos, domestic politics geared up again for elections of delegates to a constitutional convention. These campaigns distracted Philippine politicians from foreign affairs, which were never very urgent in any case. Contrary to Suharto's warning, further escalation did not follow, and with a lessened sense of urgency most ASEAN members remained passive. (Thailand was still anxious. One observer voiced the expectation that U.S. troops would be out of Vietnam before the November 1972 elections.[9])

Common diplomatic action required the more dramatic event of great-power realignment, namely, the U.S.-China rapprochement, which culminated in the July 1971 announcement that President Nixon would visit China. By September 1971 there was agreement to work out an "ASEAN approach" to the repercussions of this new relationship. The issue of China's admission to the United Nations proved difficult in part because U.S. policy was still not clear or consistent. Despite rapprochement, Washington was not voting for Peking's admission. Therefore, while Malaysia and Singapore voted for the admission, the others did not. Zopfan, however, an "ASEAN approach" to the apparent ascendancy of Communism, was both easier and imperative.

Zopfan addressed governments' concern that a vacuum caused by U.S. withdrawal would enable China to play a greater role in the region. A worst-case suspicion was that Washington was buying its way out of the Vietnam war by giving Beijing a regional sphere of influence. To prevent such an outcome the group appeared to seize upon the plan by Prime Minister Razak of Malaysia to neutralize the region by gaining the guarantees of the three major interested powers, the United States, China, and the Soviet Union.

Zopfan's invitation to these powers has "an element of making a virtue out of necessity in Malaysia's policy for the neutralization of South-East Asia."[10] The Malaysian proposal recognized both China's proximity and the Soviet Union's increased ability to project its power to the region. (A small naval task force had appeared in 1968, and naval facilities were negotiated with Mauritius, Somalia, Egypt, and India by 1971.[11]) But domestic factors persuaded this

Malaysian strategy. Malaysia's lesson from the Vietnam war was that help from a great power does not substitute for popular support.[12] This perception, reinforced by the absence of any conventional military threat and a rise in self-confidence and self-dependency, led to a policy of seeking internal security (resilience), instead of defense,[13] and neutralization. Internally, Zopfan both acknowledged and simultaneously depoliticized China; it was a way to ease tensions with the ethnic Chinese of Malaysia "and foster nation-building in the period ensuing after the political disturbances of 13 May [1969]. A policy of non-alignment would accommodate, and help to coincilate [sic] rather than exacerbate political tension arising out of communal suspicion, friction and violence."[14]

To broaden its appeal both domestically and to ASEAN partners, Malaysia represented Zopfan as a step toward independence from Britain and the United States; Ghazalie Shafie explained that it was "undignified" for leaders to "await with trepidation the outcome of elections in countries with whom they had defense arrangements."[15] Neutralization also appealed to indigenous patterns of social interaction. "They may think in terms of Malayan family attitudes: try to be friendly with all your neighbors and acquaintances for then none of them will harm you because each of them will fear the hostile reaction, not only from you but also from all the others you have befriended."[16]

Furthermore, neutralization seemed viable in light of the détente between the United States and the Soviet Union and China; it was thought that the great powers might extend their accommodation to Southeast Asia. As for the United States in particular, the ASEAN initiative served "to prime the pump" because the U.S. political situation and mood would not permit Washington to launch initiatives in this part of the world. On another level, an initiative answered the charge that ASEAN states were an inconsequential or paralyzed group. Even more important, action was needed so that the group did not unravel; Thailand was adopting more and new individualistic policies. Taking its cue from its U.S. patron, Bangkok moved closer to China and refocused its worries on the neighboring Communist regime in Cambodia. Since military support from ASEAN was not feasible, the members attempted to support Thailand with diplomatic solidarity. Zopfan thus became the first "ASEAN approach'' to the stability of the region and their association.

As such, Zopfan illustrates accommodation applied to foreign policy making. States

> were content enough to be "restrained" by the "common interests" that ASEAN represented. . . . The restraints included: (1) the requirement that all the states of the region . . . must be in agreement on the "neutralization" proposal; (2) a separate "understanding" among the ASEAN states that they would consult closely with each other, and consider each other's interests, before establishing diplomatic relations with Peking; and (3) the formation of an "ASEAN committee on neutralization" to work out details of what "neutralization" would involve and how it could be brought about.[17]

The participants, though restrained, were also committed to their sovereign rights and individual interests. Agreement and consultation were insisted upon. Zopfan was a skillful compromise; it did not take a stand against any other great or regional power, and so did not contradict any member's foreign policy. Moreover, Zopfan was low cost because it did not require any joint followup by ASEAN members; implementation was left to be worked out later. But Zopfan did give Thailand moral and political support when it was needed.

As real policy, the Zopfan initiative was stillborn. The great powers did not respond, and among ASEAN states, divisions of opinion about neutralization appeared before the ink was dry. As noted earlier, Foreign Minister Rajaratnam commented at the meeting: "We are all agreed on the concept itself. To be quite frank, we all have different approaches." By mid-1972 it was clear that there was little real support for the Zopfan plan; Singapore and Thailand publicly questioned its feasibility. And circumstances changed. During 1972 the United States adopted a more vigorous policy toward Hanoi, responding to North Vietnam's invasion of the south with the mining of Haiphong harbor and bombing increases in August and December. China also presented a new face by supporting ASEAN and pledging noninterference in domestic affairs. Consequently, with U.S. activism,[18] Thailand felt less insecure and less in need of the joint stand.

Actually, ASEAN support was taking other forms. Several bilateral summits took place for the first time, and at the AMM in April 1972, the practical and possible ASEAN approach to regional stability emerged. The ministers "also recognized the necessity of strengthening and expanding their national economies with a view to increasing the economic and political stability of the region" (Joint Communique). They went on to say, "it was necessary for member countries to develop national resilience." Conventional wisdom now became ASEAN policy.

By way of epilogue, Zopfan is still used in ASEAN diplomacy because Kuala Lumpur champions its idea, and, as an aspiration to free the region from outside interference, it is a credential of nonalignment. It has been less successfully used to reduce Hanoi's suspicions that ASEAN is an anti-Vietnam coalition.

There followed the declaration on the 1973 Arab-Israeli conflict, including support for the "lawful rights of the Palestine people." The ASEAN leaders issued a Declaration of Concord in 1976 as part of their first summit. There was no direct mention of the momentous events in Indochina in 1975; rather, it reaffirmed mutual commitment to basic ASEAN principles in that uncertain year. Since then, the declaration instrument has been used, for the most part, to make intramural or nonpolitical policy stands, such as the Declaration on the ASEAN Environment of April 1981. The most recent declaration made at the Manila summit for the most part reiterates past ASEAN stands; it did introduce a new goal of making the region a Nuclear Weapons Free Zone, though this is consistent with the larger objectives articulated in Zopfan. Declarations have been replaced by joint communiques or joint statements as the instruments articulating collective policy stands toward external problems; these are less formal, less direct instruments.

The Occupation of Cambodia

The Vietnamese occupation of Cambodia in December 1978 produced articulations of support for Thailand in the 1979 AMM Joint Communique. By July the agenda at Bali was full: the fate of Cambodia, the role of Vietnam in Indochina, the role of China in the region, and the problem of refugee outflows. But differences on these issues resulted in an ambiguous stand, appropriately characterized as "mush and steel" because it mixed tough talk and little follow-through.[19] There were expressions of indignation over the violations of principle, but they were guarded, compromising, nonprovocative, and noncommittal. Foreign Minister Romulo declared that ASEAN was on "red alert." However, this dramatic but unsubstantiated military allusion came from the Philippines, the most geographically distanced power and one that had refused the United States use of bases in its territory to aid Thailand.[20] Diplomatic solidarity apparently operates in a realm independent of military or other pragmatic commitments.

Even in the heat of the invasion crisis, even before the complication of the Chinese attack on Vietnam in February, ASEAN states had tailored solidarity to suit their individual interests. The first reaction, the joint statement of an extraordinary foreign ministers meeting in January 1979, distanced ASEAN from the Chinese position by using terminology different from Beijing's—"armed intervention" instead of "aggression." This consensus took hours of debate.[21] Differences revolved about the dangers posed by the Vietnamese action, Khmer Rouge provocations, Vietnamese rights as successors to France as sovereign in Indochina, and China's interference.

This January joint statement reflected the skillful use of international law to find a common ground. Moreover, agreement was facilitated, if not precipitated, by common perceptions that Vietnam violated its own assurances; the judgment rested simply on criteria suggested by Premier Pham Vam Dong during his October 1978 Southeast Asian tour: "I need to say one thing, that the best answer to [allegations about Vietnamese intentions] is the deed—the deed we do today, what we do tomorrow and the deed we do the day after tomorrow. And the deed will prove the pure friendship between our countries and the countries in this region."[22] Thus, despite its own recent assurances and international conventions like the UN Charter to which it had just subscribed, Vietnam violated principles of nonaggression and noninterference, threatening a decline into lawlessness. On this there was consensus, so there could be joint policy. So, in the crisis atmosphere, feelings of urgency, betrayal, and embarrassment moved ASEAN leaders to indict Vietnam for breaking its own promises "to scrupulously respect each other's independence, sovereignty and territorial integrity" (Joint Statement, January 12, 1979).

But the subsequent Chinese invasion of Vietnam in February made a common policy stand more problematic because members were again divided over the source of greater danger. Yet, though the basis of strong diplomatic action had eroded, fear and indignation about the occupation still held the consensus. The July AMM Joint Communique reaffirmed the January statements, "deploring the armed intervention against . . . Kampuchea, calling for withdrawal of the foreign forces from Kampuchean territory," and went beyond to name Vietnam more clearly, expressing "15. support for the right of the people of Kampuchea to lead their national existence free from interference by Vietnam and other foreign forces in their internal affairs." Again, intramural compromise demanded that they not lay all blame on Vietnam; "foreign forces" was a circumlocution to include Chinese support of the Khmer Rouge. More important to internal dynamics, they proclaimed unity and identity with Thailand in a common policy: "17. The Foreign Ministers called on Vietnam to demonstrate its positive attitude towards Thailand and the other ASEAN member states by withdrawing its forces from the Thai-Kampuchean border."

The refugee outflow from Vietnam greatly facilitated a common stand in 1979. The boat people landing on the western flank of ASEAN caused other ASEAN members besides Thailand to resent Hanoi. The joint communique was very direct on this issue: "22. The Foreign Ministers expressed grave concern over the deluge of illegal immigrants/displaced persons (refugees) from Indochina. . . . 23. The Foreign Ministers agreed that Vietnam is responsible for the unending exodus of illegal immigrants and has a decisive role to play in resolving the problem at source." The refugee burden irked the usually more accommodating Malaysians; some even viewed the outflow as a plan to weaken Malaysia economically and, because the refugees were ethnic Chinese, to unbalance the Federation racially. Singapore's Rajaratnam capitalized on this theme at the Bali meeting when he described the refugees as "human bombs" designed to destroy ASEAN prosperity, stability, and cohesion.[23] Malaysia's sending the refugees back out to sea showed its desperation and soon soured relations with Indonesia, which became their next destination. Yet this gave Indonesia a greater appreciation for mainland problems because it now received these second-hand refugees. Reflecting this new situation, Foreign Minister Mochtar commented, "We had to assure the Thais they would get special attention because they are bearing the brunt of the problem.''[24] And he further expressed a new mood in Jakarta, saying he was "fed up" with empty promises from Vietnam.[25] Hanoi was losing credibility with its most sympathetic ASEAN member. Thus, consensus at the 1979 AMM was built on the image of Vietnamese duplicity and intransigence and the need to settle this refugee problem.

Besides concern for law, Thai commitment, and refugee burdens, ASEAN leaders were also conscious that, in the words of Indonesian foreign minister Mochtar, ''The world is closely watching us, and the international community will analyze the results of our deliberations.''[26] Their analysis would affect ASEAN members' credibility as a bargaining force in other areas. Concern for solidarity had persuaded even the state with the "special relationship" with Vietnam, Indonesia, to join in the strong stand. Minister Mochtar was clear on this point in May when he said: ''If it were not for Thailand, the Indonesian reaction would have been more flexible.''[27]

They applied this bargaining power at the United Nations; the first ASEAN initiative in March 1979 was presented to the Security Council. As expected, the Soviet Union vetoed the resolution. But in the fall session of the General Assembly, ASEAN secured double victories: recognition of Pol Pot's Democratic Kampuchea as the government of Cambodia and passage of the "ASEAN resolution" 34/22 on the Cambodian problem. That resolution called "for the immediate withdrawal of all foreign forces from Kampuchea and calls upon all States to refrain from all acts or threats of aggression and all forms of interference in the internal affairs of States in South-East Asia." Similar to ASEAN states' first stands, Vietnam was not mentioned. Victory, however, should not be allowed to overshadow the individualism revealed during the politicking; Vietnam was even able to table one resolution on Cambodia before ASEAN's own while Indonesia looked to reduce support for a resolution on East Timor and the Philippines campaigned for a seat on the Security Council.[28]

After the initial shock faded, the deepest division became public in March 1980. Taking its name from statements released from the Hussein-Suharto summit at Kuantan, the so-called Kuantan initiative acknowledged that Vietnam had legitimate security concerns in

Indochina and supported Vietnam's true independence, that is, from all superpowers. Furthermore, the initiative included economic inducements in the form of invitations to the West and Japan to provide assistance.[29] This bold extra-ASEAN move reflected the states' sense of urgency as Thailand's government had changed again; General Prem Tinsulanond became prime minister that month. Indonesia and Malaysia feared instability that might be exploited by either Vietnam or China. Also, there was an assumption that Hanoi would respond positively before the United States, recently inflamed by the Soviet takeover of Afghanistan in December 1979, emerged from isolationism toward activism in Southeast Asia. But when the proposal was not backed by the West and resisted by Thailand, it faded away. However, the question of Thai security and ASEAN solidarity remained and, in light of Indonesian-Malaysian unilateralism and Thai instability, intramural consultations were required.

The new Thai prime minister visited his ASEAN counterparts in the weeks after assuming office. He tried to assure President Suharto that Thailand was not falling under Chinese sway and that Thailand would not let China channel arms through its territory. In general, Prem seized upon the ASEAN states' commitment to the UN resolution and used this to keep the others at a common stance.[30] He argued that a Vietnamese sphere of influence was inconsistent with the resolution's call for withdrawal of foreign troops.

Diplomatic strains did not go unnoticed by Vietnam, which next suggested that a Malaysian-Indonesian-Lao team inspect Cambodia during its elections.[31] Hanoi hoped this was a first step to gaining recognition of its fait accompli; it counted on ASEAN members' tiring of support for the infamous Khmer Rouge, on the West's ignoring the region, and on the threat of a new tide of boat people. But Hanoi lacked patience and a sense of timing. Vietnamese Foreign Minister Thach's visit to Bangkok in May was acrimonious, and he accused the Thais of collaborating with the Chinese.[32] Presumably these tactics were designed to topple the new Prem government and to play on Malaysian and Indonesian fears of China. In the end, diplomacy succumbed to expediency when Vietnam attacked the refugee camps in Thailand. This incursion by Vietnamese troops about two kilometers into Thailand for twelve hours contradicted "repeated pledges to respect the sovereignty and territorial integrity of Thailand," declared the resulting June 1980 Joint Statement, which condemned "these acts perpetrated by Vietnam" and expressed "ASEAN's firm support and solidarity with the government and people of Thailand in the preservation of Thai independence, sovereignty, and territorial integrity." The timing of the incursion was particularly embarrassing to Indonesia as Thach was in Jakarta at the time. Moreover, it took place only days before the scheduled 1980 AMM, as if to dare ASEAN states to respond.

ASEAN members closed ranks behind Thailand in a joint statement issued separately, for emphasis, from the AMM communique; it supported the "legitimate right of [Kampuchean civilians] to return to their homeland." Supporting repatriation was a significant hardening of ASEAN support for Thailand because the Vietnamese incursion seemed clearly an attempt to halt what Thach had complained about in Bangkok the week before, namely, Thai succoring of refugees during the dry season and then "sending them back as soldiers to fight inside Kampuchea during the monsoon season when guerrillas have the advantage."[33] The hardliners, who felt vindicated by the incursion, naturally supported the tougher stand; Singapore thanked Vietnam for showing its belligerence and untrustworthiness. But Indonesia and Malaysia were more frustrated; Vietnam's action made Kuantan an embarrassment, and Thailand's toleration of Vietnam in Laos seemed arbitrary. Support of Thailand was, however, sound policy; the front line showed that it could still hold up its end of the bargain, despite the concerns about its domestic politics. The Thai army accounted for itself well, and if Vietnam hoped to embarrass or discredit Thailand on the eve of the AMM, it failed.

Essentially, ASEAN members reacted to the urgency and immediacy of the issue. Invasion was not speculative or remote like the debate on long- and short-term dangers to the region. Crossing the border, the moving of the war just a mile into Thailand, demanded action, and ASEAN members knew that in this situation there could be no quibbling or Thailand would loose confidence and drift more toward China. They saw this as a real eventuality because of the domestic instability—there had been seven prime ministers in as many years—and worried about what a frightened regime might do. Yet, because some resisted confrontation, they moved onto the safe and familiar common ground of international law for a joint stand.

The invasion broke the law, and they once again condemned the sin, not the sinner ("these acts perpetrated by Vietnam"), and avoided discord on the larger role of Vietnam in the region.

Statements by the chairman of the ASEAN Standing Committee are other arrows in the quiver: the August 1980 Statement in Response to the Vientiane Proposal illustrates their usefulness in answering an initiative with solidarity, without dignifying it with a gathering of foreign ministers. After the June 1980 incursion and the common stand of ASEAN members, Vietnam adopted a less aggressive, if not more conciliatory, approach. The July 1980 Indochina Conference (a meeting of the foreign ministers of Vietnam, Laos, and the People's Republic of Kampuchea, installed by Vietnam) linked a proposal aimed at Malaysia and Indonesia to resolve peacefully "disputes in the Eastern [South China] sea" to another on the control of hostilities in Cambodia by means of a demilitarized zone (DMZ) on both sides of the border.[34] ASEAN foreign ministers stood with Bangkok and rejected this plan on the grounds that a DMZ in Thailand implied Thailand was at war with Vietnam and legitimized Vietnam's presence in Cambodia. In the name of the foreign ministers, the chair of the Standing Committee rejected the plan, proposing instead "the establishment of demilitarized peace zones in Kampuchea."

The Chairman's Statement in Response to the Ho Chi Minh City Statement (February 1981) again responded to an initiative from the Indochina Foreign Ministers' Meeting in January 1981. The Ho Chi Minh statement announced partial Vietnamese withdrawal and an offer to hold either meetings between ASEAN and the Indochina conference, or a meeting of representatives from both groupings, or a bilateral session.[35] Designed to divide ASEAN members and split them from China, the initiative countered China's support for a broader united front resistance in Cambodia; in fact, Premier Zhao Ziyang of China was in Thailand at the time of this Indochina conference. The initiative for a less-public regional conference was also viewed as an attempt to circumvent the International Conference on Kampuchea (ICK), which had been mandated by the 1980 UN General Assembly Resolution 35/6. The ASEAN chair replied, "These proposals, while presenting a seemingly conciliatory approach to the problem, ignore the root cause of the problem, the blatant breach in Kampuchea of the fundamental principles of the Non-Aligned Movement and the principles of the U.N. Charter.'' It concluded with an endorsement of the ICK forum.

The Cambodian Stalemate

The July 1984 AMM issued, in the words of one senior ASEAN official, the ''strongest, harshest, most strident'' communique to come out of any Asean annual meeting.[36] The July 9 Joint Statement on the Kampuchean Problem indicted Vietnam: ''For over five years, the ASEAN states and the international community have called upon Vietnam to cease its military occupation of Kampuchea and to join in the search for a comprehensive political settlement of the Kampuchean problem. Vietnam remains obdurate.'' This strong statement of solidarity addresses problems growing out of Vietnam's continuing occupation of Cambodia. Sustaining solidarity has been stressful; members faced confusion or apathy among external supporters for the ASEAN position, the distasteful reputation of the Khmer Rouge, which ASEAN backs, Vietnamese diplomatic initiatives, factions within the Indonesian and Thai foreign-policy making establishments, continuing apprehension about the stability of the Thai government, divisions over the role of China, and apprehensions about Sino-Soviet relations. Neither the hardline strategies of Thailand and Singapore nor the accommodationist initiatives of Indonesia and Malaysia were able to reverse or modify the Vietnamese occupation. And their conflicting perceptions pit them against each other whenever Vietnam sends a new signal.

For example, the Indochina Conference meetings in February and April 1983 offered troop withdrawals and possible future ones. More divisive was an offer to Malaysia that ASEAN discuss the question of Cambodia with Laos and Vietnam. This came to be dubbed the ''five-plus-two'' formula, which encouraged Malaysia and Indonesia to view Vietnam as willing to negotiate. The Thais, however, insisted that Vietnam was not sincere; they suspected that it would use the negotiations to gain respectability and emerge from isolation still holding Cambodia. Hanoi's tough stance toward Singapore's military support to the resistance in Cambodia, when Thach warned, ''What they can do to others, others can do to them,''[37] only reinforced the hardliners' suspicion. The formula also failed to achieve consensus as the Philippines, annoyed because it was not given proper notice before the plan was made public, resisted it.

Then, the winds shifted and bilateral Thai-Vietnamese talks seemed to move toward resolution. Foreign Minister Thach of Vietnam visited Bangkok in early June, and both sides seemed pleased and ready to talk. Thach agreed that Cambodia should be neutral, an encouraging step toward Vietnamese withdrawal.[38] Thailand also had showed a measure of flexibility in early 1983 by quietly dropping insistence that negotiations be within the International Conference on Kampuchea framework. ASEAN indicated it would settle for another form, a restricted conference.[39] Objectives outlined in the UN resolution (withdrawal, self-determination, and neutralization) remained, but the international forum for negotiation was not insisted upon. This compromise was aimed at Indonesia as much as at Vietnam, which felt that quiet diplomacy was more useful and, moreover, that an international conference was undesirable because it reduces the responsibility and role of the local powers in their own region.[40] Such concerns were salient at the time as China and the Soviet Union were resuming negotiations. Reports that Cambodia was on their agenda raised the fears of a big-power deal.[41]

The June 1983 AMM took up this new approach to the negotiations and did not mention the ICK in its joint communique. Malaysian foreign minister Ghazalie clearly stated that this omission should be seen by Hanoi as a sign of ASEAN flexibility. In addition, the AMM omitted the call for an immediate withdrawal. In September the ASEAN members held out a new approach in which they appealed for a phased withdrawal of Vietnamese troops from Cambodia, a ceasefire supervised by an international peacekeeping force, and the convocation of an international conference on the reconstruction of Indochina. No mention was made of UN resolutions or the ICK. But Hanoi changed its face and not only rejected the gesture but began using the term "irreversible" again in its description of the order in Cambodia.[42] In October the members of ASEAN demonstrated their strength at the United Nations when the credentials of the Coalition Government of Democratic Kampuchea (CGDK) were not challenged. The ASEAN resolution was passed again, and it included a new charge that Vietnam was altering the demographics of Cambodia by resettling Vietnamese in the country. This Vietnamization of Cambodia was even equated, in an address to the General Assembly, with the crimes of the Khmer Rouge.[43]

Besides erratic Vietnamese policies, ASEAN states faced moral and strategic problems growing out of the composition of the resistance forces. The main body of guerrilla forces belonged to the Khmer Rouge, the army and party of the deposed Pol Pot government of Democratic Kampuchea. Numbering sixty thousand, they represent the only effective obstacle to total Vietnamese control of the country. But some states within and outside of ASEAN want to disassociate themselves from the Khmer Rouge because of their crimes when in power. Singapore and Thailand respond with a realpolitik argument, saying one works with whatever is an effective force. To meet moral objections to the Khmer Rouge regime, Singapore and Thailand had pushed formation of a coalition of resistance forces including the Khmer Rouge, the Khmer People's National Liberation Front, and the forces loyal to Sihanouk. By June 1982 the CGDK was announced, but its member factions are extremely suspicious of each other, and their practical and military cooperation is minimal. Nevertheless, the CGDK does signal nationalist opposition to Vietnam with a more acceptable image through the person of its president, the venerable father of the nonaligned movement, Prince Sihanouk. However, it has not been able to reverse the Vietnamese occupation.

By early 1984 the Cambodian issue became more problematic for ASEAN members. The "ASEAN approach" of legal and diplomatic pressure was not influencing Vietnam. Military pressure, using the CGDK, was becoming a less and less feasible means to resolve the problem. Rather, the ongoing Cambodian conflict was allowing both China and the Soviet Union to have more involvement in the region. And this involvement was taking on larger dimensions. A second Soviet aircraft carrier, *Novorussisk*, entered the Pacific via the straits in early 1984.[44] In April a joint Vietnamese-Soviet amphibious landing maneuver was practiced on the Vietnamese coast south of Haiphong. In the next month the Chinese fleet circled the contested Spratleys Islands and then landed an amphibious exercise on Hainan Island.[45] The Sino-Soviet rivalry could now escalate in the South China Sea, and the front line would be brought to Indonesia, Malaysia, and the Philippines.

Along with this new danger, concern heightened about the stability of the Thai front line. Soviet backing of the Pak Mai, a Communist movement set up in opposition to the pro-China Communist Party of Thailand, was unsettling. On the home front, the viability of the Prem government was questioned. Since the beginning of his tenure in 1980, there had been a failed coup in April 1981, several rumors of coups since then, reports of the prime minister resigning in April 1983, his ill health, and even a symbolic no confidence vote in February 1984.

In light of these concerns, Indonesia took a more active role in regional affairs. Settling the Cambodian problem would benefit Indonesian national objectives because it would deny China a toehold in the region, free Thailand from Chinese pressures, lessen the obligation of ASEAN members to support Thailand, and set up Vietnam as a front line of defense against China.

The Indonesian initiatives included unofficial visits to Vietnam by high-level Indonesian military and political personnel. Benny Murdani, armed forces chief of staff, arrived in Hanoi in February 1984; his was the first official visit by any ASEAN member since Malaysian foreign minister Rithaudeen's in January 1980. All did not go smoothly. The Vietnamese used the occasion to highlight their shared suspicions of China and the blocking role that Vietnam plays. Defense Minister Dung of Vietnam attempted to suggest an Indonesian-Vietnamese bond when he spoke of their nations' common history of struggle against imperialism. Murdani contributed to the confusion with the comment: ''Some countries said that Vietnam is a danger to Southeast Asia, but the Indonesian Army and people do not believe it.''[46] This was later toned down by Murdani's public backing of the ASEAN diplomatic stand and an explanation that his comments were based on a purely military view, as well as his judgment that the threat is lessened by the nationalist element in Vietnamese communism.[47] Murdani would later reiterate this military view, justifying the Vietnamese invasion on grounds of national survival; he compared the Vietnamese situation to that of Israel and restated the analysis that a poor Vietnam was not threat.[48] This speech was not widely reported, perhaps because of the embarrassment of an Israel metaphor. A second Indonesian initiative took place in March during a conference in Hanoi. The head of Jakarta's

Center for Strategic and International Studies, Jusuf Wanandi, attended and subsequently commented on the requirements of Vietnamese security: Hanoi could not accept any role of the Khmer Rouge in the new Cambodia which, while neutral, must recognize Vietnamese primacy over it.[49]

Jakarta hoped that Hanoi would seize this initiative as a regional way out of the Cambodian dilemma because it was bogged down in the guerrilla quagmire, globally isolated as a pariah, and dependent on the Soviet Union. This formula granted its security needs while providing a face-saving device, the official neutrality of Cambodia, to its regional neighbors. The disadvantaged on the battlefield should not, however, expect a concession from a victor, even if they only ask for a way to capitulate.

Hanoi ignored the Indonesian formula, arrogantly disregarding the risks Jakarta had taken. In March, Foreign Minister Thach visited Indonesia, Australia, and Thailand. He took a hard line during his visit to Jakarta and made no recognition of the consideration Indonesia had tried to show Vietnam. President Suharto's process for the resolution of Cambodia included a Vietnamese and ASEAN peacekeeping force and the elimination of the Khmer Rouge from power by elections.[50] Publicly it was argued that Hanoi would have nothing to fear from elections because the people would reject the brutal Khmer Rouge. The form of elections was open and could be devised to secure the desired result, perhaps in the style of the 1969 Irian Jaya consultations, or the "ascertainments" of Sabah and Sarawak, or the integration of East Timor. But Thach demanded ASEAN members' ratification of the status quo, and he made no concession either to principles, to form, or to the risk taken by Indonesia.

The Indonesian initiative risked solidarity; if Thailand felt that Indonesia was too accommodating, it might have moved closer to China, thus widening cleavages among the members of ASEAN. Indeed, Thach saw Jakarta's formula as such a cleavage and sought to capitalize on it; he pushed the impression that Suharto and Vietnam were uniform in their shared threat perception of China.[51] However, if Hanoi had been seeking to divide, a concession to Jakarta would have widened rifts more than this disruptive ploy. But, the hard line in Hanoi won out, and diplomacy yielded to military solutions. While Thach was on tour, Vietnamese troops made an incursion into Thailand's Sisaket Province during early April. The Vietnamese occupation of a strategic hill lasted twelve days. In light of Thach's uneasy visit to Bangkok when a cold prevented him from conferring with Foreign Minister Siddhi—the *Bangkok Post* editorialized, he "sniffs an ASEAN 'rift' "[52]—an atmosphere of uncertainty was apparent.[53] Thailand called for condemnations; Singapore, Malaysia, and the Philippines responded.[54] Jakarta now resented the deliberate tension Hanoi created and the rebuff to its plan.

Finally, Foreign Minister Mochtar's trip to Moscow in April compounded the uneasiness among ASEAN members. Though it may have been originally planned to balance the expected visit of President Reagan to Indonesia, its symbolism as the first visit in ten years and the announcement of Soviet support for the Indonesian plan suggested a widening of the cleavage over China and Vietnam. Mochtar's comment that he expected ASEAN to "gradually accept" the plan[55] also violated ASEAN rules about consultation, consensus, and quiet diplomacy.

Individualism in policy, the tension of stalemate, greater Chinese and Soviet involvement in the region, the stability of the Thai government, and, most important, the Vietnamese invasion and intransigence demanded a demonstration of solidarity. The foreign ministers reacted in two statements. The July 9 Joint Statement reviewed past stands; but the July 10 Joint Communique was more pointed. The ministers noted "recurrent acts of Vietnamese aggression," intrusions and bombardments along the border, and "condemned these attacks which took place immediately after the Vietnamese Foreign Minister's visits to Jakarta and Canberra." Indignancy helped them further express their mind on the "latest so-called annual partial withdrawal of . . . troops . . . which were meant to be manoeuvres to deceive the international community, the Kampuchean people, and Vietnam's own citizens." They did not mince words on the Vietnamese settlement in fertile parts of Cambodia, calling this "Vietnamese colonization," and they rejected a Vietnamese proposal as "a propaganda ploy."

Not only did the ASEAN states speak in strong, direct language to support Thailand and express their frustration in these difficult years, they literally displayed unity—with each other and with their outside friends—in special forums. These additional instruments of solidarity, the way the states stand together, are taken up next.

8

ASEAN Diplomacy: Standing Together

> ASEAN stands more united now than at any time in its past. The Bali conference was a milestone in the sense that ASEAN political cohesion and solidarity were demonstrated, and were recognized by the world. This is the real "teeth" of the Bali Communiqué.
> —Foreign Minister Carlos Romulo

WHEN they cannot find common words, or need more time to determine them, or feel that actions speak louder, ASEAN states have used displays of solidarity. Joint policy stands, in fact, have not been the most favored tactic to bolster the process. Words live on, but a gathering works like a flash of light to catch attention and then is gone, leaving no trace and restriction on individual members. So, as Minister Romulo commented, the 1979 AMM was remembered not because of what was said but because of what was done. Since the early 1970s bilateral summits were used in a similar manner to reaffirm relationships on the western flank. On a multilateral level, ASEAN leaders have used displays of solidarity through special foreign ministers meetings, Post-Ministerial Meetings (PMMs), and summits.

Special Foreign Ministers Meetings

The gathering of chief diplomats outside the AMM in the "special foreign ministers meeting" is symbolically salient in two ways: it lends importance to an articulation that could otherwise be made by the chair of the Standing Committee, and it enables ASEAN members to express concern without an articulation. The first extraordinary gathering of foreign ministers produced the Zopfan Declaration. The policy stand was given significance by its codification as a declaration, yet this gathering of the foreign ministers, like others in July 1972 and February 1973, was above and beyond the call of annual ASEAN duty and so was itself significant. The signal underlying the instrument of the special foreign ministers meeting is voluntary, extraordinary solidarity. The first extraordinary meeting convened to signal solidarity occurred on the anniversary of the first summit in February 1977; it reaffirmed the stands and gestures made at Bali in 1976 and served as a bridge to the next summit in August 1977.

The extraordinary meetings in the troubled year of 1979 initiated more regular use of gathering as an instrument of solidarity. Along with pointed policy statements, the gathering of ministers in January during the Vietnamese invasion of Cambodia allowed ASEAN members to underline their grave concern. The meeting came only days after, and it produced a statement that echoed that made by the chairman of the ASEAN Standing Committee. The later meetings of the ASEAN foreign ministers in August and December 1979 were held in Kuala Lumpur, but the struggle for consensus on Cambodia diluted the display of solidarity. The diplomats were not so much interested in signaling as in internal cohesion. They learned in July that the search for a common-policy stand was not only difficult but also counterproductive because press coverage of the cleavages during the AMM worked against their mounting a credible display of solidarity. They gathered, however, in what were called informal sessions to reassure each other and accommodate two trends within ASEAN: those who wanted to avoid giving the impression of an alliance, and those who wanted to avoid a spotlight on their cleavages.

This new form of consultation and solidarity was needed in August 1979 soon after the July AMM. The invasion and its aftereffects, especially the refugee outflows, had been central on the Bali AMM agenda, but when the July Geneva meeting on refugees "fell short of providing an overall and lasting solution" to the problem (Joint Statement of the ASEAN Foreign Ministers Informal Meeting, August 16, 1979), they met again. The meeting was also held to discuss political action concerning Cambodia at the Nonaligned Conference in Havana. The result of this quiet session was that ASEAN states decided to oppose the seating of the Vietnamese-backed Heng Samrin regime at the next session in Havana. ASEAN diplomacy secured a partial success; that meeting ended in a draw between the wishes of Vietnam and Thailand—no Cambodian government was seated.

They met in December 1979 to draw together after individual policy stands became public; Singapore had been loud against Vietnam while Indonesia was more hopeful and willing to accept Thach's assurances. Problems also emerged from the dilemma of supporting the infamous, genocidal regime of ousted leader Pol Pot as the means of combating Vietnam's aggression. Britain brought this to a head by withdrawing recognition of Pol Pot; Vietnam was using his crimes as justification for its liberation of Cambodia. The one-day December meeting produced no new policy, but it was a display of unity. As one foreign minister commented, "There are rumours being spread that there are differences. Some people are adding to it by saying 'rift.' But we are still solidly together."[1] To accommodate Jakarta and Kuala Lumpur, the ministers designated Foreign Minister Rithauddeen of Malaysia to visit Hanoi as a representative of ASEAN. (Though he did go in January, Vietnam did not accept him as a representative and soon demanded that Thailand stop aiding the Khmer Rouge and China.)

Subsequent special meetings responded to external events or their internal repercussions. The December 1981 gathering was held to resolve strains resulting from the Cambodian occupation and to display solidarity. ASEAN members had moved to more individualistic policies after the outflow of refugees eased. In March 1980 Indonesia and Malaysia launched the short-lived Kuantan initiative, which seemed to offer Vietnam hegemony over Indochina in exchange for a rapprochement. Thailand found this approach unacceptable and demanded a return to the policy of Vietnamese withdrawal. Largely because of the timing of the invasion, the June 1980 AMM issued a common stand in support of Thailand. Vietnam floated two initiatives in July 1980 and January 1981 promising partial withdrawal and negotiations. This succeeded in splitting ASEAN members, although the ASEAN chair issued responses rejecting the offers.

On the other hand, Bangkok's use of the Cambodian resistance as a deterrent remained a point of contention with Vietnam. In late 1979 Thailand had opened a refugee camp holding 200,000, which gave it influence over these and the other 700,000 Cambodians in the border area, that is, one-fourth the estimated Cambodian population,[2] a significant lever to deal with the Vietnamese in Cambodia.

Though the ASEAN statement of June 1980 appeared to support repatriation, this Thai tactic strained relations among ASEAN states, especially Indonesia and Malaysia, who were ready to repair bridges to Vietnam. But Bangkok would not abandon its policy of military deterrents, and thus, the divisive issue of bleeding or bolstering Vietnam emerged once again among ASEAN states. Indonesia and Malaysia feared that prolonging the war only played into China's hands by bleeding Vietnam into submission—which they saw as China's first step in asserting control over a Southeast Asian sphere of interest. In contrast, Thailand and Singapore argued that bolstering Vietnam against China would result in Vietnamese expansionism. Rather, they inclined to trust China and stand up to Vietnam.

Vietnamese intransigence on the UN-sponsored International Conference on Kampuchea kept intra-ASEAN cleavages from widening. Even though the June 1981 AMM tried to send conciliatory signals to Vietnam—even Singapore's Foreign Minister Dhanabalan said that "Asean is prepared to work with Vietnam to create conditions in the region which can promote economic growth in Vietnam"[3]—Hanoi did not attend the July ICK session. Even the break by ASEAN members with China during the session (they wanted to open participation to the other Cambodian groups as well as the Khmer Rouge) did not produce a gesture from Vietnam. Rather, Hanoi stayed with its hard line, reminding Thailand that the June 1980 incursion was a consequence of its earlier repatriation policies and making reference to northeastern Thailand as the "provinces of Laos currently under Thai administration," thus strengthening the suspicion of some Thais who feel this territory is coveted by Vietnam as part of a greater Laos.[4]

While the ASEAN hawks felt vindicated in their opinion that appeasement would not work, other opinions and images also seemed fixed. Solidarity fractured in August 1981 when the Malaysian prime minister, soon after a visit from the Chinese premier, commented, "I do not think [the Vietnamese] will have much time for a lot of adventures outside Vietnam. I do not think it is their intention to invade ASEAN.''[5] Subsequently, Dr. Mahathir had to interpret this statement to reassure Thailand; he explained that when he said Vietnam is not a threat to ASEAN, he meant Malaysia, and he did not see Vietnam marching into Malaysia tomorrow. He added: ''But we understand the Vietnamese capacity to create a lot of problems for the region and for Thailand. And, of course, if Vietnam attacks Thailand it will also attack Malaysia.''[6]

Another move to split ASEAN members came from Laos in October. As a special inducement to begin talks with Indonesia and Malaysia, the Laotian foreign minister indicated that Vietnam was ready to settle the disputes with those states over territorial waters and economic zones in the South China Sea. The talks could go on to discuss the ''peace and stability of Southeast Asia.'' This time, not wanting to appear aligned against China nor resisting peace talks, ASEAN members sidestepped the initiative, saying, ''This is one carrot we can do without.''[7]

Lastly, strains arose about support for resistance forces in Cambodia. In September Deputy Prime Minister Rajaratnam of Singapore unilaterally expressed support for a united front coalition government, consisting of the Khmer Rouge, the Khmer People's National Liberation Front (KPNLF), and the Sihanoukists. Indonesia was offended by the lack of consultation—especially because Singapore was chair of the ASEAN Standing Committee when it announced the proposal—and the apparent hardening of the anti-Vietnam faction within the ASEAN process, especially as references to giving military aid were made. The tensions were high, with Foreign Minister Mochtar even suggesting that Indonesia might have to leave ASEAN over Cambodia.[8]

Resolution of the intramural tensions came at Pattaya in December 1981 with a display of solidarity. Choosing the site in Thailand (a divergence from custom, which called for meeting in the host of the next AMM), they put their solidarity on the front line. Addressing individualism, Foreign Minister Romulo explained that Foreign Minister Mochtar accepted the face-saving excuse that Singapore did not overlook or ignore partners but ''the chairman did what he could do considering the constraints of time.''[9] They agreed that military assis-

tance was beyond the scope of the ASEAN Declaration of 1967 and was
"purely a matter for the [individual] countries to decide. It is not an
ASEAN project. It is not an ASEAN exercise," said Singapore's Foreign
Minister Dhanabalan.[10] This time, without question, the chair spoke
the consensus of ASEAN members. Their policy was a compromise,
however, as they gave approval to the concept of a "loose coalition"
of resistance forces. To avoid problems in the future, Foreign Minister
Dhanabalan set out an intramural policy solution: "ASEAN foreign
ministers will meet more often whenever the opportunity presents
itself to discuss ASEAN matters, bring ourselves up to date, [and]
exchange perceptions on problems that are of concern to us."[11]

A "special meeting" in August 1982 was held to reassure Thailand
that Vietnamese foreign minister Thach's tour to Singapore, Malaysia,
and Thailand had not driven a wedge between ASEAN members and
Thailand. Thach's tour was designed to show Vietnamese reasonable-
ness. In July Thach announced a troop withdrawal from Cambodia
and promised a second withdrawal "in the near future" if Thailand
came up with a "positive response," meaning Thailand would deny
China access to supply the Khmer Rouge and set up a border safety
zone.[12] After Thach's visits, the foreign ministers met in Bangkok and
concluded that there was nothing new in the Vietnamese initiatives.[13]
(At this meeting the label "special meeting" came into use.) Solidarity
was displayed and consensus again maintained on the point that
Vietnam had illegally used force to achieve its position in Cambodia.
By invoking the UN resolution based on the United Nations Charter's
proscriptions against aggression, ASEAN ministers said nothing new;
but they displayed unity.

The special meeting held in November 1983 extended the use of
this instrument when it was scheduled to satisfy U.S. requests for a
summit on the occasion of President Reagan's tour. Though the visit
was canceled due to the Philippine destabilization following the
assassination of Benigno Aquino, the ministers—not wanting to appear subservient to U.S. whims—pushed through with the meeting.
Other items rose to the top of the agenda, namely, the Australian
government's accommodationist line with Vietnam. Australia had not
cosponsored the ASEAN resolution at the current session of the UN
General Assembly. Furthermore, Foreign Minister Hayden of Australia intended to act as facilitator between ASEAN and Vietnam. While

an anxious Singapore wanted assurances that Australia would not go too far, the others adopted a "wait-and-see approach."[14] The resulting compromise sanctioned Australia's try but warned that no impression of a dialogue via Australia should be given.

This special meeting resolved the Australian question but also revealed cleavages. The tough stands taken by Singapore during the session actually diluted the prized image of solidarity. The Cambodian issues were sent off to the SOM for more discreet consultation, in a prudent return to the use of quiet diplomacy among themselves. A special foreign ministers meeting was held again in 1986 when President Reagan stopped at Bali on his way to the Tokyo OECD Summit.

The special foreign ministers meeting in May 1984 was part of a twofold response that included the strong statements made in July 1984. The shocks, setbacks, and independent moves (as discussed in chapter 7) so distressed foreign ministers that they met only weeks before their regularly scheduled AMM in July. Soviet and Chinese naval exercises in the South China Sea, Thai initiatives to China, Vietnamese diplomatic arrogance, Indonesian initiatives to Hanoi and Moscow, and a Vietnamese incursion in Thailand's Sisaket Province called for this gesture of solidarity. Managing stress through communication is helpful, but if consultation were sufficient in itself, the July meeting or any of the other institutions, such as the Standing Committee, the SOM, or bilateral visits, could have fulfilled this need. Rather, the timing means that this was a special display of solidarity. Substantively, it prepared the way for the strong articulations heard at the AMM.

This special meeting in May went beyond a display, it condemned Vietnamese attacks on Cambodian "civilian encampments" and Vietnamese rejection of ASEAN peace proposals. Then, after supporting Thailand, the ministers addressed the apparent strains among themselves. A solution was to clarify, reaffirm, and institutionalize an intrinsic principle of their accommodation, freedom of foreign policy. The ASEAN members gave a blessing to the Indonesian role as special contact to Vietnam. This was ritualized with the codeword "interlocutor." As an ASEAN interlocutor to Vietnam, Jakarta's future initiatives to Vietnam would not give the impression that it was breaking from the ASEAN common stance. So too, Thailand could be an interlocutor to China. The result was, to paraphrase the Indonesian national motto, ASEAN diplomatic unity out of diversity of members' foreign policies.

The integrity of the process still required a clarification of Indonesian foreign-policy priorities in light of the recent Indonesian-Vietnamese exchanges. Vietnam touted a report that President Suharto, as well as General Murdani, stated "Vietnam is not a threat to the Southeast Asian nations."[15] At such times, ritual activities, like meetings and codewords, are not enough for reassurance, and at this meeting President Suharto decided that direct, personal reaffirmation was necessary. He took part in a postsession pep talk and reiterated the rationale of ASEAN cooperation, namely, good relations had brought benefits to Indonesia and, consequently, ASEAN will always have the top priority in his nation's foreign policy. Then followed the strong common stand at the July AMM.

The Cambodian situation seemed to worsen after these mid-1984 meetings. More Chinese aid to the Khmer Rouge forces, U.S. apathy or distraction, and intramural CGDK fighting—including Khmer Rouge attacks on the KPNLF in August, KPNLF squabbles with Sihanouk (for example, a demonstration during his visit to Minneapolis), and KPNLF and Sihanoukist desires to disassociate from the Khmer Rouge by changing the name of Democratic Kampuchea and redesigning the flag—were areas of concern to Thailand and other ASEAN partners. They were evidently windows of opportunity to the Vietnamese. In an attempt to capitalize on the divisions and move before increased Chinese aid made the difference, Hanoi mounted a major military offensive during the dry season (December–February).

In response, a special foreign ministers meeting was held in February 1985 to display solidarity. Once again their venue at Bangkok was part of the signal. The catalyst for the meeting was the fall of Amphil, the headquarters camp of the KPNLF in Cambodia. Foreign Minister Wu Xueqian of China spoke of the need for a "second lesson."[16] Thus, Thailand's loss of part of its resistance buffer and the danger of another Chinese attack on Vietnam, including a possible replay of Soviet-American naval confrontation, necessitated that ASEAN partners come to the Thailand's defense before China rushed in. Concurrently, since March 1984, Thailand had a perceived Vietnam as instigator behind a border dispute with Laos over ownership of three villages. Mostly viewed as an annoyance and a Vietnamese attempt to distract from the Cambodian issue, this irritant served to keep anti-Vietnamese suspicions at a high level. In addition to the display of solidarity, the special meeting went beyond the customary condemnation of the incursions and for the first time in public called "upon the international community to increase support and assistance to the Kampuchean people in their political and military struggle to liberate their homeland from foreign occupation"(Joint Statement, February 11). The foreign ministers also appealed to the Soviet Union to stop its support of these acts of aggression.

A lessening intramural tension followed: Thailand evidenced a feeling of greater security, and ASEAN partners came to have greater confidence in Thailand, more impatience with Vietnam, and perhaps a more realistic understanding of what all could expect from one another. Thailand's sense of greater security did not result from any new Vietnamese initiative; rather, Vietnam's response was aggressive, taking the Khmer Rouge stronghold of Phnom Malai soon after the February special meeting. But Bangkok's neighbors were steadfast. The new Vietnamese offensive maintained the mood and policies of the special meeting. Indonesia kept to its new hard line, evidencing this at the 1985 CSIS-IIS meeting. Support and consultation bolstered cohesion; an unofficial meeting of foreign ministers was held in Bandung during the thirtieth anniversary celebrations of the Afro-Asian conference. There a new diplomatic initiative was being discussed in terms of Malaysia's idea of "proximity talks"— wherein all concerned parties would discuss through a third party, and so the obstacle of granting recognition to Heng Samrin, Vietnam's installed regime, would be avoided. By the time of the July 1985 AMM, this idea gained more attention because of Vietnamese incursions into Thailand in May, but the attention was largely diplomatic posturing, lacking realistic expectations that a solution would follow. Its purpose was to create the appearance that ASEAN was actively concerned.

While such ASEAN diplomacy could not fully assuage Thai fears, a set of acts by other states began to build Thai confidence. Within ASEAN, the new hard line of Indonesia and the tougher stand of

Malaysia, which undertook to train sixty Sihanoukists,[17] signaled a greater appreciation of Thailand's problems. Also encouraging was the joint Sihanoukist–Khmer Rouge attack on Battambamg,[18] demonstrating that the resistance was alive and well enough to attack inside the Vietnamese-held area. This assuaged Thai fears of losing their guerrilla buffer.

Greater assurance came from actions by great powers. The dry-season offensive moved the U.S. Congress to approve U.S. $5 million in aid for the non-Communist resistance in Cambodia. Small though the amount was, it was significant as the first assistance given to an anti-Vietnamese force since 1975. This was followed by other symbolic and substantive acts. In October 1985, a Memorandum of Understanding on Logistics and Supplies was signed; it was seen as a prelude to a War Reserve Stockpile, the first in a country without a U.S. base. That plan was approved in April 1986. A final action was the change of site for the annual U.S.-Thai military exercises from southern Thailand to an area much closer to Bangkok.

Parallel acts of reassurance came from China, taking the form of a promise to do more, including shelling Vietnam. The Chinese set up a hot line to Bangkok and, in an attempt to help stabilize Thailand's economy, China bought extra rice at higher-than-market rates. By the end of 1986 the relationship evidenced a growing military dimension, with field guns and tanks being supplied to Thailand at "friendship prices," that is, well below market prices. The visit of the Crown Prince Vajiralongkorn to China served to suggest an increasing alignment. But while Thailand was feeling more secure, other ASEAN partners looked for reassurance about China. Indonesia began to counter this growing alliance with a diplomatic offensive against the source of Thailand's insecurity, the Cambodian war.

The special foreign ministers meeting in August 1987 again displayed solidarity and accommodated Thai and Indonesian policy trends. Chinese-Vietnamese border fighting in January, the disarray of the resistance forces—Prince Sihanouk was on a leave of absence as head of the CGDK, complaining that the Khmer Rouge had attacked his forces—and Thai-Lao border troubles encouraged Indonesia to revive the concept of informal "cocktail party" talks. Foreign Minister Mochtar visited Sihanouk in July and secured his cooperation in plan that called for Vietnamese withdrawal, elections, and a four-party government in Cambodia. Mochtar's subsequent visit to Hanoi resulted in "an understanding on the basis of equal footing."[19] This development was not well-accepted in Singapore, China, or Thailand, though Mochtar had consulted Bangkok before and after his trip to Hanoi. The feeling was that Vietnam was attempting to gain recognition for its Phnom Penh regime, downplay the problem from a regional matter to a civil war, and project an image of flexibility and moderation to the world.

Bangkok was especially sensitive to cracks in ASEAN at this time; Hanoi had just concluded an agreement with the United States to negotiate on Americans missing in action during the war, and Bangkok saw this as a propaganda ploy to drive a diplomatic wedge between itself and another ally. This uneasiness was reflected in *The Nation*: "The [US-Vietnam] war was over when the Paris peace accords were signed in January 1973. What could be Vietnam's urgent humanitarian concerns after 14 years? Perhaps it is time [for Thailand] to realize that there is a subtle change in American policy towards Vietnam."[20] So, in what was called a "hastily conceived conclave," the foreign ministers arrived at consensus, accepting the concept of the informal negotiations—a concession to Indonesia—but only if Vietnam enters as one of the parties. And to further reassure front-line Thailand, they gathered at the level of the state's chief diplomat. *Asiaweek*'s photograph of all six foreign ministers, smiling and arms interlocked, displayed their unity.[21]

Post-Ministerial Meetings

According to the Manila *Daily Express*, "Considering the uncertain world situation with crises in Cambodia, Afghanistan and Iran, among other areas . . . [ASEAN] had no option but to close ranks and seek friends outside the region such as Australia and New Zealand or countries in the Pacific basin like the United States and Japan."[22] The Post-Ministerial Meeting follows the ASEAN AMM, allowing opportunities to meet with and stand with outside sympathetic states. It has now become customary that the foreign ministers or other representatives of Japan, Canada, New Zealand, Australia, the European Community, and the United States attend this "Post-Minis-

terial Conference.'' The sessions with these six ''dialogue partners,'' as they are called, demonstrate that ASEAN states are not alone
and that they are valued by influential states. The sessions are
functionally important as time is allotted to give each ASEAN foreign
minister a chance to talk with each of the countries' representatives.[23] In 1984 the first joint meeting (called the ''6-plus-5'') raised
the importance of that year's gathering, as it did again in
1987. There is now a waiting list of those who have expressed
interest in being invited to the AMM.

This tactic of ''ambiguous association'' developed in the years
before 1979, the year of the first PMM. After the ASEAN states decided
to meet in their first summit, to be held in February 1976, they were
faced with strong, public Japanese and Australian interest to be
invited. This posed a dilemma because some feared that their attendance would be confrontational—that it might be seen as a U.S.-in-
spired maneuver to set up a new strategy for regional security.[24] Since
concern about confrontational appearances was behind some states'
hesitancy to hold a summit in the first place, the attendance of the two
U.S. allies was more than consensus could bear. The heads of Japan
and Australia did not attend.

For the next summit in 1977, a new approach emerged. The
leaders of Japan, Australia, and New Zealand came to Kuala Lumpur
and joined in a postsummit meeting. ASEAN members agreed on this
more measured use of outside support. Bangkok, the obvious beneficiary, argued it needed this enhanced support; under military rule
again, it worried about U.S. reliability under the new Carter administration, which had been evaluating the regime's human rights
record.[25] In July Vietnam and Laos signed a Friendship Pact that
legitimized Vietnamese troops in Laos. These pressures account for
this enhancement strategy, as indicated by a Thai diplomat at that
time: ''Thailand is . . . realistic enough to detect the inherent problem
within Asean. It is seeking outside support for Asean, particularly
from the neighboring countries of Japan, Australia, and New Zealand.''[26]

The others agreed because 1977 was an anxious year for all states,
even those not on the front line. This year saw insurgency flare up in
Mindanao, West Irian, and Acheh. Thus reminded of their common
cause, ASEAN partners had renewed motivation to accommodate.

Thailand gave more reason by cooperating with Malaysian campaigns against the CPM. Acceding to the tactic of ambiguous association was comparatively low-cost in return for the security they were gaining in the peninsula area. Another move to gather friends centered on ASEAN's identification with Third World issues. At the foreign ministers meeting in the month before the summit, the states took first-time positions calling for "withdrawal from illegally occupied Arab territories" and recognizing the "inalienable" rights of the Palestinians, as well as "majority rule in Southern Africa" (Joint Communique, July 8).[27] These gestures were part of ASEAN's propaganda war against Vietnam for influence in the Third World; they also allowed the Islamic states in ASEAN to bring home a victory in payment for their participation in the summit.

In 1978 the main ASEAN gathering was the Annual Ministerial Meeting. The context for this AMM, the year of Vietnamese smiles, did not present a sense of urgency, and Thailand did not need to make demands on ASEAN or outside parties. Foreign Minister Sonoda of Japan did attend, however.

The institution of the Post-Ministerial Meeting took its present form at the 1979 Bali AMM and in some ways was a substitute for a summit display. Attendance by the chief diplomats of the United States, Japan, Australia, New Zealand, and the European Community in the aftermath of the Vietnamese occupation of Cambodia meant that they were also displaying solidarity with Thailand. ASEAN members were glad to see the United States accept their invitation and so restore some sort of strategic balance in the region. Secretary of State Cyrus Vance came and spoke reassuringly, saying, "the United States is a Pacific power. We will stand by our commitments in the region. . . . We have made this clear to all concerned—and directly to the Soviet Union and Vietnam."[28] This was valued because of the vacillation in the Carter years.

As Cambodia is still occupied and Thailand is still threatened, the "dialogue partners" reinforcement ritual has continued. In 1980 the foreign minister of Canada joined this process, and the foreign minister of India was invited. He was cabled not to come, however, after New Delhi supported Vietnam's role in Cambodia. The dialogue partners attended in 1981, including the new U.S. secretary of state, Alexander Haig. The following year provided an exception when

Secretary Haig sent his deputy. This was viewed not as a deliberate act of deemphasis but rather a side effect of the power struggle within the U.S. administration, shown by Haig's subsequent resignation. But because it was now three years after the invasion of Cambodia, the ASEAN states had to worry about world apathy or complacency, two dynamics on Vietnam's side. Therefore, they acted to demonstrate their sense of importance, forcing the president of the European Council of Ministers to attend by expressing displeasure with a substitute.[29] Since then the dialogue partners have attended at the foreign-minister level.

In summary, talks with "dialogue partners" are unique acts of public diplomacy: the great powers of the West attend upon the deliberations of only one regional organization in a show of solidarity that converges with ASEAN's own public diplomacy. Again, no commitments are articulated or common programs begun, but endorsements like U.S. Secretary of State Shultz's "We follow your lead"[30] serve to banish isolation and enhance political standing. As Foreign Minister Romulo commented, the talks showed that ASEAN has friends and "that we can depend on these friends . . . we are not alone."[31] The primary beneficiary is Thailand, but all states in the process gain because this relationship with the great powers enhances the process and makes it more valuable. ASEAN thus becomes stronger as potential defectors would pay a higher cost.

Summits

Summits provide the most dramatic displays of solidarity, but ASEAN nations have held only three in twenty years. Moreover, the infrequency of summits over this period juxtaposed to their successful intramural record presents a paradox to unravel: how have these states supported cooperation with so few gatherings of their leaders? The answer to both inquiries begins in characterizing ASEAN summitry as an instrument of public diplomacy rather than as a substantive political process.

An important milestone in ASEAN cooperation was reached with the Zopfan Declaration of November 1971, the first collective foreign policy stand of the members. Zopfan emerged from members' shared beliefs that regional stability was endangered, and that the threat was coming from their common external milieu, namely, the U.S. withdrawal from Vietnam. Though they were concerned about possible changes in the regional distribution of power, they did not hold a summit to negotiate or proclaim this declaration. Yet members did recognize that they, as a grouping, had the responsibility and opportunity to address the problem through collective action, an important step to holding a summit. Subsequently, when regional stability was clearly threatened by full U.S. withdrawal from South Vietnam in April 1975, ASEAN heads of government took the next step in collective diplomacy—they met.

ASEAN's first two summits were held in February 1976 at Bali, Indonesia, and August 1977 at Kuala Lumpur, Malaysia. The meetings were, in many ways, two acts of a single drama. The need for consensus at the Bali summit required postponement of difficult issues to a later time; hence, the decision to hold a second summit was part of accommodation and consensus-building during the first meeting. This tactic not only allowed the group to articulate united stands in 1976, it helped to suggest ongoing solidarity through the announcement of the 1977 summit. A contemporary observer noted the solidarity imperative at the Bali summit:

> The search for consensus before the summit rather than at the summit; the signing of the Treaty of Amity, not merely its words; the cordiality of the numerous bilateral as well as multilateral contacts before and during the summit; the assertion of concord—all these added up collectively to a solidifying of the spirit of togetherness that had originally brought ASEAN together in 1967, and had sustained it over eight difficult years.[32]

The times called for solidarity; ASEAN members shared concerns about regional instability resulting from U.S. withdrawal from the Southeast Asian mainland, Hanoi's victory over South Vietnam, the establishment of Communist regimes in Laos and Cambodia, and uncertainty about the policies of China. Specifically, the summit took place because the members wanted to bolster the intramural political process that had been producing peace and stability in the ASEAN subregion for the previous nine years. While none of the attending states thought they could dictate, even collectively, the course of regional events—though the belief in the powers of collective action was heady in this golden age of OPEC—they did feel it was within their power to maintain good and cooperative relations among themselves. Much of what was done at the first summit reflects this attempt to demonstrate recommitment to each other and what they had achieved in their subregion. They restructured, strengthened, and expanded the ASEAN organization, the symbol of their good-neighborly relations; and they utilized that powerful display of solidarity, press photographs of all five leaders standing and smiling together.

But the smiles should not lead one to believe that the meeting was easily achieved. While there was consensus on the need to strengthen intramural ties, divisions of opinion about regional politics and the necessity or appropriateness of a summit lurked behind the camaraderie. Though Communist victories in Vietnam, Laos, and Cambodia brought about a sudden redistribution of power on the mainland, ASEAN states did not share an equal sense of danger. Unlike Thailand, whose geography, history, and past interactions with Vietnam made it the most suspicious and anxious ASEAN member, the others agonized over Vietnamese intentions and about appropriate responses. Some, like Indonesia and Malaysia, feeling the worst was over, did not see the necessity for joint action; they were prepared to continue the policy of wait-and-see with the new Vietnam. This policy assessment is represented in a statement of Adam Malik in July 1975: "If we look objectively at Vietnam, this country, even with their communist system, needs a peaceful time to settle their own house and make it clean. So, in our opinion, it is impossible for them at this time to export revolution. . . . To reconstruct their country, you need not one year, but maybe 10 years." This pause would allow other states time to advance economically and thus strengthen their societies.[33] Others were inclined to wait and see because they worried a summit might be read by Vietnam as a confrontational act.

Besides divisions about regional politics, several intramural issues made some reluctant moves to gather in a gesture of unity. The Indonesian seizure of the Portuguese colony, East Timor, in December 1975 occasioned an important last-minute cleavage. Some ASEAN governments, especially Malaysia, sympathized with the Indonesian fear of Timor's becoming a haven for secessionists and Communists. Singapore, however, small in size and thus concerned to uphold the principles of sovereignty and territorial integrity, felt it could not join in sanctioning Indonesia's action. It made no public condemnations, in the agreed style of quiet diplomacy, but its abstention on a UN resolution concerning Timor revealed that it was putting this national interest above ASEAN solidarity. The Timor issue served also to accent another cleavage among ASEAN members. China condemned Indonesia's action and showed sympathy for the pro-independence guerrillas, Freitilin. So while Indonesia and China were at odds, other ASEAN states, notably the Philippines, Malaysia, and Thailand, were developing relationships with China.

Along with such different perspectives on an important regional actor, other long-standing differences of opinion (which yet persist) were stumbling blocks to participation in this expression of unity. The Philippine claim to Sabah remained an irritant in Malaysian-Philippine relations. Specifically, Kuala Lumpur worried that the summit might institute planned machinery for dispute settlement which might then be used by Manila to revive the Sabah claim. Questions on economics were problematic. Singapore and the Philippines supported the concept of an ASEAN free-trade zone, but Indonesia, wishing to conserve its large domestic market to spur indigenous industry, did not.

But in the end these differences were transcended and a summit was held for some symbolic and strategic reasons important to the internal dynamics of the regional grouping. First, there was concern about ASEAN's image. Should ASEAN not meet to discuss the recent events in the region, outsiders and some members might read this as an indication of group weakness or disorganization. Moreover, this possible interpretation was made all the more likely because the leaders had not ever gathered in a group. Second, ASEAN states had some strategic concerns, including uncertainty about the United States. In addition to a report that the Pentagon was redrawing its zone of strategic interest excluding all of peninsular Southeast Asia,[34] a new U.S. foreign policy toward Asia was announced in December 1975. This Pacific Doctrine created some unease because it paid little attention to Southeast Asia and much to Japan in what was feared as a Kissingerian move to devolve responsibility onto a local power.[35] Such a role for Japan was not welcomed by former members of the Co-Prosperity Sphere, and it seemed that leaders felt "an undue closeness towards each other in the belief that such solidarity could keep them intact vis-à-vis these new challenges."[36]

Most important, security imperatives explain the summit. States to the south valued Thailand as a buffer from the Indochina front and as a partner in controlling the CPM insurgency. Now Thailand needed diplomatic support. Along with gratitude, a fear of Thai defection moved states to gather; they worried that Thailand's "bamboo diplomacy" would sway with the new prevailing wind and allow its territory to become a conduit of Vietnamese aid to guerrilla movements in the straits area. At that time there was much apprehension about Vietnamese plans for the large amounts of military supplies abandoned by the United States. For its part, Thailand felt threatened by the new balance of power in Indochina and wanted a signal from its ASEAN partners that it was not alone.

While unity was the watchword of the day, a close look reveals that the collective political stand demonstrated by that summit skillfully accommodated members' perceptions and interests; public diplomacy also indicated that solidarity was being carefully measured out. A date almost a year after the conquest of South Vietnam was chosen: By not moving with haste, the impression of alarm or alliance was diffused. Accommodation can be seen in the summit diplomacy's ambiguity. Political support for Thailand was never articulated; it was instead suggested by summit ceremonies and announcements about economic and administrative matters designed to bolster the regional organization. By issuing the Declaration of ASEAN Concord and signing a Treaty of Amity and Cooperation in Southeast Asia, by agreeing to joint-industrial projects in each country, by creating the Secretariat in Jakarta, and by expanding the scope of interaction with an announcement that the organization plays a role in political cooperation, the members restructured and strengthened the ASEAN organization and so gave support in a shadow-play style. The announcement, however, that the organization would issue a separate political communique after meetings was an important first step out of the shadows to admitting publicly (and realizing the Thai expectations of) a collective political function for ASEAN.

Nevertheless, the summit of 1976 did not directly address the tumultuous events of April 1975. As for regional instability, the ASEAN states straddled both sides; the summit's declaration, treaty, and joint communique simultaneously strengthened the association through which they supported Thailand and launched an initiative for rapprochement to Vietnam. The Treaty of Amity and Cooperation was "open for accession by other States in Southeast Asia." Its purpose was to "promote perpetual peace, everlasting amity, and cooperation among their peoples" and was a reaffirmation of the nonaggression principles found in the original 1967 accord.

This compromise was possible first because the Thais did not expect more than diplomatic assistance. Realizing that defense against Vietnam could only come from a great power, Thailand had sought out equipment and assurances from the United States and China. From ASEAN members Bangkok sought moral and diplomatic support in the struggle to keep world opinion on Thailand's side. The summit gave this kind of support; Thailand was able to show Vietnam that it had influential, organized, nonaligned, Islamic, OPEC, Third World countries as friends. Later, ASEAN members would individually give diplomatic assistance by appealing to these constituencies in support of Thailand. Last, this summit was an especially clear political signal because it was the first summit.

As for the other ASEAN partners, they were able to participate in this diplomatic gesture precisely because the meeting was only a diplomatic gesture, an end in itself; they did not fear being asked to make a greater concession, like an alliance. Moreover, the urgency of the moment helped clear any lingering hesitancies—despite less anxiety about Vietnam's intentions, the others could not deny the reality of instability in Indochina. So they had immediate reasons to accommodate their front line, which shielded them from the troubles. In the end, they chose the compromise of an ASEAN organization summit as the instrument of support because it was a way to stand by Thailand without standing against any other state.

The Kuala Lumpur summit of 1977 completed the drama of post–Vietnam war summitry. The heads of states returned, as they had announced in 1976, to deal with the projected joint economic projects and, behind this veil of economics and tenth anniversary observances, to reassess the political situation in the region. To most, the sense of urgency and danger was lessened; the Communist states of Indochina even seemed to be checking each other. The ASEAN summiteers avoided giving a confrontational impression; quite the opposite, they joined in welcoming Vietnam to the United Nations and expressed the desire for good relations with the countries of Indochina. No intention for a next summit was announced.

The view that summits largely served as instruments of intramural reassurance during crisis begins to explain why summitry did not fall into an annual pattern as is customary with other intergovernmental organizations, and specifically, why there was no meeting in 1978. Vietnam at this time pursued a policy so reassuring and accommodative that this was called the "year of smiles." But the nonoccurrence of a summit in 1979, when the conquest of Cambodia occurred, presents an inverse case, especially after prime ministers Lee and Kriangsak, and President Marcos had spoken in December 1978 of having one in the next year.[37] Since the unification of Vietnam, an internal event, albeit by a Communist government, was a catalyst for a summit, why did the conquest of Cambodia in December 1978 by Communist Vietnam not produce a summit?

One reason is some states' reluctance to use the ultimate symbol of solidarity because it might be interpreted too confrontationally. The division of opinion about events in Indochina also argued against having a gathering that might be sterile or divisive. But since the fears of Thailand demanded some concern, an earlier instrument of ASEAN solidarity—the collective political stand—was used instead. The ASEAN foreign ministers, meeting in a special session in January 1979 two weeks after the invasion, called for withdrawal of "foreign forces" and condemned the violation of Cambodia's sovereignty. The wording of this support for Thailand reveals, however, that conflicting views still needed to be accommodated; Vietnam was not named in the joint statement's important, concluding resolution.

Later in July, at the AMM, the foreign ministers addressed the Cambodian occupation more directly; by then there was a greater sense of danger resulting from the aftereffects of the occupation, namely, the Chinese attack on Vietnam, the Soviet aid infusion, the Soviet-American naval escalation in the South China Sea, and the outpouring of refugees, all of which escalated the mainland's instability to the regional, if not global, level. This time, the danger of great-power involvement and the burden of refugees brought about the indictment of Vietnamese policies; the ministers supported the right of the people of Cambodia "to lead their national existence free from interference by Vietnam and other foreign forces" and called for Vietnam to withdraw its forces from the Thai-Cambodian border to "demonstrate its positive attitude towards Thailand and the other ASEAN member states" (Joint Communique, 12th AMM). It seems at the penultimate level, and because it was not the highest level, ASEAN members found it acceptable to adopt pointed political articulations. One final factor is important. Though a summit did not take place, Thailand enjoyed an extraordinary signal of support through ASEAN. The foreign ministers gathering in 1979 was enhanced by the attendance of foreign ministers from the United States, Japan, Australia, and New Zealand along with a representative from the European Community. In sum, the Cambodian crisis did not produce a summit because other instruments of support were used.

Why were there no summits for ten years? First, from the occupation of Cambodia until the present, Thailand has been given support through the instrument of "enhanced" foreign ministers meetings, the Post-Ministerial Meetings (PMM). The ministers from the major Pacific Basin states have attended each annual meeting since 1979 almost without fail. Second, Thailand's security position has improved; insurgency is under control, and Thailand has been active in securing support from both the United States and China. While there have been indirect challenges in the form of border disputes from Hanoi's proxy, Laos, there have been no new dire developments on the mainland to serve as catalysts for summits.

Looking to a more positive occasion, Brunei's independence and accession to ASEAN in 1984 stand as curious missed opportunities for a summit, an apolitical opportunity to show support to each other. This nonoccurrence in a culture where hospitality is an art and a duty is salient. During the independence ceremonies, even though all leaders were at one locale, they did not meet as a group. The absence of even a photograph of all ASEAN leaders together, in light of their earlier deft uses of public diplomacy, highlighted the speculations about rifts over policy toward Vietnam.[38] Perhaps Brunei deserved to be the focus of its own day and not to be overshadowed by an

ASEAN event, but one might wonder why not meet at the time of Brunei's joining ASEAN or, to return to the opening question, more generally over the ten-year span.

Reluctance to have a meeting then and over the ten-year period can be traced to broad and specific disagreements that yet prevail. First, there was and still is no general feeling that summits are necessary to the maintenance of ASEAN peace and stability. This may be changing; some writers remind that political consultation may need more institutionalization and machinery as a new generation of leaders emerges.[39] But for now as in the past, ASEAN's history has shown that where there is a political will, there is an ad hoc way; and ASEAN political will is securely based on the domestic imperatives of the member governments. The ASEAN process satisfies these interests in this straightforward manner: First, when states honor their neighbor's sovereignty and refrain from interference, the result is peace and stability in the subregion. Second, the "stability of each member state and of the ASEAN region is an essential contribution to international peace and security. Each member state resolves to eliminate threats posed by subversion to its stability, thus strengthening national and ASEAN resilience" (Declaration of ASEAN Concord). One's first obligation to ASEAN members is to mind one's own business and mind it well, that is, to ensure one's neighbors a stable society. Summitry is not necessary at this primary level.

To be sure, general consultation and cooperation in interdependent security, intelligence, and economic areas are recognized as important duties. In addition, there is the duty to join in multilateral efforts in international forums. But this does not take place at the top level. Functionally, much of this is worked out by administrative and local officials, while senior-level officials meet regularly to thrash out differences in interests and policies. The annual and special foreign ministers meetings are useful to formalize or foster this process. Concurrently, the multilateral process is also bolstered by bilateral meetings between heads of government.

Having found that they can successfully manage their interdependence at ordinary and functional levels, the ASEAN members have not come to think of summitry as intrinsic to the political process. As for using a summit as another political forum, there are reservations about usefulness. Quite the contrary, such a gathering presents the participants with the challenge of resolving issues in the glare of publicity. In one sense, this was their own doing—the summit publicity was useful to their diplomatic ends in 1976—but the price was that the five had to conduct their business with the world watching. Generally, summits produce great expectations, and a meeting without some product might be viewed as discouraging or a failure. A summit would then bring to the fore all the divisive and problematic policy questions that plague the ASEAN agenda: the stalemate in Cambodia, the role of China in the region, the splits in the Khmer resistance and within the factions in the coalition, the role of the Soviet Union in Asia, the proposal for a nuclear weapons free zone in Southeast Asia, ASEAN endorsement of U.S. bases in the Philippines, relations with South Pacific states, a relationship with Papua-New Guinea, and plans to foster economic integration. On each of these points ASEAN members have different views, no impetus to accommodate, and, as a result, no reason to expect success.

The Manila summit of 1987 faced these obstacles and, in a most direct way, ASEAN's most scandalous internal cleavage, the rift over Sabah. The Mahathir administration has been less willing than earlier regimes to overlook the Sabah problem or accept less-than-total Philippine formulas for solution to the claim. More broadly, the Sabah claim strains the credibility of solidarity; Sabah unresolved means that one ASEAN member challenges another's legitimacy and territorial integrity. In such circumstances a summit, as an act of solidarity and unity, is hollow. The designated venue of the summit, Manila—a decision guided by alphabetical order—reinforced this Sabah obstacle because it required the Malaysian leader to visit the capital of his country's estranged neighbor. Unlike other ASEAN pairs who have bilateral summits, Malaysian prime ministers have promised not to visit the Philippines until the Sabah issue is resolved. Yet this was not presented as an insurmountable stumbling block. In the ASEAN spirit, Mahathir stated he would attend a summit in Manila as long it is not construed as a visit to the Philippines. Reciprocally, in an attempt to close the matter, President Aquino submitted legislation to the Congress that would exclude Sabah from the national territory of the Philippines.

Philippine domestic politics have also been a key to the absence of summits. Summit III was talked about in the early 1980s, desired by Thailand for security reasons and Ferdinand Marcos for personal interests. Capitalizing on private-sector interest for expanded economic contacts and trade, Marcos pushed for a summit in his capital to provide a foreign-policy boost for his troubled regime. The Marcos factor helps explain the absence of a Brunei summit and the distancing at the independence ceremonies. A summit was impossible in early 1984 because other leaders did not wish to identify with the Marcos regime, which was viewed as unstable and inept in the aftermath of the August 1983 assassination of Marcos's rival, Benigno Aquino. In April 1986, two months after Marcos's February departure, they agreed to meet; ASEAN partners chose the seemingly auspicious, appropriate, and neutral, twentieth anniversary year of 1987. Marcos's departure and, ironically, a less tense situation in Indochina cleared away several apprehensions about the summit planned for June 1987. That was then pushed back to December 1987, officially to allow the Philippines to recover from national legislative elections and unofficially to allow more time for intramural negotiations, both on the Sabah issue and on the general agenda. Even to the last moments, Philippine politics added uncertainty. The August 1987 coup attempt and cabinet crisis in Manila added more questions about security readiness and appropriateness. There was some worry that a summit would call attention to the Philippines' disorder and tarnish what has been the ASEAN area's reputation for stability.

The last summit took place in spite of the Philippine difficulties, the Sabah issue, and the other divisive policy points because there was again a need for a diplomatic instrument of solidarity, this time not against an external force, but now in favor of Philippine and, by extension, regional stability. The immediate context, crisis in Manila, replaced other considerations on the agenda. Having announced an anniversary summit, the first in ten years, and finding themselves in the last month of the year, the members felt constrained to have the meeting, lest others interpret the cancellation as a sign of grave difficulties in their area. Concerns about the Philippines were high; the numbers of security precautions taken by each attending leader, as well as the uncertainty about their attendance until the last days, betrayed their anxiety and, in the end, their determination. The summit was transformed from a means to an end in itself. As Foreign Minister Manglapus commented: "The very holding of the meeting is the supreme achievement of the hour."[40]

Some reflections can be made at this time. ASEAN as a political process once again owes much to Indonesian leadership. Specifically, in the words of Prime Minister Lee to President Aquino: "It was the president of Indonesia who set the example [to be in Manila]. . . . President Suharto wanted us to show united ASEAN support for your government at a time when there were attempts to destabilise your government."[41] This reflects the stabilizing role that President Suharto has played over the two decades and can be added to the list of his positive interventions, such as in the Singapore-Malaysia water talks, his May 1984 pep talk at the special foreign ministers meeting, and even reaching back into ASEAN's past to his March 1970 visit to Malaysia during the martial law period. Second, the concept of ASEAN stability through resilience may be undergoing a transformation, becoming broader or more activist. For the first time, ASEAN members have publicly and collectively sought to help stabilize a regime buffeted by domestic opposition. Besides the political gesture, it was agreed that the Philippines would take priority in disbursement of Japan's two billion dollar development fund.[42] All this suggests that the ideal of noninterference, which was tied to states' suspicions and concern for sovereignty, is being modified in the wake of twenty years of interdependence and reciprocity.

A review of the occasions when ASEAN leaders gathered indicates that summits serve as instruments of public diplomacy. They are not forums for a diplomatic process—these exist at several functional levels—but are instruments which permit members to signal a collective political stand. The utility and necessity of this ambiguous approach to solidarity, one that allows for multiple interpretations, derives from members' need to reconcile threat perceptions and policy preferences with the imperative to preserve their intramural political process. Thus, ASEAN members hold summits when external events make such gatherings necessary to defend either the political process or a member. When there is no grave danger, or when the threatened member does not feel that its defenses need come from ASEAN, there will be no gathering.

ASEAN summits are infrequent because some fear this very public form of diplomacy highlights the members' actual lack of solidarity on many issues, ironically including those economic issues for which the regional organization was founded and which served the first summit as a neutral rallying ground. Summits are not frequent because some members worry that gatherings might be misread as confrontational acts, polarizing regional politics. Not having a summit also has utility as a diplomatic signal: it diffuses the image of ASEAN as a political bloc. Summits are infrequent because they are not the only available instrument to show support and solidarity; joint policy stands, special foreign ministers meetings, and "enhanced" annual ministerial meetings are other arrows in the ASEAN quiver.

As for the future, ASEAN summits will continue to be infrequent and ad hoc because they are not intrinsic to the workings of the regional organization or the political process associated with it. Indeed, despite the rhetoric about regionalism, members seem content with those ASEAN benefits already achieved—peace, stability, and security—because these allow them to pursue independent paths, rather than pursuing greater cooperative, integrative plans. It will take a few years for a momentum to build for another gathering, and the probable occasion will be the twenty-fifth anniversary year, 1992. The site, Singapore, should prove acceptable and noncontroversial. Beyond that, when it is Bangkok's turn to be host, concerns about sending confrontational signals will make the timing of that meeting important, if the Cambodian question remains unresolved.

9
Conclusions:
The ASEAN Aggregate

We all decided many years ago that it is better to cooperate with
each other than to undermine each other.
—Singapore Foreign Minister Dhanabalan

ASEAN has an enviable vitality because its members draw benefits
from all its dimensions. As a consultative process, operating on
bilateral and multilateral levels, it facilitates accommodation; it sym-
bolizes the resultant, commonly achieved stability and prosperity; and
it is the regional organization that institutionalizes the political process. Each is a facet of ASEAN, inseparable and intertwined. The
successful association confirms their consciousness that the states are
part of a culturally interdependent entity, identified as the ASEAN
subregion. Success further realizes their aspirations for peace and
stability and so provides the incentive to participate in the ASEAN
organization, whose consultative machinery facilitates the political
process.

Symbolism is central because these states, reflecting a cultural
predisposition, prefer indirect approaches to conflictual situations.
From the start in 1967 ASEAN served as an indirect nonaggression pact
to conclude *konfrontasi* and, as states still face intramural security
problems, suspicions, and rivalries, the organization still fulfills that
function of indirect reassurance. The Association's charter holds the
promises important to managing competition. Members pledged in the
Bangkok Declaration ''that they are determined to ensure their stabil-

ity and security from external interference in any form or manifestation in order to preserve their national identities [and] to promote regional peace and stability through abiding respect for justice and the rule of law.''

The states fulfill the promises to refrain from interference and to respect each other because the regional organization unites them in a higher common interest, a peaceful and stable environment. The organization is first an escape from distasteful realities, whether they be intramural differences or problems with outsiders. The Association speaks in positive language; it points to opportunities and benefits that economics and cultural cooperation can bring. To achieve these spoken and unspoken objectives, ASEAN states willingly participate in an ''ongoing conclave,'' the political process.

Their commitment, however, rests not on hopes for the future, but on past experience, which created the common awareness that competition is futile, foolish, and costly. Specifically, states fear competition first among themselves—this is the lesson of *konfrontasi*—and then with outsiders who might exploit their vulnerabilities, namely, social cleavages, economic discontent, and insurgencies. Successful association, then, is predicated on the basic principles of restraint, respect, and responsibility. In 1967 this meant states do not interfere in other states, either by war, aid to insurgents, challenges to legitimacy, and comments about personalities. Down to the present, reciprocal restraint serves each government's domestic interests: each can focus on internal problems, such as insurgency, corruption, development, and internal political challenges. Some minimal rules follow: States will deny sanctuary to insurgents from a neighbor state and refrain from challenges to others' territorial integrity. Also, there will be no public challenges, comments, or criticisms of other regimes' legitimacy, domestic systems, conduct, policies, or style.

Besides restraint shown in tolerance, an accommodative relationship requires respect. States first show this through diplomatic acceptance, that is, they attend public consultations with their partners. ASEAN meetings and bilateral summits demonstrate both awareness of interdependence with neighbors and willingness to forgo individualism by seeking others' advice and concerns. Respect is evident in the customary approaches to decision making, consensus and ambiguity, both of which assuage the irritations of interdependence. The group makes no decision unless all agree to it, thus respecting each participant's sovereignty. A final principle of ASEAN accommodation, and one that demands the highest sensitivity to interdependence and a spirit of sacrifice, is responsibility—states must consciously consider the effects their domestic policies might have on a neighbor. Governments have come a long way in this matter of sensitivity; Singapore's 1968 execution of marines, despite President Suharto's plea, contrasts with the 1989 commutation of a caning judgment against a Thai illegal worker after the case raised popular outrage in Thailand. States may even help another government with a domestic difficulty by sharing intelligence information, advocating their partner's case with outside powers, or interceding with minority groups in that country.

Several tactics flow from the practice of these principles. Ambiguity is the handmaid of consensus; in language it allows participants to reach common stands and, subsequently, to hold their own interpretation of so-called common stands. Similarly, codewords allow participants to speak of harsh realities, threats, or understandings, and to make rallying calls in acceptable common language. So too, ''ambiguous association,'' used in displays of solidarity, shows strength and cohesion at the moment but leaves no definite restriction on the future. Other tactics are postponement, quiet diplomacy, and compartmentalization. Postponement allows the participants to avoid a divisive issue; quiet diplomacy permits governments to negotiate without external interference or domestic pressure. Compartmentalization safeguards the larger political process from bilateral disputes. And in the broadest sense of compartmentalization, the regional organization and its economic agenda serve as a veil for politics, providing participants with a neutral reason for associating.

Developed in the context of intramural relations, these principles and tactics also enable ASEAN states to determine common policies toward external actors. They are critical to the political process because the states are reluctant to pursue common foreign policy. As small, developing states, they tend to be reactive and preoccupied with domestic issues. They know that they have divergent threat perceptions and policy preferences. Nevertheless, when external crises threaten the process with disintegration and defection, they coordinate foreign policies. Such rallies go to the origins of ASEAN. When the end of colonialism presented these new nations with the challenge of dealing directly with each other, they established the ASEAN process in 1967 for these purposes. In the final phase of the Vietnam War, when they feared a power vacuum and the danger of great-power competition, ASEAN members came up with the first common initiative, Zopfan. Subsequently, with the fall of Saigon and the end of the U.S.-supplied front line in Indochina, they reaffirmed intramural relationships and symbolically shored up their own front line, Thailand, with a summit in 1976. Since the Vietnamese occupation of Cambodia in 1979, they have demonstrated solidarity through meetings and collective political stands in support of Thailand.

Giving primacy to intramural dynamics and the art of accommodation answers some questions about ASEAN politics. Common foreign-policy stands had a slow and guarded development because division of opinion and perception within the grouping made finding compromises difficult. These same factors explain why ASEAN states have not moved toward a collective defense arrangement; states differ about sources of danger, do not have sufficient military counterforce, and, in some cases, hope that the rationality of accommodation can persuade Vietnam to renounce confrontation. ASEAN's Treaty of Amity and Friendship is still open to all in Southeast Asia, including war-weary, indebted Vietnam—a prime candidate to realize that competition is futile, foolish, and costly.

ASEAN's success in multilateralism means that differences that are to be expected in a gathering of several governments have been accommodated. The important common and mutual interest, the control of insurgency, does link many members. The ASEAN process rests on the confidence engendered by the bilateral endeavors between several pairs of members to suppress insurgencies that cut across borders. The four states along the Malacca Straits developed strong bilateral ties as they cooperated in border patrol agreements and regular summits. Moving east, Indonesia and Malaysia cooperated in stabilizing Borneo. The insurgency problem again played a central but not so positive role, in linking the Philippines to the ASEAN process through its shared problem with Malaysia. Manila and Kuala Lumpur have abided by the general principles of restraint, respect, and responsibility; but the two have not moved onto a higher, more cooperative plateau like other pairs. Multilateralism has been more significant in this bilateral relationship; ASEAN partners help the two to manage their bilateral differences. Regionalism, as a conceptualization of cultural bonds and security interdependence, also helps mitigate suspicions through its positive symbolism—the "spirit of ASEAN."

This dynamic extends to all, as multilateral association takes on a life of its own. The Association dynamic, summarized as "a friend of my friend becomes my friend," provides a rationale to cooperate for those states not directly intertwined by an insurgency interdependence. Manila, Singapore, and Bangkok are brought into much more regular and close contact with each other through ASEAN than would be the case without the organization. ASEAN also creates a neutral context and forum in which smaller states, like Singapore, Brunei, and, in some respects, the Philippines, jointly deal with Indonesia. Together they feel less outclassed by the larger state without forming a potentially polarizing coalition in the region. Multilateralism is further bolstered by the appeals of regional cooperation; Europe serves as a model and the United States encourages the trend. Moreover, regionalism assuages irritations and suspicions by clothing sacrifices and policies in language of partnership, kinship, and friendship. The costs of restraint, respect, and responsibility are balanced by benefits derived from national acceptance, regional stability, and international recognition.

This intramural stability, the first achievement of ASEAN politics, is the foundation of the ASEAN process. It puts aside all charges that the early years of ASEAN were moribund; states were successful in recovering from *konfrontasi*. Second, these states concentrated on improving relationships, using gestures and approaches from their cultural milieu. As a non-Western approach, it was ad hoc; there is no precise treaty commitment concerning political or security matters, and politics are veiled by an economic-cultural organization. A consequence is that participants are open to gradual, incremental change. A negative effect, however, is that participants and observers develop different expectations of the process, most notably in the area of economics. Third, strong and cooperative bilateral ties between most contiguous neighbors—those bound in "need-suspicion'' relationships—form a skeletal foundation for the larger political process. Where insurgency interests converge, relationships are strong. But, because interdependencies vary in nature and intensity, each participant, depending on the number and importance of neighbors, has a different stake in the process. Likewise, some states are more important to the process than others. The Philippine-Malaysian cleavage has been tolerated because the stakes are not as high on the east flank, unlike the highly interdependent areas in the west—the core of ASEAN—where accommodation is essential. In brief, the ASEAN process has worked because it has satisfied participants' self-interest. However, ''self-interest is a powerful motivating force, but it comes in many shapes: short-term and long-term; narrow and broad; intelligent and stupid; and altruism may emerge when all else fails.''[1] Fortunately, ASEAN leaders have perceived their self-interest in regional terms through the ''ASEAN'' symbol, which broadens and raises individual self-interest to higher common levels. ''ASEAN'' serves as a diplomatic leitmotif helping to create long-term, broad, intelligent, and even altruistic policies among the participants. ''ASEAN'' recalls years of benefits and good faith; it reminds governments that they are interdependent—thus, the ''spirit of ASEAN'' influences national behavior. It is assisted by the framework of the ASEAN organization, which provides the context for long-term reciprocity and a means of easier communication. Together, spirit and organization speak the higher common interest; participants need and enjoy, to the envy of many, good relations with neighbors.

In sum, this symbol of unity and community insures that the political process built upon accommodation continues. ASEAN is truly a myth in the classical sense; under its facade of smiles and stories of friendship lie the basic truths. It is the acceptable public expression for cooperation between governments that have yet to overcome feelings of suspicion and rivalry in their search to control insurgency and subversion; it is the public record of good faith demonstrated over the past two decades and pledged for the future; it is a reputation of international influence and respect in diplomatic and economic bargaining forums; it is collateral backing promises of good behavior. All these images and benefits serve as higher interests to assuage potentially explosive historical, racial, religious, and economic suspicions that still divide ASEAN members. These interests are aggregated in an indirect, positive, and successful symbol, ''ASEAN.''

Accommodation Agenda

The continued success of the ASEAN process depends on member governments' ability and willingness to continue accommodation. At present incentives are strong, but new conditions or political visions may change a regime's calculation of advantage and interest, most notably, the rise of new powers, the arrival of new leaders or domestic instability, or modifications in diplomatic procedures.

External events have long placed a demand on ASEAN accommodation. The unity on the Cambodian issue rests on a convergence of perspectives that agree that Vietnam's actions violated the important principles of noninterference and renunciation of force in settling international disputes. Indonesia and Malaysia have shown from the start, however, that their priority is to resolve the problem so that great powers do not use the conflict as an entry into the region. China is their first worry, because of contiguity and history, and now more so because of its modernization program, erratic policy swings, and foothold through support of the Khmer Rouge. A newer concern is the Soviet Union, which benefited from the Vietnam war, gaining military facilities there. Since its first involvement in the region, however, Soviet policy has changed. Gorbachev's *glasnost*, initiatives to China, reduction of aid to Vietnam, and offers to withdraw forces from the region present ASEAN states with the dilemma of discerning Soviet intentions. For example, Soviet attempts at reconciliation with China, though they may aid in a Cambodian settlement, present a specter of their collaboration.

To counter Chinese or Soviet advances, ASEAN states have the familiar option of the United States as long as the U.S. military presence remains in the Philippines counterpoint to Chinese or Soviet moves. (Farther out on the horizon, some would add concern about Japan and India.) Again, the new thrust of Soviet policy is forcing these states to reevaluate customary stances. Gorbachev's 1986 Vladivostok speech seemed to open a door to Zopfan when he commented that should the United States give up bases in the

Philippines, "we wouldn't leave that unanswered."[2] ASEAN leaders are cautious and continue to prefer U.S. presence; but this option hangs on U.S. willingness and ability to shoulder the burden in light of its own domestic constraints and global strategies. The policies of the Philippines are also far from clear. As 1991 draws closer—the year the current lease on U.S. bases runs out—the issue of the U.S. presence will become more intense. Philippine nationalists target the bases as a symbol of colonialism and push for their removal; yet the majority still value this connection for sentimental and economic reasons. Indeed, both the Marcos and Aquino governments have found the bases useful in their ASEAN relationships; they underline that hosting the bases is a national and regime sacrifice made for the good of ASEAN. Since most ASEAN states continue to value the U.S. presence but are unwilling to play host themselves, they must find a way to help Manila keep the bases. In the days before the 1987 summit, Foreign Minister Manglapus called for a public stand supporting them. By pushing through with the summit, however, ASEAN partners were already granting a great favor to the Aquino regime, and the gesture was not made. A Singapore initiative in 1989 to carry part of the burden by providing facilities to the United States evoked reactions from Malaysia and Indonesia that might have been expected; they saw it as an unnecessary and dangerous invitation for more great-power interference. And of course, such a move is counter to the 1967 Bangkok Declaration and the 1971 Zopfan Declaration. In a year or two, under the pressure of the deadline, after several more years of loyal Philippine participation in demonstrations of solidarity, the request may be more difficult to put aside.

The bases also serve to reassure ASEAN states about one other major power, Japan. The countries of Southeast Asia have mixed feelings about the rise of Japan; several, like Malaysia and Singapore, look with admiration at Japanese society and technology, even to the point of imitation. They all recognize the financial power of Japan and spend time cultivating its aid and markets. But the memory of World War II lingers and is reinforced by perceived Japanese insensitivity and arrogance. ASEAN states, like China, are willing to accept and deal with Japan as a financial power, but they dread any military role. The U.S. policy encouraging Japan to shoulder some of the defense burden by patrolling one thousand miles of sea from the home islands needed great clarifications before it was accepted in Southeast Asia.

The Cambodian question also strains accommodation as states are divided in their perceptions of Vietnam. Indonesia and Malaysia have dutifully stood by their partners to maintain the image of solidarity vis-à-vis Vietnam despite their own policy preferences. But they see themselves as natural allies of Vietnam against China and share Vietnam's anxiety about China's entry into the region via the Cambodian war. On the other hand, Thailand and Singapore perceive a common cause with China against Vietnam. In effect, the ASEAN process cuts across two alliance camps. Not enough time has passed for all ASEAN states to judge the effects or sincerity of Vietnam's new policies. Its "renovation" approach to development, allowing for more private enterprise and foreign investment, signals better chances for accommodation to the pro-Vietnam in ASEAN. But those suspicious of Hanoi fear that economic success will make Vietnam a more formidable foe; this parallels the interpretation that the anti-China camp puts on Chinese modernization. Even what might be a clearer sign of good will, the Vietnamese withdrawal from Cambodia, was greeted with skepticism by hard-liners. So far ASEAN states have managed this cleavage because of the overriding intramural imperative and Vietnam's clumsy diplomacy. In the future, these factors may change.

Factions in Indonesia resent the demands of accommodation in foreign-policy making. As Indonesia is on the verge of succession, this highlights the challenge of new leadership to the process. Some in Indonesia feel either that Thailand's fears are misplaced or that Thailand is manipulative or, more generally, that Indonesia should lead instead of the "tail wagging the dog." President Suharto, who remembers *konfrontasi* and the September 30 coup, accommodates because he wants to preserve his creation, ASEAN. On the other hand, a change can be for the better. If the recent initiatives of the Chatichai government in Thailand succeed and Indochina achieves stability through mutually beneficial economic development, then this strain on the ASEAN process should be greatly decreased, and the change in leadership can be seen as benefiting accommodation.

The past suggests, however, that ASEAN success depends on Indonesia's (i.e., Suharto's) low-key leadership style and broad vision that regional stability is a national interest. If a new leader seeks to play a global role and neglects cultivation of regional relations, if he seeks to expand for reasons of prestige or to solve an insurgency, if he desires to ride the wave of fundamentalist Islam and liberate coreligionists, then it is likely the ASEAN process would disintegrate. Putting aside this type of worst-case speculation, there are signs that Indonesia is rethinking its reluctance to assume a leadership role in public or in unilateral forms. The earlier reticence had been the result, said Foreign Minister Mochtar, of a change that was "deliberate, a retreat from the special style of Sukarno which was flamboyant, almost extravagant, but without much real substance."[3] Time has passed since that era. New moves, seen in Mochtar's visits to Moscow, Africa, the South Pacific, and Muslim nations, indicate a new vision. Most especially, contacts with Vietnam concerned some ASEAN partners; but, while Indonesia has pursued its initiatives to bring about a negotiated end to the Cambodian war in the Jakarta Informal Meetings (JIM) process, it has to date accommodated its moves to Thai sensitivities.

Indonesia's two closest neighbors watch these trends toward taking up a larger role with interest. Malaysia, under Dr. Mahathir, questions the role of "little Malay brother," which bases good relations with Indonesia on common racial and cultural bonds and a policy of deference. Singapore, ever conscious of sovereignty, also has rejected any new hierarchy. Though Indonesia is the largest state and has a "sense of entitlement" as leader, its leadership must recognize that past success has resulted from observance of the rules of quiet diplomacy, low-key efforts, and giving priority to one's neighbors. A move away from these ASEAN rules could make accommodation much more difficult.

The Mahathir administration in Malaysia has also made initiatives that possibly signal a lack of appreciation for ASEAN principles. The statement that "ASEAN is not the only way to achieve peace, security and stability in South-east Asia. Other means have been utilized, including our pursuance of Zopfan" worries other ASEAN governments,[4] but so has the removal of Foreign Minister Ghazalie Shafie, whose understanding and articulation of the significance of ASEAN verged on proselytizing; tours to the South Pacific and to Islamic countries; and visions of Malaysia's leading role in Third World movements such as treaties concerning the Antarctic. These contribute to the perception that Mahathir has not realistically sorted out his foreign-policy priorities in favor of his immediate neighbors. On the other hand, Malaysia faces several domestic political preoccupations. Mahathir's leadership is challenged within the Malay community, forcing him to rebuild his political base (UMNO Baru). Defections and condemnations by present and senior UMNO leaders, including two past prime ministers, added to the fundamental cleavages already dividing Malaysia, provide strong motivations for continued adherence to the ASEAN process.

All ASEAN states are subject to the emergence of new leaders who may have priorities or less appreciation of ASEAN procedures. To date leaders have shared an understanding of the benefits of mutual accommodation because they lived through the periods of confrontation and insurgency. The challenge from a new generation of leaders who will come to power by orderly succession will be more subtle than a revolutionary upheaval, which might clearly and quickly show a state's withdrawal. Two ASEAN leaders have ruled since the process was initiated, and one is head of its largest member. Suharto speaks of the need for *regenerasi*, showing his concern that the next generation does not have memories of the difficult years. Reacting to a reporter's detachment about the troubles and hardships in Singapore's early years and to the dangers derived from the next generation's ignorance of the lessons of the 1960s, Prime Minister Lee said:

> If this young man is representative of his generation, I fear his generation will have to pay to learn the facts of life in a multi-racial, multi-lingual, and multi-religious society situated in South-east Asia.
> For turbulence, turmoil and troubles come fast and thick if one tinkers with this mixture, believing it to be non-explosive because nothing has gone wrong for so long.[5]

Applying this lesson to regional politics, the fear is that the next generation would take "ASEAN"—peace—for granted or presume that its rules and guidelines were unnecessary or could be flouted with impunity for reasons of short-run expediency.

Both Lee and Mahathir must deal with the fruits of their successful economies: they have an educated middle class that wants civil and political liberties. Crackdowns on the press in Malaysia, Singapore, and Indonesia derive from leaders' policies of enforced toleration and fear of instability. As Prime Minister Lee warned: "You write in the Singapore papers like you write in the American papers, and, I tell you, you are at war."[6] Freedoms of speech and press can, of course, run counter to the personal interests of an authoritarian ruler; but incidents show that these freedoms have damaged intramural ASEAN relations. As long as newspapers remain under government control, there is less danger of comments, taken as insults, being made about other ASEAN leaders and societies. The rule of silence has been as important to ASEAN politics as to domestic politics, and the question remains how the ASEAN process, like the member societies, will weather the transition to democracy.

Equally challenging is economic development. While Singapore, Malaysia, and Thailand have management problems derived from successful economic strategies, the Philippines presents concern unhappily from the other end of the spectrum. For many it represents a control group validating the "resilience" theory that economic prosperity can legitimize a regime and defeat an insurgency, namely, as a result of Marcos's mismanagement, insurgency has grown and the regime was toppled. Now that several years have given distance and perspective on the "revolution" of 1986, more realistic questions about the Aquino administration and the nation's future are coming to the fore. Essentially, stability hinges on the landowning oligarchy's ability to find the political will to sacrifice class and personal interests by initiating reforms and by rejecting the fractious politics of the past. ASEAN partners have advised the resilience approach and made the self-sacrifice at the Manila summit of allowing the Philippines priority in Japanese aid. The divisive campaigning already begun by the leading presidential candidates for the 1991 election, however, does not indicate that the traditional Philippine elites feel a sense of emergency or duty.

Development and democracy are important factors in evaluating the stability of Malaysia, a core state intrinsic to the success of the ASEAN process. The economic recession of the early 1980s added to the Mahathir regime's concerns about middle-class demands for a more open political system. His crackdown on the press has served to discourage them and contribute to brain drain. More dangerous to this "society on a razor's edge" is the need to satisfy Malay economic demands and Chinese sense of justice in the government's developmental plans. Then too, the government must manage the ideological challenge from fundamentalist Islam; acceding to its demands will only widen the Malay–non-Malay cleavages in that society. Unless Malaysia is managed by an accommodationist regime among its races, it is hard to imagine its government following such a foreign policy with its neighbors. And because it is the geographic center of the region, physically linking all ASEAN members, its stability is most critical to ASEAN.

In sum, assuming the ASEAN member states will produce moderate regimes in the mold of the past twenty years, confidence can be had in the stability of this consultative process as governments change. Unless a regime change involves a radical change of ideology, like communism or extremist Islam, succeeding administrations can be expected to adhere to ASEAN principles. Confidence is based on leaders' continued appreciation of ASEAN's contribution to their primary security interest, control of interdependent insurgency. For example, while Ferdinand Marcos may have had regime interests motivating his participation in the process, national interests like the control of the Mindanao insurgency and good relations with large Indonesia are valid reasons for his successor to continue in the ASEAN process. Similarly, a post-Suharto regime is likely to be preoccupied with internal economic and demographic problems and continue to see a cordon sanitaire along its northern borders as a national interest. Optimism is justified by observing that this rationality behind ASEAN has been transferred over several changes of administrations in Malaysia and Thailand. Finally, as leadership will probably change at individual times, there will be opportunity in ASEAN consultations for the old guard to pass on the "ASEAN" rationale to the next generation.

Notes

Chapter 1

1. ASEAN Secretariat, *16th Asean Ministerial Meeting*, Bangkok, June, 24–28, 1983, p. 24.

2. *Times Journal* (Manila) July 8, 1979.

3. Ghazalie Shafie, Malaysian Ministry of Foreign Affairs, "Detente and ASEAN: A Malaysian View," speech on January 12, 1983.

4. Michael Leifer, *Dilemmas of Statehood in Southeast Asia* (Vancouver: University of British Colombia Press, 1972), p. 132; cf. Laurence Stifel, "ASEAN Cooperation and Economic Growth in Southeast Asia," *Asia Pacific Community* 4 (1979): 113–46; Ryokichi Hirono, "Towards Increased Intra-ASEAN Economic Cooperation," *Asia-Pacific Community* 3 (1978-79): 92–118.

5. Paisal Sricharatchanya, "A Free-For-None," *Far East Economic Review (FEER)*, September 26, 1985, p. 76.

6. Ghazalie Shafie, *Regionalism in Southeast Asia* (Jakarta: CSIS, 1974), p. 18.

7. *New Nation* (Singapore), February 18, 1978.

8. Address to 15th Asean Ministerial Meeting, Singapore, June 14, 1982.

9. Russell Fifield, *National and Regional Interests in Asean* (Singapore: ISEAS, 1974), p. 13.

10. Prem Tinsulanond, "Opening Address," *16th Asean Ministerial Meeting*, p. 10.

11. Joseph Nye, *Peace in Parts* (Boston: Little, Brown, 1971), p. 186.

12. John Stremlau, "The Foreign Policies of Developing Countries in the 1980s" in *The Foreign Policy Priorities of Third World States*, ed. Stremlau (Boulder: Westview, 1982), pp. 8–9.

13. Ibid., p. 2.

14. Alex Josey, "The Government and the 'New Left,' " *FEER*, December 6, 1974, p. 32.

15. Michael Haas, "The 'Asian Way' to Peace," *Pacific Community* 4, 4 (July 1973): 511; Arnfinn Jorgensen-Dahl, "The Significance of ASEAN," *World Review* 19, 3 (August 1980): 55, and *Regional Organization and Order in Southeast Asia* (London: Macmillan, 1982).

16. Terry Nardin, "The Moral Basis of the Law of War," *Journal of International Affairs* 37, 2 (Winter 1984): 300.

17. Ernst Haas, Robert Butterworth, and Joseph Nye, *Conflict Management by International Organizations* (Morristown: General Learning Press, 1972), p. 215.

18. Estrella Solidum, *Towards a Southeast Asian Community* (Quezon City: University of the Philippines, 1974), p. 174.

19. James Schuber, "Toward a 'Working Peace System' in Asia: Organizational Growth and State Participation in Asian Regionalism," *International Organization* 32, 2 (Spring 1978): 457.

20. Justus M. van der Kroef, "Maphilindo: Illusion or Reality," *FEER*, September 5, 1963, p. 641.

21. Ghazalie Shafie, "Think ASEAN," *Foreign Affairs Malaysia* 16, 2 (June 1983): 237.

22. Leifer, *Dilemmas*, p. 150.

23. Ferdinand Marcos in Benjamin Domingo, *The Making of Filipino Foreign Policy* (Manila: Foreign Service Institute, 1983), p. 282.

24. Warner Levi, "Political Culture and Integration in Southeast Asia," in *Regional International Organizations: Structures and Functions*, ed. Paul Tharp (New York: St. Martin's, 1971), p. 76.

25. W. W. Rostow, *The United States and the Regional Organization of Asia and the Pacific* (Austin: University of Texas, 1986), p. 12.

26. Harvey Stockwin, "Interview with Tun Abdul Razak," *FEER*, June 9, 1966, p. 41.

Chapter 2

1. Ghazalie Shafie, speech on occasion of presentation of International Dag Hammarskjöld Award, January 12, 1983, mimeo.

2. *FEER*, November 21, 1963, p. 380.

3. David Crane, "Penang Trade Hit," *FEER*, January 30, 1964, p. 191.

4. Ghazalie Shafie, "Indochina Crisis: The Threat to ASEAN and the Implication of the Crisis," *Foreign Affairs Malaysia* 16, 1 (March 1983): 74; Michael Leifer, *Indonesia's Foreign Policy* (London: Allen & Unwin, 1983), pp. 74–80; Franklin Weinstein, *Indonesia Abandons Confrontation* (Ithaca: Cornell, 1969); J. A. C. Mackie, *Konfrontasi: The Indonesian-Malaysian Dispute 1963–66* (Kuala Lumpur, 1974).

5. Harvey Stockwin, "And Now—Konfusi," *FEER*, April 21, 1966, p.

143; Chin Kin Wah, *The Defence of Malaysia and Singapore* (Cambridge: Cambridge University Press, 1983), p. 119.

6. Peter Boyce, *Malaysia and Singapore in International Diplomacy* (Sydney: Sydney University Press, 1968), p. 106.

7. Harvey Stockwin, "The Dangers Within," *FEER*, August 18, 1966, p. 298.

8. Harvey Stockwin, "Border Questions," *FEER*, October 20, 1966, p. 120.

9. Leifer, *Indonesia's Foreign Policy*, p. 173.

10. Boyce, *Malaysia and Singapore*, p. 90.

11. *Facts on File* 1966, p. 159.

12. Bernard Gordon, "Common Defence Considerations and Integration in Southeast Asia" in *Regional International Organizations*, ed. Tharp, pp. 246–47.

13. Bob Reece, "Seeking the Stragglers," *FEER*, July 10, 1969, p. 118.

14. *Djakarta Times*, December 23, 1969.

15. *New Straits Times*, July 6, 1981.

16. *New York Times*, January 27, 1981.

17. *Asiaweek*, November 27, 1981.

18. *Indonesian Times*, July 17, 1984.

19. *Straits Times* (Singapore), September 18, 1979.

20. *Malaysian Digest*, December 1986.

21. Note from Dr. Adam Malik to Mr. Lee Kuan Yew, dated April 1966, in Boyce, *Malaysia and Singapore*, p. 106.

22. R. William Liddle, "1977 Indonesian Election and New Order Legitimacy," *Southeast Asian Affairs 1978* (Singapore: ISEAS, 1979).

23. Harsja Bachtiar, "The Indonesian Nation: Some Problems of Integration and Disintegration" (Singapore: ISEAS, 1974).

24. Robert Cribb, "Elections in Jakarta," *Asian Survey* 24, 6 (June 1984): 656.

25. Liddle, "1977 Indonesian Election," p. 122.

26. Ameer Ali, "Islamic Revivalism in Harmony and Conflict," *Asian Survey* 24, 3 (March 1984): 310.

27. James Clad, "The Media's Proper Role," *FEER*, October 3, 1985, p. 34.

28. Anthony Polsky, "A Modest Booster," *FEER*, March 26, 1970, p. 7.

29. Lau Teik Soon, "Malaysia-Singapore Relations: Crises of Adjustment 1965–68," *Journal of Southeast Asian History* 10, 1 (March 1969): 173.

30. K. Das, "Crackdown Critics," *FEER*, April 17, 1981, p. 8.

31. Suhaini Aznam, "Saying the Unsayable," *FEER*, September 25, 1986, p. 14.

32. Suhaini Aznam, "Cool Word from the King," *FEER*, October 23,

1986, p. 19; "A Melting Pot Simmers," *FEER*, November 20, 1986, p. 34.

33. Suhaini Aznam, "An Act of Approval," *FEER*, December 18, 1986, p. 46.

34. Suhaini Aznam, "The Language of Politics," *FEER*, October 29, 1987, p. 21.

35. Nono Anwar Makarim, "Indonesia's Next Nationalisms," *Pacific Community* (January 1973): 291.

36. *Straits Times*, July 24, 1984.

Chapter 3

1. Harvey Stockwin, "Crisis in Malaysia," *FEER*, July 22, 1965, p. 188.

2. *FEER*, May 20, 1965, p. 344.

3. Anthony Oei, "Native Rights," *FEER*, June 10, 1965, p. 499.

4. Robert Gamer, "The Lee Kuan Yew Style," *FEER*, November 11, 1965, p. 287.

5. Seah Chee Meow, "Singapore's Position in Asean Co-Operation," in *Singapore's Position in Asean Cooperation*, ed. Lim, Seah, and Shaw (Tokyo: Institute of Developing Economies, 1979), p. 62.

6. "The Search for Exclusivity," *FEER*, March 28, 1968, p. 593.

7. James Morgan, "Non-aligned Alignment," *FEER*, September 19, 1970, p. 6.

8. Anthony Polsky, "Asia's Little Israel," *FEER*, September 11, 1969, p. 655.

9. Robyn Lim, "Conclusion: East-West and North-South," in *Understanding ASEAN*, ed. Alison Broinowski (Hong Kong: Macmillan, 1982), p. 249.

10. *FEER*, December 3, 1982, p. 11.

11. Robert Rau, "Singapore's National Security Policy," *Spectrum* 3, 3 (April 1975): 42.

12. Lau, "Malaysia-Singapore Relations," p. 173.

13. Chan Heng Chee, "Singapore's Foreign Policy 1965–68," *Journal of Southeast Asian History* 10, 1 (March 1969): 179.

14. Linda Y. C. Lim, "Singapore's Success: The Myth of the Free Market Economy," *Asian Survey* 23, 6 (June 1983): 752.

15. Ibid., p. 754.

16. Ian Buruma, "Singapore," *New York Times Magazine*, June 12, 1988, p. 25.

17. Seah Chee Meow, "Singapore's Foreign Policy in Southeast Asia: Options for National Survival" *Pacific Community* 4, 4 (July 1973): 539.

18. Franklin Weinstein, "The Meaning of National Security in Southeast Asia," in *Southeast Asia in a Changing World*, ed. Matsumuto Shigekazu (Tokyo: Institute of Developing Economies, 1980), p. 33.

19. Helmut Collis, "The Role of Indonesia in Asian Regionalism," paper given at the 5th Annual ASPAC June 24–27, Oaxtepec, Mexico, 1972, p. 17.

20. V. G. Kulkaini, "An Ever Growing Thirst," *FEER*, October 3, 1985, p. 21.

21. "Enough of a Lesson," *FEER*, December 11, 1986, p. 52.

22. Interview with Inspector General of Police, Tan Sri Mohammed Hariff Omar, *Straits Times*, December 19, 1981.

23. *Straits Times*, December 7, 1981.

24. Ibid., August 20, 1982.

25. Seah Chee Meow, "Singapore's Foreign Policy," p. 82.

26. *Straits Times*, October 13, 1978.

27. John Sterling, "ASEAN: The Anti-Domino Factor," *Asian Affairs* 7, 5 (May–June 1980): 277.

28. *New Nation*, July 14, 1980.

29. *FEER*, October 10, 1985; Lam Lai Sing, "Singapore's Role in China's Offshore Oil Venture," *Asia Pacific Community* 28 (Spring 1985): 120–21.

30. Dan Coggin, "Indonesia's Isolating Tactics," *FEER*, September 19, 1975, p. 10; *Straits Times*, September 1, 1975.

31. *Straits Times*, May 21, 1979.

32. Ibid., September 8, 1982.

33. Ho Kwong Ping, "ASEAN: The Five Countries" in *Understanding ASEAN*, ed. Broinowski, p. 214.

34. *Straits Times*, August 20, 1982 reprinting an editorial from *Sinar Harapan* (Indonesia).

35. Peter Carey, "Indonesia in the 1980s," *Asian Affairs* (London) 16 (June 1985): 127.

36. Astri Suhkre, "Irredentism Contained: The Thai-Muslim Case," *Comparative Politics* 7, 5 (January 1975): 190.

Chapter 4

1. M. Ladd Thomas, *Political Violence in the Muslim Provinces of Southern Thailand*, Occasional Paper 28 (Singapore: ISEAS, 1975), p. 26.

2. Boyce, *Malaysia and Singapore*, p. 229.

3. Surin Pitsuwan, "Issues Affecting Border Security Between Malaysia and Thailand," Monograph Series No. 4 (Bangkok: Thammasat Research Center, 1983), p. 33.

4. *New Straits Times*, May 18, 1976.

5. *Straits Times*, February 13, 1976.

6. Ibid., March 6, 1977.

7. K. Das, "Back in Hot Pursuit," *FEER*, March 18, 1977, p. 10.

8. *Straits Times*, February 15, 1977.

9. Chaiwat Satha-Anand, *Islam and Violence: A Case Study of Violent Events in the Four Southern Provinces, Thailand, 1976–81* (Bangkok: Thai Khadi Research Institute, Thammasat University, 1983), p. 12.

10. *FEER*, February 19, 1982, p. 7.

11. *New Straits Times*, November 26, 1981.

12. Chaiwat Satha-Anand, *Islam and Violence*, p. 19.

13. *Straits Times*, October 29, 1976.

14. Ibid., June 17, 1981.

15. Surin Pitsuwan, "Issues Affecting Border Security," p. 31.

16. Ibid., p. 43.

17. *Asiaweek*, September 17, 1982.

18. *New York Times*, April 30, 1982.

19. *New Straits Times*, September 4, 1982.

20. *Asiaweek*, December 24, 1982.

21. Paisal Sricharatchanya, "Malaysian Reds Under Fire," *FEER*, May 23, 1985, p. 51.

22. *Straits Times*, September 14, 1974.

23. Ibid., June 16, 1979.

24. *New Straits Times*, October 25, 1979.

25. *Straits Times*, November 11, 1979.

26. Ibid., November 19, 1979.

27. *New York Times*, December 29, 1983.

28. *New Straits Times*, October 29, 1983.

29. *Star*, October 30, 1983.

30. Derek Davies, "1971: Toward Multi-Polar Balance," *FEER*, January 1, 1972, p. 25.

31. Pang Cheng Lian, *New Nation*, October 19, 1973.

32. *New Straits Times*, May 7, 1975.

33. *Straits Times*, July 26, 1975.

34. Singapore *Herald*, August 25, 1970, as quoted in Robert Rau, "Singapore's National Security Policy," *Spectrum* 3, 3 (April 1975): 39.

35. *New Straits Times*, July 10, 1983; *Star*, January 1, 1984.

36. Yong Mun Cheong, "Indonesian Questions of Stability," *Southeast Asian Affairs 1978* (Singapore: ISEAS, 1979), p. 113.

37. *Straits Times*, February 9, 1977.

38. *Bangkok Post*, July 7, 1977.

39. *New Nation*, February 18, 1978.

40. *Straits Times*, February 18, 1978, report of *Kompas* (Indonesia).

41. Michael Richardson, "Keeping Up the Momentum," *FEER*, March 10, 1978, p. 16.

42. *Daily Express* (Manila), June 17, 1979.

43. *Straits Times*, May 25, 1975.

44. *FEER*, March 19, 1973.

Chapter 5

1. *FBIS*, AFP, December 15, 1987.
2. Cf. Martin Meadows, "The Philippine Claim to North Borneo," *Political Science Quarterly* 77 (September 1962).
3. *Asiaweek*, December 3, 1982.
4. *New Straits Times*, April 19, 1976.
5. Harold Maynard, "Views of the Indonesian and Philippine Military Elites," in *The Military and Security in the Third World: Domestic and International Impacts*, ed. S. Simon (Boulder: Westview, 1978), p. 148; Yuwono Sudarsono, "Problems of Internal Stability in the ASEAN Countries" in *Asia and the Western Pacific*, ed. Hedley Bull (Melbourne: Nelson, 1975), p. 82.
6. *Straits Times* (Kuala Lumpur), December 6, 1969.
7. Carl Trocki, "Islam: Threat to ASEAN Regional Unity?" *Current History* 78, 456 (April 1980): 181.
8. *Asiaweek*, December 3, 1982.
9. Ibid., March 9, 1984.
10. *Straits Times*, November 24, 1981.
11. *New Straits Times*, December 6, 1981.
12. *Star*, April 17, 1982.
13. *FEER*, August 13, 1976, p. 5.
14. *Asiaweek*, March 11, 1983.
15. Ibid., December 3, 1982.
16. *Straits Times*, July 12, 1984.
17. *FEER*, November 13, 1986, p. 13.
18. Rodney Tasker, "Cobbling a Constitution," *FEER*, August 21, 1986, p. 19.
19. *Asiaweek*, December 3, 1982.
20. Ibid., August 23, 1987, p. 25.
21. Astri Suhkre and Lela Noble, "Muslims in the Philippines and Thailand," in *Ethnic Conflict in International Relations*, ed. Suhkre and Noble (New York: Praeger, 1977), p. 183.
22. Ibid., p. 210.
23. Trocki, "Islam," p. 181.
24. Suhaini Aznam, "Sabah as a Tightrope," *FEER*, June 6, 1985, p. 14; May 30, 1985.
25. Bernardo Ronquillo, "Backdoor Entry," *FEER*, April 1, 1965, p. 10.
26. Suhkre and Noble, "Muslims," p. 210.
27. Robyn Lim, "The Philippines and the Foundation of Asean" *Review of Indonesian and Malayan Affairs* 7, 1 (January–June 1973): 16.
28. *FEER*, October 10, 1963, p. 4.
29. Philippines, Department of Public Information, *Menado Talks*, 1974.

30. *New Nation*, May 25, 1977; *Bulletin Today* (Manila), May 28, 1977.

31. *Straits Times*, May 28, 1977.

32. Ibid., July 14, 1977.

33. Ibid., January 9, 1982.

34. Seah Chee Meow, "The Muslim Issue and Implications for ASEAN," *Pacific Community* 6, 1 (October 1974): 154.

35. *New Straits Times*, August 9, 1984.

36. David Joel Steinberg, *The Philippines: A Singular and A Plural Place* (Boulder: Westview, 1982), p. 61.

37. Diosdada Macapagal, *The Philippines Turns East* (Manila: Mac Publishing, 1966), p. 235.

38. *Times Journal* (Manila), May 28, 1984.

39. *Bulletin Today* (Manila), January 18, 1974.

40. *Bulletin Today*, January 19, 1977.

41. *New Nation*, July 21, 1980; *FEER*, June 2, 1978; Brian Crozier, *Southeast Asia in Turmoil* (Middlesex: Penguin, 1968), p. 157.

42. Michael Leifer, "Decolonialization and International Status: The Experience of Brunei," *International Affairs* (London) 54, 2 (April 1978): 11–12.

43. Lim Joo-Jock, "Brunei: Prospects for a 'Protectorate,' " *Southeast Asian Affairs 1976* (Singapore: ISEAS, 1976), p. 163.

44. *New York Times*, February 18, 1981; Ruth Leger Sivard, *World Military and Social Expenditures* (Washington, D.C.: World Priorities, 1985), p. 36.

45. *Straits Times*, July 30, 1984.

46. *New York Times*, October 7, 1982.

47. *FEER*, July 28, 1983, p. 13.

48. *Indonesian Observer*, July 14, 1984.

49. *Indonesian Times*, July 18, 1984.

50. Ibid., July 21, 1984.

51. *New York Times*, April 18, 1988.

52. Rodney Tasker and Guy Sacerdoti, "A Prod for Marcos from Suharto and Hussein," *FEER*, June 2, 1978, p. 12.

53. *New Straits Times*, February 12, 1979.

54. *Straits Times*, July 2, 1979.

55. *Star*, June 8, 1983.

56. Timothy Ong Teck Mong, "Modern Brunei: Some Important Issues," *Southeast Asian Affairs 1983* (Singapore: ISEAS, 1983), p. 83.

57. A. R. Sutopo, "Independent Brunei Joins Asean," *Indonesian Quarterly* 12, 1 (January 1984): 12; also Pushpa Thambipillai, "Brunei in Asean: The Viable Choice?" *Southeast Asian Affairs 1982* (Singapore: ISEAS, 1982).

58. *Indonesian Observer*, July 11, 1984.

59. Ralph Premdas, "The Organisasi Papua Merdeka in Irian Jaya,"

Asian Survey 25, 10 (October 1985): 1063.

60. J. A. C. Mackie, "Does Indonesia Have Expansionist Designs on PNG?" in *The Indonesia-PNG Border*, ed. R. J. May (Canberra: ANU Press, 1979), p. 63.

61. *Straits Times*, July 29, 1984.

62. *New Straits Times*, February 15, 1984.

63. Ian Andrews, "Border Cooperation," FEER, November 13, 1986, p. 58.

64. *Indonesian Observer*, July 11, 1984.

Chapter 6

1. *Straits Times*, December 17, 1981; *New Straits Times*, December 17, 1981; FEER, May 25, 1979.

2. *Straits Times*, January 17, 1977.

3. Noordin Sopiee, "ASEAN—Making Peace, Producing Security," *New Straits Times*, August 9, 1984.

4. Ghazalie Shafie, speech at the Fletcher School, November 11, 1981, p. 20.

5. Thomas Schelling, *The Strategy of Conflict* (New York: Oxford University Press, 1963), p. 74.

6. *Straits Times*, June 10, 1975.

7. Michael Leifer, "South-East Asia," in *Foreign Policy Making in Developing States*, ed. Christopher Clapham (London: Saxon House, 1977), p. 17.

8. Harsja Bachtiar, *The Indonesian Nation: Some Problems of Integration and Disintegration* (Singapore: ISEAS, 1974), p. 12.

9. Wang Gungwu, "Introduction: Asean Between Tradition and Modernity" in *Understanding ASEAN*, ed. Broinowski, p. 3.

10. Howard Warshawsky, "From Confrontation to Cooperation: The Influence of Domestic Forces on Indonesian Foreign Policy" (Ann Arbor: University Microfilms, 1974), p. 286.

11. *World Paper*, March 1982.

12. Robert Pringle, *Indonesia and the Philippines* (New York: Columbia University Press, 1980), p. 45.

13. Ghazalie Shafie, "Towards a Pacific Basin Community—A Malaysian Perception," paper presented at Pattaya Conference, December 1979, p. 94.

14. Ali Moertopo, "Opening Address," in *Regionalism in Southeast Asia* (Jakarta: CSIS, 1974), p. 15.

15. *Straits Times*, December 19, 1981.

16. *Asiaweek*, January 30, 1981.

17. *Straits Times*, September 14, 1974.

18. Ibid., July 26, 1975.

19. *Malaysian Digest*, February 28, 1983.

20. *Straits Times*, March 7, 1984.

21. Ghazalie Shafie, "Asean's Response to Security Issues in Southeast Asia," in *Regionalism in Southeast Asia*, p. 31.

22. Ali Moertopo, *Indonesia in Regional and International Cooperation: Principles of Implementation and Construction* (Jakarta: CSIS, 1973), p. 11; Goh Cheng Teik, "The Kampuchean Key," *Asiaweek*, July 13, 1979, p. 48.

23. Alejandro Melchor, Jr., "Security Issues in Southeast Asia," in *Conference Papers* (Jakarta: CSIS, 1973), p. 41.

24. Peter Lyons, *War and Peace in Southeast Asia* (London: Oxford University Press, 1969), p. 182.

25. "Both Have Returned," editorial in *Sinar Harapan*, FBIS *Asia and Pacific*, February 29, 1984.

26. *Bulletin Today* (Manila), May 17, 1980.

27. Harold Crouch, *The Army and Politics in Indonesia* (Ithaca: Cornell University Press, 1978), p. 339.

28. Bernhard Dahm, *History of Indonesia in the Twentieth Century* (London: Praeger, 1971), p. 212.

29. Donald Weatherbee, "Southeast Asia in 1982: Marking Time," *Southeast Asian Affairs 1982* (Singapore: ISEAS, 1983), p. 13; Jusuf Wanandi, *The Nation Review* (Bangkok), December 2, 1981.

30. Harvey Stockwin, "Interview with Tun Abdul Razak," FEER, June 9, 1966, 41.

31. *New Straits Times*, July 26, 1975.

32. Ibid., December 3, 1980.

33. *Straits Times*, December 27, 1979.

34. Ibid., July 7, 1982; *Asiaweek*, July 23, 1982.

35. *New Straits Times*, September 20, 1982.

36. *Straits Times*, August 9, 1983.

37. As quoted in "Straightening Out the ASEAN Line," *Asiaweek*, May 18, 1984, p. 14.

38. Arnfinn Jorgensen-Dahl, "The Emerging External Policies of the Association of Southeast Asian Nations (ASEAN)," *Australian Journal of Politics and History* 24, 1 (April 1978): 46.

39. J. Soedjati Djiwandono, "Asean Regionalism and the Role of the USA," *Indonesian Quarterly* 12, 1 (January 1984): 64.

40. *Straits Times*, June 14, 1980.

41. Ibid., July 5, 1980.

42. Attributed to a ranking Indonesian official in *Asian Wall Street Journal*, July 3, 1979.

43. Rodney Tasker, "Diplomacy Loses Its Power," *FEER*, March 9, 1979, p. 17.

44. Paisal Sricharatchanya, "Hearts But Not Minds," *FEER*, August 28, 1981, p. 15.

45. Mochtar Kusumaatmadja, address at Columbia University, New York, October 28, 1985.

46. Guy Sacerdoti, "This Is the Captain Speaking," *FEER*, August 22, 1980, p. 28.

47. Guy Parker, "The ASEAN Energy Scene," *Asian Survey* 19, 6 (June 1979): 637.

48. *Asian Wall Street Journal*, July 6, 1979.

49. Nick Seaward, "The Price of Progress," *FEER*, June 13, 1985, p. 106.

50. *Business Day* (Manila), June 14, 1984.

51. *New Nation*, June 12, 1974.

52. "Rattling the Sabre Again," *FEER*, December 24, 1976, p. 7.

53. *FEER*, February 8, 1968.

54. *New Straits Times*, August 9, 1984.

55. Ibid., July 27, 1984.

56. *Asiaweek*, July 13, 1979.

57. *New Straits Times*, April 18, 1983.

Chapter 7

1. Allan Gyngell, "Looking Outwards: ASEAN's External Relations" in *Understanding ASEAN*, ed. Alison Broinowski (Hong Kong: Macmillan, 1982), p. 115.

2. *New York Times*, January 14, 1968.

3. Frances Starner, "Through Malik's Eyes," *FEER*, September 5, 1968, p. 468; S. M. Ali, "Bridging the Gap," *FEER*, February 8, 1968, p. 228.

4. Richard Nixon, "Asia After Viet Nam," *Foreign Affairs* 46, 1 (October 1967): 114.

5. *New York Times*, September 9, 1969.

6. Peter Simms, "Communism in Malaysia and Singapore," *Southeast Asian Spectrum* 3, 2 (January 1975): 42.

7. T. D. Allman, "No Gordian Knot," *FEER*, November 14, 1970, p. 30.

8. *New York Times*, May 24, 1970.

9. Somsakdi Xuto, "Prospects for Security and Stability in Southeast Asia," *Pacific Community* 3, 1 (October 1971): 118.

10. Noordin Sopiee, "The 'Neutralization' of South-East Asia," in *Asia and the Western Pacific*, ed. Hedley Bull (Melbourne: Nelson, 1975), p. 136.

11. Ali Moertopo, "The Indian Ocean: Strategic and Security Problems," *Indonesian Quarterly* 5, 2 (April 1977): 33, 36.

12. Noordin Sopiee, "The 'Neutralization' of South-East Asia," p. 136.

13. Bruce Ross Larson, ed., *Issues in Contemporary Malaysia* (Kuala Lumpur: Heinemann, 1977), p. 164.

14. Murugesu Pathmanathan, *Readings in Malaysia's Foreign Policy* (Kuala Lumpur: University of Malaya, 1979), pp. 127–28.

15. *Straits Times* (Kuala Lumpur), August 27, 1972.

16. Ferenc Vali, *Politics of the Indian Ocean* (New York: Free Press, 1976), p. 78.

17. Peter Polomka, "Indonesia's Future and South-East Asia," Adelphi Papers no. 104 (London: Institute for Strategic Studies, 1974), p. 26.

18. Arnold Abrams, "Back in Business," *FEER*, August 26, 1972, p. 21. One U.S. official commented that the Thais have "been urging us for years to bomb the dykes."

19. "Mush and Steel at Bali," *Asiaweek*, July 13, 1979.

20. *Bangkok Post*, February 5, 1979, as cited in John Funston, "The Third Indochina War and Southeast Asia," *Contemporary Southeast Asia* 1, 3 (December 1979): 281.

21. Rodney Tasker, "Condemnation but no Confrontation," *FEER*, January 26, 1979, p. 25.

22. K. Das and Peter Weintraub, "ASEAN Waits for Action from Dong," *FEER*, October 27, 1978, p. 13.

23. *Asiaweek*, July 13, 1979.

24. David Jenkins, "An Island in the Stream," *FEER*, May 25, 1979, p. 19.

25. *Bulletin Today* (Manila), June 27, 1979.

26. Rodney Tasker, "Reason, Sanity and Stout Hearts," *FEER*, July 13, 1979, p. 11.

27. David Jenkins, "Maintaining an Even Keel," *FEER*, June 1, 1979, p. 23.

28. *FEER*, November 16, 1979, p. 7.

29. K. Das, "The Kuantan Principle," *FEER*, April 4, 1980, p. 13.

30. Richard Nations, "Revolving Door Diplomacy," *FEER*, May 16, 1980, p. 12.

31. Nayan Chanda, "Hanoi's Signal Invitation," *FEER*, May 23, 1980, p. 17.

32. Richard Nations, "A Dialogue of the Deaf," *FEER*, May 30, 1980, p. 18.

33. Derek Davies, "Victory for the Hardline Hawks," *FEER*, July 4, 1980, p. 13.

34. Nayan Chanda, "The Ball is Back in Bangkok's Court," *FEER*, July 25, 1980, p. 8.

35. Nayan Chanda, "Hanoi on the Offensive," *FEER*, January 30, 1981, pp. 12–13.

36. Rodney Tasker, "ASEAN Toughs It Up," *FEER*, July 26, 1984, p. 32.

37. Derek Davies, "Standing by a Friend," *FEER*, April 14, 1983, p. 15.

38. *New York Times*, June 10, 1983.

39. *New Straits Times*, June 27, 1983.

40. Juwono Sudarsono, "Security in Southeast Asia: The Circle of Conflict," *Indonesian Quarterly* 10, 2 (April 1982): 19.

41. *Washington Post*, January 17, 1983.

42. *FEER*, October 13, 1983, p. 12; Rodney Tasker, "Ready—and Waiting," *FEER*, September 29, 1983, p. 24.

43. *Malaysian Digest*, October 31, 1983.

44. Robert Horn, "Southeast Asian Perceptions of U.S. Foreign Policy," *Asian Survey* 15, 6 (June 1985): 685.

45. Chang Pao-min, "Sino-Vietnamese Territorial Disputes," *Asia-Pacific Community* 28 (Spring 1985): 86.

46. Nayan Chanda, "ASEAN's Odd Man Out," *FEER*, March 1, 1984, p. 8.

47. Susumu Awanohara, "Murdani's Modification," *FEER*, March 8, 1984, p. 36.

48. Susumu Awanohara, "A Soldier Out of Step," *FEER*, March 29, 1984, p. 16.

49. Susumu Awanohara, "The Pace Quickens," *FEER*, March 15, 1984, p. 15.

50. Susumu Awanohara, "A Soldier Out of Step," p. 16.

51. Susumu Awanohara, "Up Against the Wall," *FEER*, March 22, 1984, p. 12.

52. *Bangkok Post*, March 5, 1984.

53. Rodney Tasker, "Feeling the Chill," *FEER*, April 5, 1984, p. 18.

54. Rodney Tasker, "Seeking Diplomatic Support," *FEER*, April 12, 1984, p. 14.

55. *New York Times*, April 23, 1984.

Chapter 8

1. "Groping for an Initiative," *Asiaweek*, December 28, 1979, p. 12.

2. Richard Nations, "Battle for the Hearts and Stomachs," *FEER*, December 7, 1979, p. 14.

3. Nayan Chanda, "Haig Turns the Screw," *FEER*, June 26, 1981, p. 11.

4. John McBeth, "Hanoi Blurs the Focus," *FEER*, June 12, 1981, p. 13.

5. K. Das, "Threat? What Threat?" *FEER*, August 21, 1981, p. 14.

6. Paisal Sricharatchanya, "Hearts But Not Minds," *FEER*, August 28, 1981, p. 14.

7. Nayan Chanda, "A Surrogate Siren's Song," *FEER*, October 23, 1981, p. 42.

8. Paisal Sricharatchanya, "Paper Over the Cracks," *FEER*, December 18, 1981, p. 8.

9. "Pol Pot Tries Another Face Lift," *Asiaweek*, December 18, 1981, p. 14.

10. *Indonesian Times*, December 5, 1981, cited in Huynh Kim Khanh and Hans Indorf, "Southeast Asia 1981: Two Currents Running," *Southeast Asian Affairs 1982* (Singapore: ISEAS, 1982), p. 22.

11. Paisal Sricharatchanya, "Paper Over the Cracks," *FEER*, December 18, 1981, p. 8.

12. Della Denman, "Withdrawal Symptoms," *FEER*, July 16, 1982, p. 10.

13. John McBeth, "The Smiling Five," *FEER*, August 13, 1982, p. 14.

14. Nayan Chanda, "Head-On with Hayden," *FEER*, November 24, 1983, p. 34.

15. Hanoi International Service in English, *FBIS Asia and Pacific*, February 29, 1984.

16. Richard Nations, "Hanoi's Slow Learners," *FEER*, February 7, 1985, p. 10.

17. *FEER*, July 10, 1986, p. 9.

18. Rodney Tasker, "The Reality of Coalition," *FEER*, July 10, 1986, p. 11.

19. Murray Hiebert, "Mochtar Cocktail Party," *FEER*, August 13, 1987, p. 34

20. *The Nation* (Bangkok), quoted in "Knocking on Vietnam's Door," *Asiaweek*, August 16, 1987, p. 15.

21. "Is the Cocktail Party Over?" *Asiaweek*, August 30, 1987, p. 17.

22. *Daily Express* (Manila), March 13, 1980.

23. *Indonesian Observer*, July 12, 1984.

24. *Asiaweek*, July 2, 1976.

25. Richard Nations, "What Price Human Rights?" *FEER*, July 22, 1977, p. 14.

26. Sarasin Viraphol, "Directions in Thai Policy," Occasional Paper 40 (Singapore: ISEAS, 1976), p. 31.

27. *Asiaweek*, July 22, 1977.

28. "New Growls from China," *Asiaweek*, July 20, 1979, p. 19.

29. *Asiaweek*, June 25, 1982.

30. Rodney Tasker, "Ready for Reagan," *FEER*, July 14, 1983, p. 12.

31. *Daily Express* (Manila), July 5, 1979.

32. Harvey Stockwin, "The Bali Summit," *FEER*, March 5, 1979, p. 11.

33. "Interview/ Adam Malik—After Vietnam," *FEER*, July 4, 1975, p. 30.

34. Seah Chee Meow, "Asean and the Changing Power Balance in South-East Asia," *Spectrum* 4, 1 (October 1975): 36.

35 Sarasin Viraphol, "Directions in Thai Policy," p. 31.

36. Seah Chee Meow, "Singapore's Position in ASEAN Cooperation," in *Singapore's Position in ASEAN Cooperation*, ed. Lim, Seah, and Shaw, p. 73.

37. *Straits Times*, December 10, 12, 13, 1978.

38. "Welcome to the Club," *FEER*, March 8, 1984, p. 18.

39. Jusuf Wanandi, "ASEAN: Time for More Political Cooperation," *FEER*, June 11, 1987, p. 48.

40. *New York Times*, December 16, 1987.

41. Rodney Tasker, "18 Minute Solidarity," *FEER*, December 24, 1987, p. 8.

42. James Clad, "Something for Everyone," *FEER* , December 31, 1987.

Chapter 9

1. Leonard Silk, "Getting Back to the Real World," *New York Times*, November 16, 1983.

2. "Taking Aim at the Bases," *Asiaweek*, August 10, 1986, p. 14.

3. *New York Times*, April 22, 1984.

4. James Clad, "Lizards and Alligators," *FEER*, January 31, 1985, p. 32.

5. *Singapore Monitor*, July 25, 1984.

6. *New York Times*, July 10, 1988.

Selected Bibliography

Books

Boyce, Peter. *Malaysia and Singapore in International Diplomacy*. Sydney: Sydney University Press, 1968.

Buszynski, Lesek. *SEATO: The Failure of an Alliance Strategy*. Singapore: Singapore University Press, 1983.

Chin Kin Wah. *The Defense of Malaysia and Singapore*. Cambridge: Cambridge University Press, 1983.

Comber, Leon. *13 May 1969. A Historical Survey of Sino-Malay Relations*. Kuala Lumpur: Heinemann Asia, 1983.

Crouch, Harold. *The Army and Politics in Indonesia*. Ithaca: Cornell University Press, 1978.

Crozier, Brian. *Southeast Asia in Turmoil*. Middlesex: Penguin, 1968.

Dahm, Bernhard. *History of Indonesia in the Twentieth Century*. London: Praeger, 1971.

Domingo, Benjamin. *The Making of Filipino Foreign Policy*. Manila: Foreign Service Institute, 1983.

Gullick, J. M. *Malaysia and Its Neighbors*. New York: Barnes and Noble, 1967.

Haas, Ernst, Robert Butterworth, and Joseph Nye. *Conflict Management by International Organizations*. Morristown: General Learning Press, 1972.

Jorgensen-Dahl, Arfinn. *Regional Organization and Order in Southeast Asia*. London: Macmillan, 1982.

Leifer, Michael. *Dilemmas of Statehood in Southeast Asia*. Vancouver: University of British Colombia Press, 1972.

————. *Foreign Relations of the New States*. Victoria: Longman, 1974.

Levi, Werner. *The Challenge of World Politics in South and Southeast Asia*. Englewood Cliffs: Prentice Hall, 1968.

Lim Joo Jock. *Geo-Strategy and the South China Sea Basin*. Singapore: Singapore University Press, 1979.

Lyon, Peter. *War and Peace in Southeast Asia*. London: Oxford University Press, 1969.

Macapagal, Diosdado. *The Philippines Turns East*. Manila: Mac, 1966.

McDonald, Hamish. *Suharto's Indonesia*. Blackburn, Victoria: Dominion Press, 1980.

Mackie, J. A. C. *Konfrontasi: The Indonesian-Malaysian Dispute 1963-1966*. Kuala Lumpur: Oxford, 1974.

May, Brian. *The Indonesian Tragedy*. London: Routledge and Kegan Paul, 1978.

Meyer, Milton Walter. *A Diplomatic History of the Philippine Republic*. Honolulu: University of Hawaii Press, 1965.

Morrison, Charles and Astri Suhrke. *Strategies of Survival: The Foreign Policy Dilemmas of Smaller Asian States*. New York: St. Martin's Press, 1979.

Mortimer, Robert. *The Third World Coalition in International Politics*. Boulder: Westview, 1984.

Nye, Joseph. *International Regionalism*. Boston: Little, Brown, 1968.

———. *Peace in Parts*. Boston: Little, Brown, 1971.

Pathmanathan, Murugesu. *Readings in Malaysia's Foreign Policy*. Kuala Lumpur: University of Malaya, 1979.

Phuangkasem, Corrine. *Thailand's Foreign Relations 1964–80*. Singapore: ISEAS, 1985.

Pringle, Robert. *Indonesia and the Philippines*. New York: Columbia University Press, 1980.

Rabushka, Alvin. *Race and Politics in Urban Malaya*. Stanford: Hoover Institute Press, 1973.

Rajendran, M. *ASEAN's Foreign Relations*. Kuala Lumpur: Arenabuku, 1985.

Rickels, M. C. *A History of Modern Indonesia*. Bloomington: Indiana University Press, 1981.

Ross-Larson, Bruce. *Issues in Contemporary Malaysia*. Kuala Lumpur: Heineman, 1977.

Saravanamuttu, J. *The Dilemma of Independence: Two Decades of Malaysia's Foreign Policy 1957–1977*. Penang: Universiti Sains Malaysia, 1983.

Simon, Sheldon. *The ASEAN States and Regional Security*. Stanford: Hoover Institute Press, 1982.

Solidum, Estrella. *Bilateral Summitry in ASEAN*. Manila: Foreign Service Institute, 1982.

———. *Towards a Southeast Asian Community*. Quezon City: University of the Philippines Press, 1974.

Steinberg, David Joel. *The Philippines: A Singular and a Plural Place*. Boulder: Westview, 1982.

Wanandi, Jusuf. *Security Dimensions of the Asia-Pacific Region in the 1980s*. Jakarta: CSIS, 1979.

Weinstein, Franklin. *Indonesia Abandons Confrontation.* Ithaca: Cornell University Press, 1969.
Wilairat, Kawin. *Singapore's Foreign Policy: The First Decade.* Singapore: ISEAS, 1975.
Wong, John. *ASEAN Economies in Perspective.* Philadelphia: Institute for the Study of Human Needs, 1979.
Wu, Yuan-li. *The Strategic Land Ridge.* Standford: Hoover Institute Press, 1975.
Zacher, Mark, and R. Stephen Milne, eds. *Conflict and Stability in Southeast Asia.* New York: Anchor, 1974.

Articles and Papers

Ali Moertopo. "Indonesia in Regional and International Cooperation: Principles of Implementation and Construction." Jakarta: Center for Strategic and International Studies (CSIS), 1973.
———. "International Politics in Asia and the Pacific: Complexities and Uncertainties." In *New Foundations for Asean and Pacific Security,* ed. Joyce Larson. New York: National Strategy Information Center, 1980.
———. "The Indian Ocean: Strategic and Security Problems." *Indonesian Quarterly* 5, 2 (April 1977).
———. "Keynote Address." Conference on New Foundations Asian and Pacific Security, December 1979, Pattaya, Thailand. New York: National Strategy Information Center (hereafter Pattaya Conference).
———. "Opening Address." *Regionalism in Southeast Asia.* Jakarta: CSIS, 1974.
———. "Political, Economic, and Social Development of Southeast Asia with Particular Emphasis on the Future of ASEAN." *Indonesian Quarterly* 4, 2–4 (1976).
Ameer, Ali. "Islamic Revivalism in Harmony and Conflict." *Asian Survey* 24, 3 (March 1984).
Bachtiar, Harsja W. "The Armed Forces in Indonesian Society." *Asian Defence* (May 1982).
———. "The Indonesian Nation: Some Problems of Integration and Disintegration." Singapore: ISEAS, 1974.
Barnett, Robert. "ASEAN's Unguarded Coasts." *Contemporary Southeast Asia* 38 (Spring 1980).
Bellows, Thomas. "Proxy War in Indochina." *Asian Affairs* 7, 1 (September 1979).
Beresford, Melanie, Bob Catley, and Francis Pilkington. "America's New Pacific Rim Strategy." *Journal of Contemporary Asia* 9, 1 (1979).
Brackman, Arnold. "Indonesia: The Critical Years 1976–78." *Conflict Studies* 49 (September 1974).

Bui Diem. "A New Kind of War in Southeast Asia." *Asian Affairs* 6, 5 (May 1979).

Bull, Hedley. "The New Balance of Power in Asia and the Pacific." *Foreign Affairs* 49 (July 1971).

Buszynski, Les, "Vietnam Confronts China." *Asian Survey* (August 1980).

———. "Vietnam's ASEAN Diplomacy: Recent Moves." *World Today* 39, 3 (March 1983).

Carey, Peter. "Indonesia in the 1980s." *Asian Affairs* (London) 16, 3 (June 1985).

Catley, Bob. "The Development of Underdevelopment in Southeast Asia." *Journal of Contemporary Asia* 6, 1 (1976).

Chaiwat Satha-Anand. "Islam and Violence: A Case Study of Violent Events in the Four Southern Provinces, Thailand 1976–81." Bangkok: Thai Khadi Research Institute, Thammassat University, 1983.

Chan Heng Chee, "The Interests and Role of Asean in the Indochina Conflict." International Conference on Indochina and Problems of Security and Stability in Southeast Asia, Chulalongkorn University, Bangkok, June 1980.

———. "Singapore's Foreign Policy 1965–68." *Journal of Southeast Asian History* 10, 1 (March 1969).

Chang, C. Y. "ASEAN's Proposed Neutrality: China's Response." *Contemporary Southeast Asia* 1, 3 (December 1979).

———. "The Sino-Vietnam Rift: Political Impact on Relations with Southeast Asia." *Contemporary Southeast Asia* 4, 4 (March 1983).

Chang, Pao-min. "Sino-Vietnamese Territorial Disputes." *Asia-Pacific Community* 28 (Spring 1985).

Cheow, Eric Teo Chu. "New Omnidirectional Overtures in Thai Foreign Policy." *Asian Survey* (July 1986).

Chia Siow Yue, "ASEAN Economic Cooperation." *Contemporary Southeast Asia* 2, 2 (September 1980).

Chin Kin Wah. "The Five Power Defence Arrangements and AMDA." Singapore: ISEAS Occasional Paper 23, 1974.

———. "A New Assertiveness in Malaysian Foreign Policy." In *Southeast Asian Affairs 1982*. Singapore: ISEAS, 1982.

Cohen, Raymond. "Threat Perception in International Crises." *American Political Science Review* 93, 1 (1978).

Collis, Helmut. "The Role of Indonesia in Asian Regionalism." 5th annual ASPAC, June 24–27, Oaxtepec, Mexico, 1972.

Cribb, Robert. "Elections in Jakarta." *Asian Survey* 24, 6 (June 1984).

Crosbie, A. J. "Brunei: The Constraints on a Small State." In *Southeast Asian Affairs 1978*. Singapore: ISEAS, 1978.

Darling, Frank. "Thailand in the 1980s." *Current History* (December 1980).

Dawson, Alan. "Implications of a Long Term Conflict on Thai-Vietnamese

Relations." ISIS Workshop on the Future of ASEAN-Vietnamese Relations, February 1983. Bangkok: Chulalongkorn University Press.

Dikhit Dhiravegin. "ASEAN and the Major Powers: Today and Tomorrow." Monograph no. 7. Bangkok: Research Center, Faculty of Political Science, Thammasat University, 1984.

Djiwandono, J. Soedjati. "The Asean After the Bali Summit." *Indonesian Quarterly* 4, 2–4 (1976).

———. "Asean Regionalism and the Role of the USA." *Indonesian Quarterly* 12, 1 (January 1984).

Drummond, Stuart. "ASEAN: The Growth of an Economic Dimension." *World Today* (January 1979).

Duncanson, Dennis. "Vietnam in the New Balance of Power." *Asian Affairs* (London) (October 1973).

Eckel, Paul E. "SEATO: An Ailing Alliance." *World Affairs* 134, 2 (Fall 1971).

Fifield, Russell H. "ASEAN: Image and Reality." *Asian Survey* 19, 12 (December 1979).

———. "ASEAN: The Perils of Viability." *Contemporary Southeast Asia* 2, 3 (December 1980).

———. "National and Regional Interests in ASEAN." Singapore: ISEAS, 1979.

———. "Power Relations Among the Southeast Asian States." *Asian Affairs* 4, 3 (January 1977).

FitzGerald, C. P. "The Power Structure in Asia Since the Vietnam War." *Pacific Community* (April 1978).

Frost, Frank. "The Origins and Evolution of ASEAN." *World Review* 19, 3 (August 1980).

Fuad Hassan. "ASEAN: Is There any Economic, Social, Ethnic or Political Basis for the Development of ASEAN?" ISEAS-IISS Conference of Southeast Asian Security, Singapore, May 1974.

Funnell, Victor. "China and ASEAN: The Changing Face of Southeast Asia." *World Today* (July 1975).

Funston, John. "The Third Indochina War and Southeast Asia." *Contemporary Southeast Asia* 1, 3 (December 1979).

Galbraith, Francis. "Southeast Asian Policy After the Vietnam War." *Asian Affairs* 2, 6 (July 1975).

Ghazalie Shafie. "Asean's Response to Security Issues in Southeast Asia." *Regionalism in Southeast Asia.* Jakarta: CSIS, 1974.

———. "Indochina Crisis: The Threat to ASEAN and the Implications of the Crisis." *Foreign Affairs Malaysia* 16, 1 (March 1983).

———. "The Neutralization of Southeast Asia." *Pacific Community* 3, 1 (October 1971).

———. "Think ASEAN." *Foreign Affairs Malaysia* 16, 2 (June 1983).

————. "Towards a Pacific Basin Community—A Malaysian Perception," Pattaya Conference.

Girling, J. L. S. "The Guam Doctrine." *International Affairs* (January 1970).

————. "Southeast Asia and the Great Powers." *Pacific Community* (January 1978).

————. "Soviet Attitudes Toward Southeast Asia." *World Today* (May 1973).

Goh Keng Swee. "Vietnam and Big Power Rivalry." In *Asian Security in the 1980s: Problems and Policies for a Time of Transition*, ed. Richard Solomon. Santa Monica: Rand, 1979.

Gordon, Bernard. "Asian Perspectives on Security: The ASEAN Region." *Asian Forum* 8, 4 (Autumn 1976).

————. "Common Defence Considerations and Integration in Southeast Asia." In *Regional International Organizations: Structures and Functions*, ed. Paul Tharp. New York: St. Martin's, 1971.

————. "Problems of Regional Cooperation in Southeast Asia." *World Politics* 16 (January 1964).

————. "Regionalism and Instability in Southeast Asia." *Orbis* 10, 2 (Summer 1966).

Gurtov, Melvin. "The Nixon Doctrine and Southeast Asia." *Pacific Community* (October 1972).

Gyngell, Allan. "Looking Outwards: ASEAN's External Relations." In *Understanding ASEAN*, ed. Alison Broinowski. Hong Kong: Macmillan, 1982.

Haas, Michael. "The 'Asian Way' to Peace." *Pacific Community* 4, 4 (July 1973).

Haddad, William. "Japan, the Fukuda Doctrine, and ASEAN." *Contemporary Southeast Asia* 2, 1 (June 1980).

Hamzah, B. A. "Brunei Joins ASEAN: Its Expectations." *Asia-Pacific Community* 24 (Spring 1984).

Hawkins, David. "Britain and Malaysia Another View: Was the Decision to Withdraw Entirely Voluntary or Was Britain Pushed a Little?" *Asian Survey* 9, 7 (July 1969).

Hernandez, Carolina. "The Role of the Military in Contemporary Philippine Society." *Diliman Review* 32, 1 (January–February 1984).

Hill, H. Monte. "Community Formation within ASEAN." *International Organization* (Spring 1978).

Hirono, Ryokichi. "Towards Increased Intra-ASEAN Economic Cooperation." *Asia-Pacific Community* 3 (Winter 1978–79).

Ho Kwong Ping. "ASEAN: The Five Countries." in *Understanding ASEAN*, ed. Alison Broinowski. Hong Kong: Macmillan, 1982.

Horn, Robert C. "Moscow and Peking in Post-Indochina Southeast Asia." *Asian Affairs* 4, 1 (September 1976).

————. "Moscow's Southeast Asian Offensive." *Asian Affairs* 2, 4 (March 1975).

————. "Southeast Asian Perceptions of U.S. Foreign Policy." *Asian Survey* 15, 6 (June 1985).

————. "Soviet-Vietnamese Relations and the Future of Southeast Asia." *Pacific Affairs* (1978).

Huynh Kim Khanh and Hans Indorf. "Southeast Asia in 1981: Two Currents Running." In *Southeast Asian Affairs 1982*. Singapore: Institute of Southeast Asian Studies (ISEAS), 1982.

Indorf, Hans. "Some Speculation on a Second Blueprint for ASEAN." *Contemporary Southeast Asia* 3, 2 (September 1981).

Irvine, Roger. "The Formative Years of ASEAN: 1967–75." In *Understanding ASEAN*, ed. Alison Broinowski. Hong Kong: Macmillan, 1982.

Jacobs, G. "Vietnam's Threat Potential to ASEAN." *Asian Defence* (May 1982).

Jorgensen-Dahl, Arfinn. "The Emerging External Policies of the Association of Southeast Asian Nations (ASEAN)." *Australian Journal of Politics and History* 24, 1 (April 1978).

————. "Extra-Regional Influences on Regional Cooperation in Southeast Asia." *Pacific Community* 8, 3 (April 1977).

————. "Forces of Fragmentation in the International System: Case of Ethnonationalism." *Orbis* 19, 2 (Summer 1975).

————. "The Significance of ASEAN." *World Review* 19, 3 (August 1980).

Kattenburg, Paul. "South-East Asia Reconsidered." *Southeast Asian Spectrum* 4, 2 (January 1976).

Koh, T. T. B., and Lau Teik Soon. "Regional Cooperation in South-East Asia." In *Asia and the Western Pacific*, ed. Hedley Bull. Melbourne: Nelson, 1975.

Lau Teck Soon. "Malaysia-Singapore Relations: Crises of Adjustment 1965–68." *Journal of Southeast Asian History* X:1 (March 1969).

————. "Overseas Chinese and ASEAN-China Diplomatic Relations." *Philippine Sociological Review* 24, 1–4 (1976).

Lee Boon Hok. "Reconciling Survival Ideology with Achievement Concept." In *Southeast Asian Affairs 1978*. Singapore: ISEAS, 1979.

Lee Lai To. "Deng Xiaoping's ASEAN Tour: A Perspective on Sino-Southeast Asian Relations." *Contemporary Southeast Asia* 3, 1 (June 1981).

Lee Yong Leng. "The Razor's Edge Boundaries and Border Disputes in Southeast Asia." Singapore: ISEAS, 1980.

Leifer, Michael. "The ASEAN States: No Common Outlook." *International Affairs* 49, 4 (October 1973).

————. "China and Southeast Asia." *Pacific Community* (October 1977).

————. "Decolonization and International Status: The Experience of Brunei." *International Affairs* (London) 54, 2 (April 1978).

————. "The Security of Sea-lanes in South-East Asia." *Survival* 25, 1 (1983).

————."Some Southeast Asian Attitudes." *International Affairs* (January 1966).

————. "South-East Asia." In *Foreign Policy Making in Developing States*, ed. Christopher Clapham. London: Saxon House, 1977.

Levi, Werner. "Political Culture in Southeast Asia." In *Regional International Organizations: Structures and Functions*, ed. Paul Tharp. New York: St. Martin's, 1971.

Liddle, R. William. "1977 Indonesian Election and New Order Legitimacy." In *Southeast Asian Affairs 1978*. Singapore: ISEAS, 1979.

Lim Chong Yah. "Singapore's Position in Asean Economic Co-Operation." In *Singapore's Position in Asean Cooperation*, ed. Lim, Seah, and Shaw. Tokyo: Institute of Developing Economies, 1979.

Lim Joo Jock. "Brunei: Prospects for a 'Protectorate.' " In *Southeast Asian Affairs 1976*. Singapore: ISEAS, 1977.

————. "The Indochina Situation and the Superpowers in Southeast Asia." In *New Foundations for Asean and Pacific Security*, ed. Joyce Larson. New York: National Strategy Information Center, 1980.

Lim, Linda Y. C. "Singapore's Success: The Myth of the Free Market Economy." *Asian Survey* 13, 6 (June 1983).

Lim, Robyn. "The Philippines and the Foundation of Asean." *Review of Indonesian and Malayan Affairs* 7, 1 (January–June 1973).

————. "Conclusion." In *Understanding ASEAN*, ed. Alison Broinowski. Hong Kong: Macmillan, 1982.

Lim Teck Ghee. "Southeast Asian Perceptions of Japan and the Japanese." In *Japan as an Economic Power and Its Implications for Southeast Asia*. Singapore: Singapore University Press, 1974.

Linz, Juan. "An Authoritarian Regime: Spain." In *Mass Politics*, ed. Allardt and Rokkan. New York: Free Press, 1970.

Lyon, Peter. "ASEAN and the Future of Regionalism." In *New Directions in the International Relations of Southeast Asia*, ed. Lau Teik Soon. Singapore: ISEAS, 1973.

McCloud, Donald. "Indonesian Foreign Policy in Southeast Asia: A Study of the Patterns of Behavior." Ann Arbor: Xerox University Microfilms, 1975.

Mackie, J. A. C. "Does Indonesia Have Expansionist Designs on PNG?" In *The Indonesian-PNG Border*, ed. R. J. May. Canberra: ANU Press, 1979.

Maynard, Harold. "Views of the Indonesian and Philippine Military Elites." In *The Military and Security in the Third World: Domestic and International Impacts*, ed. Sheldon Simon. Boulder: Westview, 1978.

Meadows, Martin. "The Philippine Claim to North Borneo." *Political Science Quarterly* 77 (September 1962).

Melchor, Alejandro Jr. "Security Issues in Southeast Asia." Jakarta: CSIS, 1973.

Mendenhall, Joseph. "Laos: Vietnam's Stepping Stone to Thailand." *Conflict* 2, 2 (1980).

Mount, Frank. "The Prussians of Southeast Asia: Can They Be Stopped?" *Asian Affairs* 6, 6 (July 1979).

Nardin, Terry. "The Moral Basis of the Law of War." *Journal of International Affairs* 37, 2 (Winter 1984).

Nguyin, Manh Hung. "The Sino-Vietnamese Conflict." *Asian Survey* (November 1979).

Nixon, Richard. "Asia After Viet Nam." *Foreign Affairs* 46, 1 (October 1967).

Noble, Lela Garner. "Ethnicity and Philippine-Malaysian Relations." *Asian Survey* (May 1975).

Nono Anwar Makarim. "Indonesia's Next Nationalisms." *Pacific Community* (January 1973).

Noordin Sopiee. "The 'Neutralization' of South-East Asia." In *Asia and the Western Pacific*, ed. Hedley Bull. Melbourne: Nelson, 1975.

Nuechterlein, Donald. "Prospects for Regional Security in Southeast Asia." *Asian Survey* (September 1968).

———. "US National Interests in Southeast Asia: A Reappraisal." *Asian Survey* (November 1971).

Obaod ul Hag. "The Changing Balance of Power in the Pacific and Its Implications for Southeast Asia." *Pacific Community* (April 1975).

Ong Teck Mong, Timothy. "Modern Brunei: Some Important Issues." In *Southeast Asian Affairs 1983*. Singapore: ISEAS, 1983.

Osborn George. "Asean Security: Dominoes Revisited." In *Southeast Asian Affairs 1978*. Singapore: ISEAS, 1979.

Osborne, Milton. "Post Vietnam: The End of an Era in Southeast Asia?" *International Affairs* (January 1969).

Parker, F. Charles. "Vietnam and Soviet Asian Strategy." *Asian Affairs* 4, 2 (November 1976).

Pauker, Guy. "The ASEAN Energy Scene." *Asian Survey* 19, 6 (June 1979).

———. "Indonesia in 1980: Regime Fatigue?" *Asian Survey* 21, 2 (February 1982).

Polomka, Peter. "Indonesia's Future and South-East Asia." Adelphi Papers no. 104. London: Institute for Strategic Studies, 1974.

Porter, Gareth. "The Great Power Triangle in Southeast Asia." *Current History* 79, 461 (December 1980).

———. "Storms over Indochina: A Political Primer." *Indochina Issues* 25 (May 1982).

———. "Vietnam Plays a Negotiating Card." *Indochina Issues* 29 (October 1982).

Pranee Saipiroon. "ASEAN Governments' Attitudes Towards Regional Security 1975–79." Bangkok: Institute of Asian Studies, Chulalongkorn University, 1982.

Premdas, Ralph. "The Organisasi Papua Merdeka in Irian Jaya." *Asian Survey* 15, 10 (October 1985).

Ramos, Narcisso. "ASA and the Philippines." *Foreign Affairs Review* 5, 1 (January–June 1966).

Rau, Robert. "The Role of Singapore in ASEAN." *Contemporary Southeast Asia* 3, 2 (September 1981).

———. "Singapore's National Security Policy." *Southeast Asian Spectrum* 3, 3 (April 1975).

Regional Security Developments and Stability in Southeast Asia. Singapore: ISEAS, 1980.

Reyes, Narcisso. "ASEAN's Achilles Heel." *Foreign Service Institute Record* (Manila) 4 (1983).

Robinson, Thomas. "The Soviet Union and Asia in 1980." *Asian Survey* 21, 1 (January 1981).

Sarasin Viraphol. "Directions in Thai Foreign Policy." Occasional Paper no. 40. Singapore: ISEAS, 1976.

———. "Domestic Considerations of Thai Policies Towards the Indochina States." ISIS Workshop on Future ASEAN-Vietnamese Relations, February 1983.

Schuber, James. "Towards a 'Working Peace System' in Asia: Organizational Growth and State Participation in Asian Regionalism." *International Organization* 32, 2 (September 1978).

Seah Chee Meow, "Asean and the Changing Power Balance in South-East Asia." *Southeast Asian Spectrum* 4, 1 (October 1975).

———. "The Muslim Issue and Implications for ASEAN." *Pacific Community* 6, 1 (October 1974).

———. "Singapore's Foreign Policy in Southeast Asia: Options for National Survival." *Pacific Community* 4, 4 (July 1973).

———. "Singapore's Position in Asean Co-Operation." In *Singapore's Position in Asean Cooperation*, ed. Lim, Seah, and Shaw. Tokyo: Institute of Developing Economies, 1979.

Seah Chee Meow and Seah, Linda. "Japan-ASEAN Relations: New Perspectives on an Old Theme." *Pacific Community* (October 1977).

Shee Poon Kim. "The ASEAN States' Relations with the Socialist Republic of Vietnam." Occasional Paper no. 39. Department of Political Science, National University of Singapore, 1980.

———. "A Decade of ASEAN, 1967–1977." *Asian Survey* 17, 8 (August 1977).

Silverstein, Joseph. "The Military and Foreign Policy in Burma and Indonesia." *Asian Survey* 12, 3 (March 1982).

Simms, Peter. "Communism in Malaysia and Singapore." *Southeast Asian Spectrum* 3, 2 (January 1975).

Simon, Sheldon. "The ASEAN States: Obstacles to Security Cooperation." *Orbis* (Summer 1978).

———. "China, Vietnam and ASEAN: The Politics of Polarization." *Asian Survey* (December 1979).

Soedjatmoko. "An Indonesian Perspective on Security Trends in East Asia." In *Asian Security in the 1980's: Problems and Policies for a Time of Transition*, ed. Richard Solomon. Santa Monica: Rand, 1979.

Soesastro, Hadi. "ASEAN and North-South Trade Issues." *Indonesian Quarterly* 11, 3 (July 1983).

Solidum, Estrella. "ASEAN and Security." *Foreign Service Institute Record* (Manila) 4.

Solomon, Robert L. "Boundary Concepts and Practices in Southeast Asia." *World Politics* 23, 1 (October 1970).

Sompong Sucharitkul. "Policy Planning for the Security of Southeast Asia," Pattaya Conference.

Somsakdi Xuto. "Prospects for Security and Stability in Southeast Asia." *Pacific Community* 3, 1 (October 1971).

Sorenson, John. "The Social Bases of Instability in Southeast Asia." *Asian Survey* (July 1969).

Sterling, John. "ASEAN: The Anti Domino Factor." *Asian Affairs* 7, 5 (May–June 1980).

———. "Thailand and ASEAN in a Dangerous World." *Asian Affairs* 6, 5 (May 1979).

Stifel, Lawrence. "ASEAN Cooperation and Economic Growth in Southeast Asia." *Asia-Pacific Community* 4 (1979).

Stremlau, John. "The Foreign Policies of Developing Countries in the 1980s." In *The Foreign Policy Priorities of Third World States*, ed. John Stremlau. Boulder: Westview, 1982.

Sudarsono, Juwuno, "Political Aspects of Regionalism: ASEAN." *Indonesian Quarterly* 11, 3 (July 1983).

———. "Problems of Internal Stability on the ASEAN countries." In *Asia and the Western Pacific*, ed. Hedley Bull. Melbourne: Nelson, 1975.

———. "Security in Southeast Asia: The Circle of Conflict." *Indonesian Quarterly* 10, 2 (April 1982).

Suhkre, Astri. "Indochinese Refugees: Impact on ASEAN and U.S. Policy." *Contemporary Southeast Asia* 3, 1 (June 1981).

———. "Irredentism Contained: The Thai-Muslim Case." *Comparative Politics* 7, 2 (January 1975).

Suhkre, Astri, and Lela Noble. "Muslims in the Philippines and Thailand." In *Ethnic Conflict in International Relations*, ed. Suhkre and Noble. New York: Praeger, 1977.

Sukhumbhand Paribatra. "The H'mong of Ban Vinai: A Future Factor in Thailand's Security Equation." *ISIS Bulletin* 1, 1 (July 1982).

Surachai Sirikrai. "Japan-ASEAN Relations: The Pacific Basin Cooperation." Monograph no. 3. Bangkok: Thamasat Research Center, 1982.

Surin Pitsuwan. "Issues Affecting Border Security Between Malaysia and Thailand." Monograph Series no. 4. Bangkok: Thammasat Research Center, 1983.

Sutopo, A. R., "Independent Brunei Joins Asean." *Indonesian Quarterly* 12, 1 (January 1984).

Sycip, David. "Views on ASEAN." *Foreign Service Institute Record* 4.

Tanham, George. "Some Insurgency Lessons from Southeast Asia." *Orbis* 16, 3 (Fall 1972).

Thambipillai, Pusha. "Brunei in Asean: The Viable Choice?" In *Southeast Asian Affairs 1982*. Singapore: ISEAS, 1982.

————. "Malaysia: Twenty-Five and Pragmatic." In *Southeast Asian Affairs 1983*. Singapore: ISEAS, 1983.

Thanat Khoman. "Conflict and Cooperation in Southeast Asia: The New Chapter." In *New Foundations for Asean and Pacific Security*, ed. Joyce Larson. New York: National Strategy Information Center, 1980.

————. "The New Equation of World Power and Its Impact on Southeast Asia." *Orbis* 20, 3 (Fall 1976).

Thayer, Carlyle. "Vietnam: Beleaguered Outpost of Socialism." *Current History* (December 1980).

Thomas, M. Ladd. "The Malayan Communist Insurgency." *Asian Affairs* 4, 5 (May–June 1977).

————. "Political Violence in the Muslim Provinces of Southern Thailand." Occasional Paper no. 28. Singapore: ISEAS, 1975.

Tilman, Robert O. "Asia, ASEAN, and America in the Eighties: The Agonies of Maturing Relationships." *Contemporary Southeast Asia* 2, 4 (March 1981).

Ton Thay Thien. "New Confrontations in Southeast Asia." *Asian Affairs* 6, 2 (November 1978).

Tow, William. "Japan's Rearmament: The ASEAN Factor." *Asia-Pacific Community* 23 (Winter 1984).

Trager, Frank. "After Vietnam: Dominoes and Collective Security." *Asian Affairs* 2, 5 (May 1975).

————. "Domestic Instability in Southeast Asia." *Orbis* 19, 3 (Fall 1975).

Trocki, Carl. "Islam: Threat to ASEAN Regional Unity?" *Current History* 78, 456 (April 1980).

Turley, William, and Jeffrey Race. "The Third Indochina War." *Foreign Policy* 38 (Spring 1980).

Upadit Pachariyangkun. "The Strategic Outlook for Thailand in the 1980s." In *New Foundations for Asean and Pacific Security*, ed. Joyce Larson.

New York: National Strategy Information Center, 1980.

van der Kroef, Justus. "ASEAN, Hanoi, and the Kampuchean Conflict: Between 'Kuantan' and a 'Third Alternative.' " *Asian Survey* 21, 5 (May 1981).

————. "Hanoi and ASEAN: Is Co-existence Possible?" *Contemporary Southeast Asia* 1, 2 (September 1979).

————. "The Indochina Tangle: The Elements of Conflict and Compromise." *Asian Survey* 20, 5 (May 1980).

————. "Indonesia and East Timor: The Politics of Phased Annexation." *Solidarity* (Manila) 5, 5–6 (September 1976).

————. "Normalizing Relations with the PRC: Indonesia's Rituals of Ambiguity." *Contemporary Southeast Asia* 3, 3 (December 1981).

————. "Indonesia: Strategic Perceptions and Foreign Policy." *Asian Affairs* 2, 3 (January 1975).

————. "Southeast Asia: New Patterns of Conflict and Cooperation." *World Affairs* 138, 3 (Winter 1975–76).

van Dijk, Cees. "The ASEAN Summit Meeting." *Review of Indonesian and Malayan Affairs* 10, 2 (July–December 1976).

van Praagh, David. "The Outlook for Thailand." *Asian Affairs* 4, 5 (May 1977).

Wanandi, Jusuf. "Dimensions of Southeast Asian Security." *Contemporary Southeast Asia* 1, 4 (March 1980).

————. "Impacts of the Conflict in Indochina upon ASEAN's Security." *Conflict* 2, 1 (1980).

————. "The Internal and External Dimensions of Southeast Asian Security." In *New Foundations for Asean and Pacific Security*, ed. Joyce Larson. New York: National Strategy Information Center, 1980.

————. "Third World Conflict and International Security: A Third World Perspective." *Conflict* 3, 1 (1981).

Wang Gungwu. "China and the Region in Relation to Chinese Minorities." *Contemporary Southeast Asia* 1, 1 (May 1979).

————. "Introduction: Asean Between Tradition and Modernity." In *Understanding ASEAN*, ed. A. Broinowski. Hong Kong: Macmillan, 1982.

Warshawsky, Howard. "From Confrontation to Cooperation: The Influence of Domestic Forces on Indonesian Foreign Policy." Ann Arbor: University Microfilms, 1974.

Weatherbee, Donald. "ASEAN Security Cooperation and Resource Protection." Bangkok: Faculty of Political Science, Chulalongkorn University, 1981.

————. "Southeast Asia in 1982: Marking Time." In *Southeast Asian Affairs 1982*. Singapore: ISEAS, 1982.

Weinstein, Franklin. "The Meaning of National Security in Southeast Asia." In *Southeast Asia in a Changing World*, ed. Shigekazu Matsumuto.

Tokyo: Institute of Developing Economies, 1980.

———. "The Uses of Foreign Policy in Indonesia." Ann Arbor: Xerox University Microfilms, 1972.

Wills, Raymond. "Intra-regional Cooperation in ASEAN." *Asia Pacific Community* 24 (Spring 1984).

Wilson, Dick. "Future Relations ASEAN and Indochina." *Asia Pacific Community* 1 (Summer 1978).

———. "The New Role of Vietnam in East Asian Politics." *Asian Affairs* (London) (February 1977).

Withaya Sucharithanarugse. "Thailand in 1982: The Year of Living in Anxiety." In *Southeast Asian Affairs 1983*. Singapore: ISEAS, 1983.

Yamakage, Susumu. "Asean's Political Cooperation, 1966–77." Discussion Paper no. 109. Centre of Southeast Asian Studies, Kyoto University, 1980.

Yong Mun Cheong. "Indonesian Questions of Stability." In *Southeast Asian Affairs 1978*. Singapore: ISEAS, 1979.

Zartman, William. "Africa as a Subordinate State System in International Relations." *International Organization* 21 (Summer 1967).

Documents

ASEAN Secretariat. *15th ASEAN Ministerial Meeting*. June 1982.

———. *16th ASEAN Ministerial Meeting*. June 1983.

———. *10 Years of ASEAN*. April 1978.

Malaysia. Ministry of Foreign Affairs. "ASEAN: Contributor to Stability and Development." Speech by Ghazalie Shafie, November 11, 1981.

———. "Detente and ASEAN: A Malaysian View." Speech by Ghazalie Shafie, January 12, 1983.

Philippines. Department of Public Information. *Menando Talks*. 1974.

Thailand. Ministry of Foreign Affairs. *ASEAN Documents*. 1983.

Index

accommodation: basis of ASEAN
process, 5–10, 49; consultation
principles and tactics, 91–107,
156–57, 164; as "need-
suspicion," 45; at origins of
ASEAN, 10–17; between
sovereignty and solidarity, 102;
as "specific bargaining
situation," 50; strains on, 161–67
accommodation, bilateral:
Indonesia-Malaysia, 16–33;
Indonesia-Philippines, 77–80;
Indonesia-PNG, 88–89;
Indonesia-Singapore, 45–50;
Indonesia-Thailand, 65–68;
Malaysia-Brunei, 83–88;
Malaysia-Philippines, 69–77;
Malaysia-Singapore, 34–45;
Malaysia-Thailand, 51–62;
Singapore-Thailand, 62–65
accountability in consultative
process, 91–92
Acheh, 27, 32, 140
Afghanistan invasion, 119
Agnew, Spiro, 111
Ali Moertopo, 95, 97
Alliance government (Malaysia), 28
ambiguity: in accommodation,
104–107; in consensus, 157; in
domestic politics, 107; in
"nuances," 102; in solidarity,
153; in support for Thailand, 146
ambiguous association, 146, 157
Amity, Treaty of: as accommodation
to Vietnam, 105, 147, 158;

Amity, Treaty of (*continued*)
instrument of solidarity, 143,
146; role in ASEAN-Brunei
relations, 88
Amphil, causes special meeting, 136
Annual visits, 90
Aquino, Benigno, 73, 82, 134
Asian Forum, 77
Association of Southeast Asia
(ASA), 12–15
Association of Southeast Asian
Nations (ASEAN):
accommodation to Brunei,
83–89, 149; accommodation to
Vietnam, 134; core, 18, 34, 69;
east flank, 18, 69; Marcos on
value of, 15; meanings of, 3–5,
155, 160–61; myth of, 96;
origins of, 10–17; west flank,
18, 51, 68. *See also* conflict
management
ASEAN Annual Ministerial Meeting
(AMM): as consultation
instrument, 91, 150; as display
of solidarity, 122; drops ICK,
123; offers accommodation to
Vietnam, 132; reaction to
Vietnamese incursion, 120;
response to Cambodian
occupation, 115; supports
"proximity talks," 137; teaches
importance of quiet diplomacy,
130
"ASEAN approach," 112
ASEAN consciousness, basis of, 96